Proactive Law for Managers

Proactive Law for Managers

A Hidden Source of Competitive Advantage

GEORGE SIEDEL
University of Michigan

and

HELENA HAAPIO
Lexpert Ltd

Routledge
Taylor & Francis Group
LONDON AND NEW YORK

First published in paperback 2024

First published 2011 by Gower Publishing

Published 2016 by Routledge
4 Park Square, Milton Park, Abingdon, Oxon OX14 4RN

and by Routledge
605 Third Avenue, New York, NY 10158

Routledge is an imprint of the Taylor & Francis Group, an informa business

Gower Applied Business Research
Our programme provides leaders, practitioners, scholars and researchers with thought provoking, cutting edge books that combine conceptual insights, interdisciplinary rigour and practical relevance in key areas of business and management.

British Library Cataloguing in Publication Data
Siedel, George J.
Proactive law for managers : a hidden source of competitive advantage.
1. Business enterprises—Law and legislation. 2. Corporate governance. 3. Organizational change. 4. Competition.
I. Title II. Haapio, Helena.
658.1'2—dc22

Library of Congress Cataloging-in-Publication Data
Siedel, George J.
Proactive law for managers : a hidden source of competitive advantage / George Siedel and Helena Haapio.
p. cm.
Includes index.
ISBN 978-1-4094-0100-1 (hardback : alk. paper) — ISBN 978-1-4094-0101-8 (ebook)
1. Business law—United States. 2. Industrial management—United States. 3. Competition—United States. I. Haapio, Helena. II. Title.

KF390.B84S558 2010
340.02'4658—dc22

2010025553

ISBN: 978-1-4094-0100-1 (hbk)
ISBN: 978-1-03-292832-6 (pbk)
ISBN: 978-1-315-60224-0 (ebk)

DOI: 10.4324/9781315602240

Contents

List of Illustrations

Figures

Exhibits

Endorsements for Proactive Law for Managers

Market volatility, regulatory uncertainty, the complexity of international relationships ... these are critical issues for today's business managers and they demand innovative, flexible approaches to traditional legal solutions. This book offers unique ideas and insights that will significantly enhance the ability to compete and win.

Tim Cummins, President, International Association for Contract & Commercial Management

Using the frameworks provided in Proactive Law for Managers, *our company has been able to seek new business advantages as we deal with a diverse range of legal—and non-legal—issues. Now, instead of waiting to confront legal issues only when we are faced with a legal problem, we take a more holistic, comprehensive approach to the law by using the Manager's Legal Plan™, and the other practical tools outlined in this book, to develop and merge legal strategies into good business practices and focus on using them to gain a competitive advantage. It empowers our executives to address these concerns and pursue contracts and negotiations using a fresh and dynamic and absolutely essential business mindset and approach.*

This book challenges each of us to envision a considerably more productive state for our firm, one that requires our managers to proactively step in and take charge of business matters that have legal components or potential legal problems rather than simply delegating these issues to our legal department.

Proactive Law for Managers *is a fundamental book that addresses a critical component of any business and offers a comprehensive, step-by-step guide and other invaluable tools on a plethora of legal issues to gain a competitive advantage in your firm. It is a must-read for any manager and ultimately, it is essential for business success and should be incorporated into every company's legal and business strategy.'*

Alyssa R. Martina, President and Publisher, Metro Parent Publishing Group

For far too long, managers have tended to look at the law as a constraint on their activities. The odd thing is that money, plant and equipment can all be constraints, but managers tend to look at them as resources too. George Siedel and Helena Haapio do a great service to managers by brilliantly demonstrating how law, too, can be a tool for competitive advantage.

Timothy L. Fort, Ph.D., J.D., Executive Director, Institute for Corporate Responsibility, Lindner-Gambal Professor of Business Ethics, George Washington University, USA

In today's hyper-competitive business world, securing the upper hand is imperative for survival. Although many business students and professionals do not always consider creating a legal plan as a means of gaining an advantage, the Siedel/Haapio book vividly opens the readers' minds as to how this can be achieved.

Robert J. Aalberts, J.D., M.A., Ernst Lied Professor of Legal Studies, University of Nevada, USA

George Siedel and Helena Haapio have written a wonderful tutorial on how to conduct a well structured review of a company's (global) legal risks and opportunities, and then develop a proactive business law strategy to maximize management's return on legal investment dollars.

Tom Highley, CEO of Tenon Limited, Auckland, New Zealand

Proactive Law for Managers ... *provides an excellent framework to help managers and business students think more clearly about potential legal issues as well as issues that have already entered the legal arena. The four-step process, called the "Manager's Legal Plan™," expands the executive's perspective beyond just dealing with an immediate legal problem to a more comprehensive understanding of the broad implications of legal trends and company responsibilities. The book incorporates many practical applications to common problems facing managers, such as product liability, contract negotiations, and protection of intellectual property. The authors argue that, when acting upon such a broad understanding, the firm will more effectively create and sustain its competitive advantage. I wholeheartedly agree and recommend this book to managers and students who want to deal more proactively with legal challenges.*

Dr. Jeanne M. Logsdon, Regents Professor & Rust Professor of Business Ethics, Anderson School of Management, University of New Mexico, USA

Acknowledgments

The authors want to acknowledge the contributions of Leila Hamhoum, Executive Assistant, Lexpert Ltd, to the successful completion of this book. The authors thank Martin West for encouraging us to publish this book. Martin is Commissioning Editor for Gower Applied Research, which publishes books that emphasize the practical benefits to business that can arise from the intersection between theory and practice. Thanks also to Rachel Lynch, Managing Director, Ashgate Publishing, and to the Gower team within Ashgate for their professional support. This team includes Jonathan Norman, Publishing Director; Emily Ruskell, Production Editor; Sue White, Marketing Manager; and Donna Shanks, Assistant Commissioning Editor. In addition to the Gower team, Charlotte Parkins provided valuable advice while proofreading the book.

We owe a special debt of gratitude to managers with whom we have worked in Asia, Europe, the United States and South America. The Manager's Legal Plan™ is the result of their advice and encouragement and this book reflects their success in achieving competitive advantage for their companies. We are also indebted to professors who have used the Manager's Legal Plan™ in the classroom for their enthusiasm in introducing students to this new framework for business success.

George J. Siedel
Helena Haapio

About the Authors

George J. Siedel

George J. Siedel is Williamson Family Professor of Business Administration and Thurnau Professor of Business Law at the Ross School of Business, University of Michigan. After completing graduate legal studies at the University of Michigan and Cambridge University, he worked as an attorney in a professional corporation. Siedel has also served on several boards of directors and as Associate Dean for Executive Education at the Ross School of Business. His research focuses on international business, negotiation, dispute prevention, and dispute resolution.

The author of numerous books and articles, Siedel has received several research awards, including the Faculty Recognition Award from the University of Michigan and the following awards from the Academy of Legal Studies in Business: the Maurer Award, the Ralph Bunche Award, and the Hoeber Award. The Center for International Business Education and Research selected a case he authored for its annual International Case Writing Award. His research has been cited by appellate courts in the United States and abroad, including the High Court of Australia. Siedel has served as Visiting Professor of Business Law at Stanford University, Visiting Professor of Business Administration at Harvard University, and Parsons Fellow at the University of Sydney. He has been elected a Visiting Fellow at Cambridge University's Wolfson College and as a Life Fellow of the Michigan State Bar Foundation. As a Fulbright Scholar, he held a Distinguished Chair in the Humanities and Social Sciences.

Helena Haapio

Helena Haapio works as International Contract Counsel for Lexpert Ltd (www.lexpert.com) based in Helsinki, Finland. She helps corporate clients become more successful in cross-border contractual ventures by using a *proactive approach*, one that helps them use contracts to achieve better business results and stay out of legal trouble. After completing legal studies at the University of Turku and Cambridge University, Haapio served for several years as in-house Legal Counsel for Wärtsilä Group companies in Finland, Norway, Sweden, and the US, and for three years as General Counsel for one of the Group's Divisions. Her responsibilities included drafting and negotiating contracts for complex international projects, acquisitions, joint ventures, distributorships, sales and licensing transactions. She also arranged in-house training in related fields and was nominated "Export Educator of the Year" by the Finnish Institute for International Trade.

Haapio's current research focuses on proactive contracting as a means to bridge business and law. She is the co-author of *Industrial Services and Service Contracts—A Proactive Approach* (The Federation of Finnish Technology Industries, Helsinki, 2009) and the editor of *A Proactive Approach to Contracting and Law* (IACCM and Turku University of Applied Sciences, Turku, 2008). Her articles have appeared in *ACCA Docket, Contract Management,*

Contracting Excellence, and various other business and professional publications. She is a member of the International Association for Contract and Commercial Management (IACCM, www.iaccm.com) Advisory Council and the founder and co-ordinator of IACCM Finland. She is actively involved in the development of the Nordic School of Proactive Law (www.proactivelaw.org) and of the ProActive ThinkTank (www.proactivethinktank.com) and acted as Expert in drawing up the European Economic and Social Committee (EESC) Opinion on the Proactive Law Approach. She regularly conducts corporate in-house training workshops in various parts of the world. She also acts as arbitrator in cross-border contract disputes.

Foreword

Today's networked world has caused an explosion in the number and variety of trading relationships. Increasingly, companies transact business across cultural and geographic boundaries and rely upon intangible services for their operational effectiveness. This "voyage into the unknown" brings with it new risks and exposes the weakness of traditional mechanisms for forming and managing commercial relationships.

In this still emerging world, the potential for misunderstanding and for disagreements over performance management has spiraled. And it is against this background that the "school" of proactive law and contracting has emerged. In the old world, "the contract" was a document that frequently saw the light of day only if something went wrong. This reactive approach focused on protecting the parties against the consequences of their actions or inactions—a focus made more extreme by the dominance of US litigation practices in shaping world trade.

The proactive approach invites a paradigm shift. It offers a method focused on success, one directed at prevention rather than cure. The approach recognizes that economic value, cycle times, and innovation—all critical weapons in today's highly competitive global economy—are directly influenced by contracts. The goal is to help the parties reach their goals and secure success while reducing the likelihood of problems and disputes. Market volatility, regulatory uncertainty, the complexity of international relationships ... these are critical issues for today's business managers and they demand innovative, flexible approaches to traditional legal solutions. This book offers unique ideas and insights that will significantly enhance the ability to compete and win.

Tim Cummins, President,
International Association for Contract and Commercial Management (IACCM)

Preface

This book is for managers who have responsibility for the success of their organizations. It's about discovering competitive advantage in the law and even in the legal challenges of doing business—discovering how a lawsuit against your firm can help you develop more profitable products and practices, how governmental restrictions might actually work to your firm's advantage, and why contracts are much more than a formality. For example, because your contracts are not only legal tools but are also management tools, your contracting process can become an important source of competitive advantage. In other words, this book can help you to revolutionize your business strategies related to law and contracts.

At the heart of this book is the Manager's Legal Plan™, a four-step process by which you can better defend against costly and wasteful litigation while turning your contracts and legal resources into competitive assets. The four steps are as follows:

Step One: Understand the law. This starts with an understanding of the legal dimensions of business. It goes beyond having legal resources available when an issue labeled "legal" arises. It involves recognizing the legal aspects of business, exercising informed judgment when managing them, and knowing when professional legal help is (and is not) required.

Step Two: Know how to cope with legal problems and learn from them. If you do face a legal problem, the book takes you through the choices of "fight or flight": fighting or settling cases, ceasing or moving operations, or possibly seeking law reform. The book will explain how increasing globalization of law is greatly reshaping these choices. Even if you are fortunate enough not to face legal problems yourself, you can learn from legal concerns of others and use those learnings for the next step.

Step Three: Develop business strategies and solutions to prevent future problems. This step prompts you to think along three basic domains of prevention: first, prevent the cause from arising; second, prevent the cause from doing harm; and third, if harm occurs, limit the damage. Here legal solutions take a backseat to business solutions. For example, once a dispute over termination of an employment agreement has been resolved, your company's recruiting, contract and pre-termination practices should be reviewed, your company documents (including sample contracts and termination letters) should be revised, and your employees should receive training and support that will prevent them from taking actions that could result in business failure and unexpected liability.

Step Four: Climb to the balcony to see the big picture and become more proactive. This step takes you well beyond the usual responses to legal challenges and helps you adopt a wider view of the legal dimensions of business. With the broader perspective provided by your view from "the balcony," you can see things differently. This starts with changing the belief that "the law" relates only to legal problems or someone threatening to sue, leading you from being reactive to becoming proactive. This step encourages you to focus not only on preventing what is not desirable, such as future legal problems and their causes, but also to promote what is desirable and to create and enhance future business opportunities. By incorporating legal issues into the normal strategic and operational aspects of the business you can reframe issues and find new sources of innovative solutions. You may even note that what originally appeared to be a legal concern or a necessary evil may in fact represent a broader business opportunity that may enable you to gain new competitive advantage.

While these four steps address key concerns that arise in business operations and management decision making, this book is not meant to supply direction on how to handle legal issues; nor is it intended to provide or replace legal or other expert advice. Appropriate legal or other professional advice should always be obtained and relied upon before taking or omitting to take action in respect of any specific problem.

The book opens in Chapter 1 with a description of the Manager's Legal Plan™. This is followed in Chapters 2 to 4 with examples of how you can use the plan to address important stakeholder (customers, employees, and society at large) concerns. Chapter 2 deals with your customers, showing how you can not only prevent future legal problems and excessive liability exposure but also how product liability provides an opportunity for new product innovation. Chapter 3 deals with employees and shows how the Manager's Legal Plan™ enables you to attract and retain key talent while avoiding employment pitfalls. The chapter uses examples from two quite different legal systems, the European Union and the United States. Chapter 4 deals with government. For example, the chapter shows how stringent environmental regulations can create opportunities for competitive advantage through new business models and new product development.

Chapter 5 deals with innovation and intangible assets. To sustain your competitive advantage and thrive long term, you must know how to protect your valuable ideas. The chapter focuses on the important role intellectual property rights (IPR) play in today's business and how you can use them to seize strategic control of innovations, gain a legal monopoly, and attract new partners. Chapter 6 deals with contracts and contracting. The chapter shows their profound impact on business success and how you as a manager can design your contracts and contracting processes so that they promote business success while preventing problems.

Chapter 7 addresses a wide variety of management resources and tools that you can use to create competitive advantage while also encouraging ethical decision making within your company. This chapter, along with Chapters 1–4, have been adapted from chapters in *Using the Law for Competitive Advantage* by George J. Siedel (Wiley, New York, 2002). Special thanks to Professor Jeanne M. Logsdon, Regents Professor & Rust Professor of Business Ethics, Anderson School of Management, University of New Mexico, whose original suggestion led to the publication of *Proactive Law for Managers*.

This book is based on our work with managers, legal professionals, and academic thought leaders from North and South America, Europe, the Middle East, Asia, and Africa. This work, combined with our review of cutting-edge research, has led to three insights regarding the relationship between law and business. First, the legal environment is rapidly changing in response to the globalization of business. For example, there has been significant convergence of the law relating to contracts, environmental protection, and securities regulation.

Second, managers have an increasing appreciation for the importance of law. For example, an analysis of program evaluations completed by over 900 senior managers attending University of Michigan executive programs revealed that law is one of three most important subjects (along with finance and human resources) among business school required courses. The reason is obvious: law touches almost every aspect of a manager's work.

Third, the combination of legal change and the ubiquity of law have created new opportunities for competitive advantage. Specifically, savvy managers can use the law to reduce their costs, develop products and services that are unique and/or priced lower than those of competitors, collaborate to innovate, and create value for their customers that is superior to the value offered by competitors. But to achieve competitive advantage, these managers need a plan.

This book provides the plan, the four-step Manager's Legal Plan™ designed for managers who have responsibility for their companies' success. The plan described in this book is also useful to business school students whose goal is to develop business leadership skills or to start a business, to corporate attorneys who work with managers in the pursuit of competitive advantage, and to law students who plan to specialize in business law.

CHAPTER 1 Seize Competitive Advantage: A Legal Plan for Managers

Congratulations! Last year the chief executive officer of your company named you general manager of one of the firm's most important divisions. Your first year as head of the division has been a success, as you have exceeded the goals set by corporate headquarters.

Condolences! You have no time to savor your early success. You and the CEO recently analyzed current business trends. You both anticipate that the market for your products will become much more competitive, especially with a recent increase in foreign competition. The CEO emphasizes that your division must gain competitive advantage over rival companies in order to survive.

Beyond concerns about the survival of your division, you have other worries. If you fail as leader of the division, in the current economic climate you may be unable to find a general manager position at another company. You also feel responsible for the division's employees. The division is the largest employer in your town, and a shutdown would devastate the local economy, as well as the families of your employees.

As you plan for the coming year, you develop a list of your goals. High on your list are access to, and retention of, key talent; the ability to adapt to change; the strength of your brand and reputation, and high-quality customer service. To this list you add a personal goal—managing time and stress—because your work increasingly pulls you away from your family and you have little time for recreation.

You then list key obstacles that might prevent you from achieving your goals (while also increasing your stress levels). Among these you list several legal concerns. For instance, you are worried about a lawsuit that might have a significant impact on the company and on you personally. A year ago, when you took over leadership of the division, you fired an employee of your division's US subsidiary company who was not performing up to your expectations. The employee has now sued you and the company, claiming breach of contract. The employee also claims that you defamed him by making untrue statements about his performance. As a result of this lawsuit, you are reluctant to terminate other poor performers, for fear that they might also file suit.

If it is any consolation, you have lots of company among managers at firms around the world. Achieving competitive advantage is critical to the success and even the survival of companies that cross a variety of industries and cultures. Managers at these companies share many of the goals you listed. Like you, they need to strike a balance between surviving immediate market conditions and making certain their companies endure and succeed over the long term. In fact, talent, agility, reputation, and customer service top the list of managers worldwide. According to the PricewaterhouseCoopers Annual Global CEO Survey 2009,[1] more than 90 percent of CEOs believe that these four features are important or critical to long-term growth. In this survey, covering over 1,100 CEOs from more than 50 countries, PricewaterhouseCoopers found that the following are considered to be the critical drivers of long-term success by managers worldwide:

EXHIBIT 1.1 CRITICAL DRIVERS OF LONG-TERM SUCCESS[2]

1. Access to, and retention of, key talent
2. Ability to adapt to change
3. Strength of your brand and reputation
4. High-quality customer service
5. Customer or market intelligence
6. Technological innovation
7. Efficient sourcing or supply chain management
8. Access to capital
9. Ability to implement successful collaborative business partnerships
10. Strength of your corporate social responsibility programs
11. Access to affordable natural resources (for example, raw materials, water, energy)

The concerns faced by managers worldwide are increasingly similar. They relate to trends and issues such as globalization, outsourcing, networking, ethics, and social responsibility. The PricewaterhouseCoopers survey shows that after the financial crisis that began in 2008 many CEOs around the world were fighting threats to their companies' survival. The scale of the damage was not all that took senior executives and government ministers by surprise; so did the fact that the world markets were much more closely connected than most people had believed.[3] As businesses try to survive immediate market conditions, they are also trying to make certain that they endure and succeed over the long term. CEOs have long believed that critical sources of competitive advantage take years, not quarters, to build.[4]

Concern over the impact of the law in general has emerged as one of the most important factors in the external environment in which business operates. It is estimated that in the United States, Fortune 500 executives spend 20–25 percent of their time on litigation-related matters.[5] It is no wonder that business executives attending management development programs rank law among the three most important business topics, along with human resources and finance.[6] Yet law, as Wharton Professor G. Richard Shell explains in his book *Make the Rules or Your Rivals Will*, "is perhaps the most hidden of all competitive strategy tools. Many in business fear getting tangled up with lawyers, lobbyists, and bureaucrats, so they keep their distance from legal matters. But it is just this aversion that makes legal knowledge such a rich source of competitive advantage for those who take the time to understand how legal systems really work. Someone, after all, is going to make the rules. The only question is who."[7]

John Seeley Brown, Director of Xerox Research Center, once observed that "Managers don't make products; they make sense."[8] In your leadership role, as you attempt to make sense of legal challenges in your competitive environment, it is easy to become mesmerized by the complexity of the issues, looking much like a deer in the headlights. In a sense, the goal of this book is to provide a plan, called the Manager's Legal Plan™, that will enable you to cross the legal highways that intersect your business strategies—maximizing your opportunities while minimizing the risk of being struck down by unexpected legal liability. In a broader sense, however, the goal is to help you recognize the ways in which the law can work for you as a competitive strategy tool and as an enabler, rather than work against you as an obstacle. Along the way, you may notice that the law—even the so-called legal problems—can in reality be opportunities for competitive advantage.

This chapter will introduce the Manager's Legal Plan™ by first explaining the business concept of competitive advantage. The chapter will next describe the traditional approach used by many managers when confronted with the law (the law being too often, incorrectly, understood as meaning legal problems). The traditional, *reactive* approach will then be contrasted with a different, *proactive* approach that enables you to use the law and your legal capabilities to prevent problems, promote successful business, and achieve competitive advantage. The chapter will close with a brief overview of the remaining chapters in the book.

The Essence of Competitive Advantage

The concept of competitive advantage is central to business success around the world. The definition of competitive advantage is straightforward: Your goal in business is to gain an *advantage* over your *competitors*. If you were a college basketball coach, you would try to gain advantage over competitors by recruiting athletes who are taller and faster than players on opposing teams. You would attempt to develop game plans that maximize your strengths and exploit your opponents' weaknesses. You would develop a training program and organize practices to improve the performance of your athletes. In other words, your goals as a coach would be similar to the goals in Exhibit 1.1: talent, agility, and reputation. In order to succeed, you and your team need to master the rules of the game—something so self-evident that you probably do not even think about it.

Of course, college basketball teams and businesses use different measures of success. In college basketball, the success of a coach is determined primarily by whether fans are satisfied with the number of games that the team wins during the season. In business, a manager must also satisfy the fans (customers) but must do so in a manner that produces profits for the firm's owners.

As a result, a company seeking competitive advantage must create value for its customers that is superior to the value offered by its competitors. Superior value, as Harvard Professor Michael Porter explains in his book *Competitive Advantage*,[9] "stems from offering lower prices than competitors for equivalent benefits or providing unique benefits that more than offset a higher price." The amount that buyers are willing to pay for this value must exceed the company's costs in order for the firm to be profitable. As Porter puts it, "Competitive advantage grows fundamentally out of value a firm is able to create for its buyers that exceeds the firm's cost of creating it."[10]

In order to create value in today's economy, companies can no longer rely on merely internal resources; they must use external resources as well. They may spend 50 percent or more of their revenue to acquire the goods and services necessary to conduct their business. New technologies have enabled networking, outsourcing, and alliances across borders in a way that was not possible earlier. Competitive advantage can no longer be built on the position of individual companies within one industry or country: the ability to leverage external resources and the creation of value in collaboration with other companies has become a key source of competitive advantage.[11] It has been said that *companies* no longer compete; *supply chains* and *business networks* compete.

When considering competitive advantage, we thus must take into account not only individual companies and their resources and capabilities but also those of the companies they work with, as well as the relationships between them. And we need to have expertise in the rules that apply, whether those rules are made by regulators or by private actors through their contracts.

In today's business environment of increased inter-corporate dependency, complexity, and uncertainty, companies must take good care of their relationships. They must detect and strengthen weak links in their supply chains and manage their projects and transactions well. Contracts and contracting practices can help them in this enterprise. This book will present contracts in this context, as self-made rules of the game and as tools that can be used proactively for business success and problem prevention. This is particularly relevant for you as a manager, as a large part of the negotiation and drafting of business contracts is actually carried out by managers and not lawyers.

As we will see in the chapters that follow, law can play an important role in all these aspects. Business, law, and contracts are intertwined, and the latter two can increase or decrease business costs, liabilities, and risks. If contracts fail, apart from the legal issues, there are business and relationship issues. If a contract dispute arises, business performance will suffer and a lot is at stake, including good-will and reputation.

As a solution to the challenges faced by today's managers, the chapters that follow will introduce a *proactive* approach and related competencies that help prevent problems, promote successful business relationships, and secure sustainable competitive advantage.

If all companies took full advantage of their contracts and legal resources, any resulting advantage over the competition would disappear. However, because law and contracts are an almost untapped source of competitive advantage that will continue to be misunderstood by many managers, selected companies should be able to leverage their contracts and legal resources into a source of competitive advantage.

Strategy scholars have long known that companies gain competitive advantage by developing hard-to-imitate core competencies. By applying the Manager's Legal Plan™ to complement your company's technological, marketing, sourcing, and other capabilities, you as a manager can create for your company competitive advantage that is sustainable over the long term.

The Challenge: the Conventional, Reactive Approach to Law—"Flight or Fight"

In the vocabulary of many managers, the word "law" implies legal problems that must be solved by legal means. Some managers seem to think about the law only when approached—or threatened—by lawyers. They then want their lawyer to get them out of legal trouble.

Such a reactive approach to legal matters contains many pitfalls. It may lead you to start with a mindset that separates legal issues from the normal strategic and operational aspects of the business. Too often, legal concerns are treated as problems to be resolved as quickly as possible so that attention can be focused on business goals. This attitude overlooks the fundamental point that, even if legal matters are viewed as problems, they affect the business goals of both you and your competitors. The companies and managers that can best resolve these problems create an opportunity to seize competitive advantage. As later chapters will illustrate, proactive managers ask the question: How can this situation create an opportunity to gain an advantage over our competitors?

Given the current approach that too often separates legal and business concerns, managers typically engage in a two-step process when addressing their legal concerns. The first step is to meet with an attorney to discuss their rights and obligations. For instance, in responding to an alleged breach of contract or product liability lawsuit, you would first meet with your attorney to determine whether the claim has any merit. During the course of your conversation, the attorney would explain the issues involved and would also discuss whether the claimant might win in court, the potential damages, and the costs of the litigation.

Following the briefing by an attorney, the second step is to activate the flight-or-fight responses that have developed in humans over millions of years and allow us to survive in dangerous situations. In a legal sense, there are two basic flight options for your company (see Figure 1.1). First, flight might involve settlement of the case. Second, if certain types of cases are so common that they prevent your company from achieving its objectives, then flight might involve, for instance, ceasing certain operations or moving them to another country. Class actions, employment laws, or environmental burdens might cause you to consider such measures.

The fight response also includes two basic options. One option is to fight individual claims in court on a case-by-case basis. The other option is to take the fight to a different level and fight to reform laws that have a detrimental impact on business. For instance, in addition to fighting individual customs duty, tax, or workers' compensation cases, your company might push for legal reform that would change the customs duties or taxes or reduce the financial burden of workers' compensation.

For reasons stated in the sections that follow, the traditional flight or fight responses have become more difficult—or in some situations impossible—to execute successfully. Thus, in a global economy, the flight or fight approach to legal concerns is often no longer realistic.

	Specific Cases	*Broader Concerns*
Flight	Settle	Move Business
Fight	Litigate	Law Reform

Figure 1.1 Conventional approach to legal problems

DIFFICULTIES WITH THE "FLIGHT" RESPONSE

Both of the characteristic flight responses can lead to problems in the current environment. Sometimes, neither settlement of a specific case nor movement of your business makes sense.

The strategy of settling specific cases

Flight from litigation through settlement of a specific case often appears to be a logical course of action. This may be the case even when it is likely that your company will win if the case goes to trial. While in most countries the winning party is entitled to recover its litigation costs, this is not the case in the US. If you can settle a case for $50,000 and it will cost you $100,000 to litigate the case even if you win, common sense tells you to settle.

The total cost of settlement might be much higher than litigation costs when, by settling the case, you signal to potential plaintiffs (and their attorneys) that you are willing to pay to settle future cases in order to avoid a trial even when you have a winning case. Professor John Coffee of Columbia Law School, in commenting on a 2001 Merrill Lynch settlement with a client who lost money on a stock market investment, put it this way: "[Settlement] is like putting out warm milk for a stray cat that meows. You get 30 more cats the next night. This will create an incentive for others" to sue.[12]

The strategy of ceasing or moving certain operations of the company

When certain types of liability, such as liability resulting from class actions, tax or labor laws, or environmental regulation, become burdensome, it is tempting to consider the flight option of ceasing certain operations or moving them to another country. Under traditional notions of *comparative* advantage, certain countries have a comparative advantage over others as a result of cost advantages, including legal costs. But in a global economy, countries face difficulty in achieving comparative legal advantage for two reasons illustrated by Figure 1.2: (1) the cross-border movement of goods, services, and investments, and (2) the increasing convergence of legal rules and regulations.

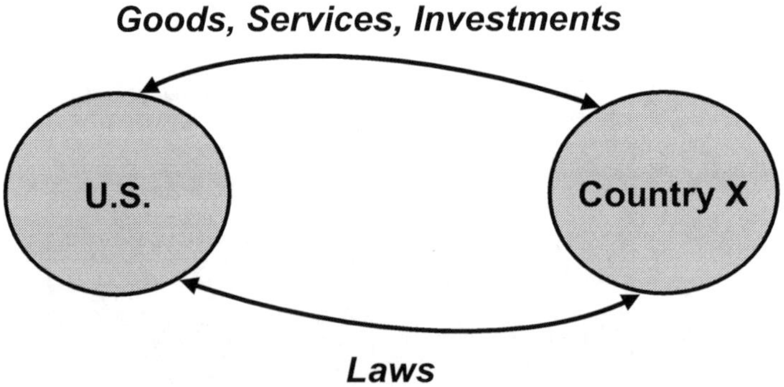

Figure 1.2 Decline of comparative advantage

Cross-border movement of goods, services, and investments

The movement of goods, services, and investments across borders means that you can be subject to regulation and liability in other countries regardless of where the goods and services are produced. For example, if you are operating a plant in Country X and your goods are exported to the US (see Figure 1.2), you are subject to liability for injuries caused by your goods in the US. This can be the case even if you did not export the goods yourself. You may, for instance, have sold components to another company in your country (or in a third country), and this other company may have incorporated them into equipment that was later exported.

The rationale for this liability was explained in a 1988 Nevada case involving the band Judas Priest. One evening two young men went to an empty churchyard and attempted to commit suicide. The first man succeeded, after propping a sawed-off shotgun under his chin and pulling the trigger. The second man somehow survived a similar suicide attempt, but suffered severe injuries. The survivor and the mother of the decedent filed a lawsuit in Nevada against the members of Judas Priest, who were residents of Great Britain. They claimed that the suicidal actions were caused by one of the band's albums, *Stained Class.*

Before deciding whether the band was liable, the Nevada court first had to determine whether it had the right to hear a case involving residents of another country. The court determined that the courts of Nevada could hear cases like this because "the band members consciously and deliberately chose to develop a world-wide market."[13]

In today's global economy, where electronic commerce facilitates global product reach, companies increasingly choose "to develop a world-wide market." As a result, they must be prepared to defend lawsuits in other countries, even those that they eventually win—as did the members of Judas Priest. In many cases, their products must meet the regulatory requirements of other countries. In other words, in a world where the mantra "think globally, act locally" applies to law as well as to other aspects of business, the option of flight to a country with minimal legal requirements might no longer be available.

Convergence of legal rules

Laws increasingly move across borders, resulting in convergence of the legal rules that govern business practice. The European Union (EU) has harmonized many of the laws of its Member States. In many cases, US rules and regulations have spread to other countries. An article in *The Economist* on a new California law begins by describing this legal migration pattern: "California today, America tomorrow—and the rest of the world the day after."[14] However, Figure 1.2 illustrates that law reform moves in two directions, as laws in the EU and in countries elsewhere also influence legal developments in the US.

Law can be divided into two broad categories—substantive and procedural—both of which have been affected by convergence in recent years. *Substantive law* deals with the substance of the law—the legal rules and regulations that govern business operations and management decision making. *Procedural law* is the body of law relating to the enforcement of substantive law.

The following examples illustrate the convergence of substantive law:

1. *Sales law.* The United Nations Convention on Contracts for the International Sale of Goods, the CISG (also known as the Vienna Convention, the UNCITRAL Convention, and "the uniform international sales law") establishes a uniform set of rules for

contracts involving buyers and sellers of goods from different countries. These rules have now been adopted by more than 70 countries accounting for more than three-quarters of all world trade. By reducing legal differences from one country to another, the CISG lowers contract law barriers to international trade.

Adopted by a diplomatic conference in Vienna in 1980, the CISG establishes a comprehensive set of rules governing the formation of contracts for the international sale of goods, the obligations of the buyer and seller, remedies for breach of contract, and other aspects of the contract. To find CISG texts in different languages, a map, and list of contracting states, guides, articles, CISG-Advisory Council's opinions relating to the interpretation and application of the CISG, or cases on the CISG, you can go to the Pace University School of Law CISG database.[15] This award-winning database is compiled from submissions by many contributors. The Section "Applying the CISG" containing "Guides for Managers and Counsel" and "Drafting CISG Contracts" is particularly valuable for managers and practitioners.

2. *Contract law.* Beyond the sale of goods, there has been convergence of general contract law, especially in the EU. The European Parliament and Council have consistently affirmed the need for greater coherence in order to ensure the proper functioning of the internal market. The European Commission has undertaken a series of initiatives aimed at increasing the overall coherence of European contract law.[16]

   The Commission on European Contract Law, chaired by Professor Ole Lando, has prepared the Principles of European Contract Law (PECL).[17] The Rome I Regulation on the law applicable to contractual obligations seeks to ensure that the courts of all EU Member States apply the same rules to disputes related to contractual obligations in case of a conflict of laws.[18]
3. *Product liability laws.* Product liability, your company's liability for bodily injury or property damage caused by your products, will be discussed in Chapter 2. As noted in that chapter, product liability is no longer a US specialty but has spread to the EU and to the Pacific Rim, including Australia, China, the Philippines, and Japan. Describing product liability laws in Europe in an article entitled "Sue everywhere," *Forbes* magazine notes that "savvy companies are starting to realize they face a whole new continent of potential plaintiffs."[19] European legislation parallels the laws of the EU Member States in order to ensure a high level of consumer protection against damage caused to health or property by a defective product.[20]
4. *Environmental law, securities regulation,* and *anti-corruption law.* Environmental regulation and potential liability has spread throughout the world. Countries around the world have come to realize that fair and consistent regulation is necessary if companies are to have faith in the market and investors in securities transactions. Extraterritorial law is frequently also embedded in international conventions, such as the Organisation for Economic Co-operation and Development (OECD) Anti-Bribery Convention, in International Chamber of Commerce (ICC) Rules of Conduct, and in codes of conduct adopted by multinational companies.[21]

Procedural law, as noted previously, deals with the enforcement of substantive law. Historically, six features of the legal process distinguished the United States from the rest of the world. In recent years convergence has had an impact on these features in two ways. First, the impact of some features (see the first three items on the following list) has been diminished by law reform in the United States. Second, other features (the second half of the list) have been exported to other countries.

1. *Jury trials*. Unlike most countries in the world, the US still allows litigants the option of a jury trial in civil lawsuits. However, the right to jury trial has diminished as a result of a combination of factors, including an increase in the use of arbitration, requirements that judges hear certain types of cases, and dismissal of cases by judges before they reach a jury.
2. *Punitive damages*. The US is unusual in allowing plaintiffs to recover punitive damages when defendants have engaged in egregious behavior. Over the past several years, however, Supreme Court decisions and state legislation have limited punitive damages.
3. *Legal expenses*. Unlike other countries, which typically use a "loser pays" approach, in the US the winning party must pay most of its own legal costs. This traditional American rule is being eroded as new legislation in the US frequently provides that the loser must pay the winner's full legal costs.
4. *Contingency fees*. In the US, contingency fee agreements—whereby the payment to a lawyer is contingent on the outcome of the case—are legal. For example, if you agree to pay your attorney a 30 percent contingency fee and the jury awards you $10 million, the lawyer's fee is $3 million. If the jury decides that you are not entitled to damages, the attorney receives nothing (30 percent of 0). Other countries have joined the US in allowing contingency fees, including Canada, the United Kingdom, Japan, and China.
5. *Discovery*. Discovery is the process used by attorneys to locate evidence and witnesses for use at trial. For instance, the opposing lawyer has the right to search through your business records for evidence that might be relevant to the case. E-mail has been an especially fruitful source of evidence. In one case, after Atlantic Richfield Company (ARCO) sold its solar energy subsidiary to Siemens, ARCO employee e-mail messages such as the following were discovered: "We will attempt to finesse past Siemens the fact that we have had a great amount of trouble in successfully transitioning technology from the laboratory to the manufacturing floor." These e-mail messages contributed to a Siemens lawsuit requesting $146 million in damages.[22] In recent years, other countries have moved closer to US-style discovery. In Japan, for example, rules adopted in 1998 make it easier to obtain evidence from the opposing side.
6. *Class actions*. If your company illegally overcharges a customer $10 for your product, it is unlikely that the customer will bother filing suit for such a small amount of damages. But if the company overcharges a million customers, a lawsuit filed on behalf of these customers—called a class action—converts a $10 claim to a $10 million dollar lawsuit (or possibly $30 million if damages are trebled, as they might be in the US in this type of case). Critics of class actions claim that the real winners in class actions are attorneys, whose 30 percent contingency fee would net them millions of dollars. Their clients, on the other hand, would receive the price of lunch (70 percent of $10, or of $30 as a best case) *before* expenses were taken out of their share. Despite their controversial nature, class actions are now allowed in a number of other countries, including Australia, Canada, the United Kingdom, Sweden, Finland, China, and Japan.

We have examined several examples of the convergence of substantive and procedural law. It is said that a butterfly flapping its wings in the US can cause a typhoon in Asia. Similar to this "butterfly effect," convergence of the law causes a legal development in one country to change business practice elsewhere. Several years ago, for instance, an elderly woman sued McDonald's in the US after she was burned when she spilled her cup of McDonald's coffee. The woman was awarded close to $3 million, although she later settled the case for substantially less. After this case was resolved, one of the authors traveled to Argentina to address the national association of corporate lawyers. While in Buenos Aires, he visited a local McDonald's and purchased a cup of coffee. Printed in four places on the small cup in bright red letters were warnings that the coffee was hot: "PRECAUCION: CALIENTE!" These warnings were no doubt prompted by a legal decision in a country that, while far away in a geographic sense, has become much closer legally to the rest of the world.

DIFFICULTIES WITH THE "FIGHT" RESPONSE

Flight from legal concerns—through settlement of specific cases or movement of business operations to a supposedly friendlier legal environment—is often expensive and unrealistic in a global economy. The other option engrained into our genetic code is to stand and fight. There are two legal contexts for legal battles, each representing a different form of regulation of business: specific cases, in which court decisions represent a form of business regulation, and larger legislative and regulatory arenas in which law reform battles are fought.

The option of fighting specific cases has already been covered in discussing the settlement of cases. That discussion noted problems with litigating individual cases. Litigation costs are substantial, and a cost-benefit analysis can cause your company to settle even when you are confident that you would win at trial. And beyond the cost of settling individual cases, there is a risk that settlement will encourage future litigation.

This section will concentrate on the larger arenas in which the battle for law reform takes place. At first glance, law reform would seem to offer an opportunity to secure competitive advantage by lowering a company's legal costs. However, the outcome of law reform often benefits all companies, whether or not they invested their time and money in the reform effort.

Even when all companies in a particular industry contribute equally to law reform that benefits only their industry (in other words, when there are initially no "free riders"), the reform might provide little or no competitive advantage to your company. For instance, a reduction in environmental burdens might make the industry as a whole more profitable, but companies will not share equally in these profits. And the increased profitability of the industry may well attract new competition, "free riders" from the outside.

Efforts to improve the legal system are often noble and necessary to improve the national economy. Before your company invests resources in reform initiatives, however, you should carefully analyze the goal of law reform. If your goal is to serve a higher purpose, such as benefiting society, then your efforts might be justified. But if your goal is to increase your own competitive advantage, you should carefully answer the question: "What's in it for my company?"

In some cases a change in the law may provide your company with direct competitive advantage. For instance, time limits protecting intellectual property (IP) are sometimes extended in a way that protects specific products. In 1998, the life of copyrighted works was extended from 75 to 95 years, a change supported by Disney Corporation to protect its exclusive rights to Donald Duck and Mickey Mouse. Suddenly Disney competitors were playing on a different field. In the words of Wharton Professor G. Richard Shell: "There has been a lot of legislative maneuvering to gain competitive advantage. To use a football analogy, it's like making first and goal and suddenly finding they have lengthened the field by 30 yards."[23] But in other situations, where there are no specific benefits, it is easy for companies to become so enthusiastic about a cause that they overlook the fact that the benefits do not provide competitive advantage.

Thus all four conventional approaches to legal problems depicted in Figure 1.1 are flawed:

- Settling of specific cases can encourage future litigation.
- Ceasing or moving your company's operations is often unhelpful, given the global convergence of law.
- Fighting specific cases is often not cost-effective.
- Investing in law reform might benefit your industry or the country in general without creating competitive advantage for your company.

A Way to Meet the Challenges: the Proactive Approach

Traditionally, the steps in providing legal care have resembled those of medical care: diagnosis, treatment, and referral—all steps that happen after a client or a patient has a problem. Care has been *reactive*. You get sick, you seek treatment. You encounter a dispute, you turn to a lawyer. We need to move away from that model and, instead, adopt a *proactive* approach.

Being proactive is the opposite of being reactive or passive. The word proactive implies acting in anticipation, taking control, and self-initiation.[24] These elements are all part of the proactive approach to law (also known as *Proactive Law*), which includes two further aspects of proactivity: a *promotive* dimension (promoting what is desirable; encouraging good behavior) and a *preventive* dimension (preventing what is not desirable; keeping legal risks from materializing).

Traditionally, the focus in the legal field has been on the *past*. Legal research has been mainly concerned with *failures*—shortcomings, delays, and failures to comply with the law. The focus of the *proactive* approach is different; it is on the *future*. The approach is focused on *success* rather than failure. It is about taking the initiative to promote and strengthen factors that drive success.

The idea of proactivity in law—or legal foresight—is not new in itself. It has been known for years that the earlier a dispute or a potential dispute is addressed, the better the chances of a fair and prompt solution. Most contract lawyers and in-house counsel actually practice future-oriented law: they help clients to plan and structure transactions and manage risk.

In the context of practicing law, the idea of prevention was first introduced by Louis M. Brown, a US law professor and legal practitioner recognized as the "Father of Preventive Law." In an effort to help people minimize the risk of legal trouble and maximize legal benefits, he published the treatise *Preventive Law* in 1950, followed by numerous other books and articles on the topic.[25] In this treatise, he states a simple but profound truth that has not lost any of its value in more than 50 years: "It usually costs less to avoid getting into trouble than to pay for getting out of trouble."[26]

The approach specifically called *Proactive Law* emerged in Finland in the 1990s. Its origins are in *Proactive Contracting*.[27] Originally, the goal was to provide a framework for integrating legal foresight into the tangible practice of everyday business and to merge good contract, legal, project, quality and risk management practices with Preventive Law.[28] In response to a need to further develop practical methods and legal theories in this emerging field, the *Nordic School of Proactive Law* was established in 2004.[29] In 2009, the importance of the work of the Nordic School of Proactive Law was recognized in the EU, in the Opinion of the European Economic and Social Committee (EESC) on "The proactive law approach: a further step towards better regulation at EU level" published on July 28, 2009 in the *Official Journal of the European Union*.[30]

Both the preventive and promotive approaches to law have similarities with preventive medicine: a branch of medical science dealing with methods (such as vaccination) of preventing the occurrence of disease. Using the analogy of health care and preventive medicine, the *Proactive Law* approach can be said to combine aspects of health promotion with those of disease prevention: the goal is to help individuals and businesses stay in good "legal health" and avoid the "disease" of legal uncertainties, disputes, and litigation.

Today, a growing number of legal professionals—especially in-house counsel—have begun to adopt the *proactive* approach. They are concerned about how to promote better performance and sound business practices. They want to aid in the prevention and prompt resolution of issues that can adversely impact relationships. Whether working on their clients' sell-side or on the buy-side, they care about a commercially justifiable allocation of risks. In contracting, they seek to secure success through incentives for good performance and arrangements where rights, responsibilities, risks, and remedies are effectively identified and realistically assessed, shared, and managed.

In traditional *litigation*, it is essential for the lawyer to predict what *a court* will do. In *preventive* and *promotive law*, it is essential to predict what *people* will do. Here, the core is not about applying legal rules to facts that happened in the past, but about applying sound legal practices to create future facts and to plan a future course of conduct. As noted by Edward A. Dauer, a pioneer of Preventive Law: "Litigation law is mostly law. Preventive law is mostly facts. And the critical time for preventive lawyering is when those facts are first being born. As a lawyer speaking to business people, I would have one request of them: Please let us be involved in the making of those facts."[31]

The immediate purpose of preventing disputes is to reduce the staggering burden of wasted time and money caused by conflict, and to avoid the fracturing of carefully-created business relationships. At the same time, a proactive/preventive approach to law can produce the additional benefit of improving business efficiency and creating competitive advantage—provided that you, the manager, take the lead. As Wharton Professor G. Richard Shell states in his book *Make the Rules or Your Rivals Will*, you are the decision maker, as strategic decisions (for example, whether to sue or settle) are made by business leaders who see their legal options against a broad background of pricing, marketing, advertising, resource allocation, and production issues. While you need legal professionals, "[i]n conducting competitive legal strategy, you are the commander in chief."[32]

The Manager's Legal Plan™

Managers faced with myriad business concerns frequently take a reactive approach to the law. Given their reactive stance, it is not surprising that managers often view law as an obstacle rather than an enabler and that they tend to mentally separate the law from the issues that are considered more central to competitive advantage.

No wonder managers often feel incapable of creating a plan for dealing with legal matters. But every plan does not have to be great or flawless; even an imperfect plan can be better than nothing. Albert Szent-Gyorti, Nobel Laureate in medicine, tells the story of a military reconnaissance team that was lost in the Swiss Alps following a snowstorm. The soldiers had given up hope of returning to their main unit alive when one of them discovered a map in their equipment. Having the map calmed the soldiers and, with the sense of direction provided by the map, they found their main unit. Upon their return, they showed the map to their lieutenant, who discovered that it was a map of the Pyrenees, rather than the Alps.[33]

This story illustrates that a leader does not need a perfect legal or strategic plan to calm employees and get them moving in the right direction. When a manager is faced with a confusing situation, be it a rapidly changing legal environment or new forms of competition, simply having a plan is often enough to inspire action that can lead to positive results. As noted by Karl Weick of the Ross School of Business at the University of Michigan, one of the world's leading organizational theorists: "Followers are often lost and even the leader is not sure where to go. All the leaders know is that the plan or the map they have in front of them are not sufficient to get them out. What the leader has to do, when faced with this situation, is instill some confidence in people, get them moving in some general direction, and be sure they look closely at cues created by their actions so that they learn where they were and get some better idea of where they are and where they want to be."[34]

In today's business environment, skill at using legal tools for competitive advantage is a requirement—not an option—in business.[35] Taking informed action is better than the paralysis that can result when managers encounter legal aspects of business. In this spirit, the following four-step Manager's Legal Plan™ is intended to enable managers to move from a reactive approach to an ability to actively and proactively use the law to uncover and develop new forms of competitive advantage.

STEP ONE: UNDERSTAND THE LAW

This step starts with an interest in and a basic understanding of the legal dimensions of business. It goes beyond having legal resources available when an issue labeled "legal" arises. It involves recognizing the legal aspects of business, exercising informed judgment when managing them, and knowing when professional legal help is (and is not) required.

As discussed in later chapters, an obvious reason for this broader perspective is to prevent future litigation and to promote your company's legal health. Beyond this goal, the broader view is essential to your career growth. As you move higher in the organization you will increasingly face business decisions that have legal implications. You will also discuss legal matters with a variety of parties, including customers, suppliers, employees, government officials, the media, shareholders, the board of directors, and creditors.

According to Ben Heineman, Senior Vice President of General Electric, "People who lead corporations need to have an appreciation for the whole public side of their job as they go higher and higher up the ladder. Law [is] a significant part of any corporate entity's life."[36] A former CEO of General Motors reputedly put it more bluntly: "My lawyer and I go steady."

The fields of law you will need to understand will of course depend on your company and your industry. In highly regulated industries you will need to master the core regulations that have an impact on your business. Depending on your industry, you may benefit greatly from learning about IP, such as patents, copyrights, trademarks, or semiconductor chip protection, which you might use to obtain a legal monopoly for your company's products or services, fend off rivals, and earn royalties. In manufacturing, you may want to learn about sales and warranty laws and how you can pass on obligations to your suppliers.

Understanding the law and acquiring legal capabilities involve both gaining your own legal knowledge and learning how to manage and work with legal professionals. One of your most important resources is a lawyer who has the ability to guide and coach you. A survey of CEOs by the Association of Corporate Counsel (ACC) concluded that the most important role of a corporate attorney is that of an educator on legal issues.[37] The study of business law is also an important facet of a manager's formal education. In some countries, including the US, the legal environment of business is a key component of undergraduate, MBA, and executive education. In other countries, the importance of understanding business law is highlighted by the fact that legal education is a popular alternative to a business education for students who intend to become managers.

STEP TWO: KNOW HOW TO COPE WITH LEGAL PROBLEMS AND LEARN FROM THEM

If you do face a legal problem, you have the choices of "fight or flight": fighting or settling cases, ceasing or moving operations, or possibly seeking legal reforms as summarized in Figure 1.1. While resort to one of these solutions is often inevitable, you should keep in mind their limitations in the global economy, as described earlier in this chapter. Once you have resolved your legal problems, you do not want to leave it at that: the third step in the Manager's Legal Plan™ reminds you that you will want to learn from your experience for the future.

If you are fortunate enough not to face legal problems yourself, you can still learn from problems encountered by others and use those learnings for the next step. There are many cases and examples that are highly educational as you, for example, develop and implement your strategic marketing plans.

STEP THREE: DEVELOP BUSINESS STRATEGIES AND SOLUTIONS TO PREVENT FUTURE PROBLEMS

The third step in the Manager's Legal Plan™ goes beyond the traditional approaches by searching for business strategies and solutions to prevent legal problems. From a business perspective, many disputes should be settled rather than litigated at Step Two and, better still, they should be resolved before they become legal disputes. But best of all, they should be prevented. Often, it is possible to plan on three different levels of prevention *before* things go wrong: first, how to prevent the cause from arising; second, how to prevent the cause from doing harm; and, third, if harm occurs, how to limit the damage.

The third step in the Manager's Legal Plan™ prompts you to apply sound business judgment when faced with legal decisions. Even when addressing a litigation decision, you do not want to become so focused on the legal issues that you forget to use a financial analysis that includes calculation of net present value and opportunity costs in making settlement decisions. But Step Three goes beyond applying business tools to litigation. For example, a manager confronted with wrongful discharge litigation should take actions that move beyond the narrow decision to settle or fight. You should review the company's hiring practices, revise company documents, and provide employees with training that will prevent them from making statements that could result in liability.

STEP FOUR: CLIMB TO THE BALCONY TO SEE THE BIG PICTURE AND BECOME MORE PROACTIVE

It may be tempting to conclude the Manager's Legal Plan™ at Step Three. After all, once you have completed the three steps, you have a broad understanding of the law, you know how to cope with and learn from legal problems, and you have applied best business practices in an attempt to resolve legal problems and prevent them from reoccurring.

However, one step remains, beginning with the following questions: Are you framing the situation correctly? Do you see the big picture? Mental frames that help us simplify and organize the complexity in our world are necessary for rational decision making. But simplification often comes at a cost. In viewing the world through a particular window, such as the window provided by a legal problem, we see only part of the landscape. In narrowing the scope of our vision, we risk what decision researchers call frame blindness, which is similar to the blind spot in a car's rearview mirror. By failing to take into account the entire picture when making decisions, we often overlook the best options.[38]

Your challenge as a manager, when dealing with a problem that appears to relate narrowly to a particular function—whether law or marketing or finance or manufacturing—is to step back from the details of the problem in an attempt to broaden the frame. This book will provide numerous examples of the art of reframing issues and seeing things in a new light.

In his book *Getting Past No*, author William Ury uses the phrase "going to the balcony" as a metaphor for the mental detachment that is necessary when you are attacked or rebuffed by the other side during a negotiation.[39] In your role as a manager, a trip to the balcony can give you a broader perspective of the entire playing field without the blind spots that hinder your decision making when you are closer to the action. This broader perspective may enable you to reframe what you originally thought was a legal problem as a business opportunity. Or it may enable you to reframe the way in which you approach your next new deal or contract. This, in turn, will allow you to generate new options for discovering new value with and for your customers to gain competitive advantage. Though you may be unable to reframe every legal problem that you face, the attempt should at least encourage you and others in your organization to think about where you are and where you want to be.

This step starts with changing the belief that "the law" relates only to legal problems or someone threatening to sue, leading you from being reactive to becoming proactive. This step encourages you to focus not only on preventing what is not desirable, such as future legal problems and their causes, but also on promoting what is desirable to enhance future opportunities.

The law and your contracts have the ability to help you strengthen your customer relationships and protect your commercial transactions. They help you define property rights and allow you to seize strategic control of innovations. All of these are critical to your ability to create and capture value and to your success in the market. From Coca-Cola's secret formula to Nike's Swoosh, hundreds of billions of dollars hinge on the legal strategies used to protect and exploit IP.[40] As much if not more is likely to hinge on the relational capital and intangible assets embedded in contracts.

Law is perhaps the most hidden of all competitive strategy tools.[41] It is sometimes complex, and not all managers like to deal with it—or with lawyers. The Manager's Legal Plan™ is designed so that you as a manager will not fall into the trap of neglecting law as a competitive tool. By using the Manager's Legal Plan™ along with deal maps, decision trees, and other visualization tools, you may see alternatives, connections, and potential rewards—or gaps and potential risks—that you didn't know existed, and can act accordingly. By incorporating legal issues into the normal strategic and operational aspects of your business you can reframe issues and find new sources of innovative solutions and new competitive advantage.

How this Book is Organized

The chapters that follow will apply the four steps of the Manager's Legal Plan™ to issues that relate to various stakeholders—parties with an interest in your company. In creating value for the owners of your company, the shareholders, you must manage relationships with a variety of other stakeholders in a cost-effective manner. Especially important among them are your customers, your suppliers, your employees, and society at large, represented by government. The Manager's Legal Plan™ will be used to explore the most controversial legal problems relating to these stakeholders.

Chapter 2 will focus on product liability, as well as hidden new product opportunities represented by this type of litigation. Chapter 3 will show how the Manager's Legal Plan™ enables you to secure access to key talent (employees and others) while avoiding employment pitfalls. Chapter 4 will deal with government and use examples of environmental regulations to show how these can create opportunities for competitive advantage. Chapter 5 will focus on the important role intangible assets and IP play in your business and how you can use these to seize strategic control of innovations and sustainable strategic advantage. Chapter 6 deals with contracts and contracting, showing their profound impact on business success and how you as a manager can design your contracts and contracting processes so that they promote business success and prevent problems.

Each of these chapters will offer concrete examples of ways in which the Manager's Legal Plan™ can generate opportunities for competitive advantage.

Beyond the issues covered in Chapters 2 through 6, several generic matters apply to a wide variety of legal aspects of business. For instance, given the importance of the law to business success, how can you ensure that you have the best legal resources and that you are maximizing the value of your legal talent? What tools are available for you to control and resolve disputes and how can you use systems design to best apply these tools? And how can your use of the law to achieve competitive advantage encourage ethical decision making within your company? These questions will be addressed in Chapter 7.

Chapter Summary

Law plays an important role in achieving competitive advantage. For example, law allows companies to seize strategic control of innovations and gain a legal monopoly through intellectual property rights (IPR). Law allows companies to "make their own laws" through their contracts in business-to-business relationships, and enforces those contracts. However, many managers do not actively think about the law until faced with a lawsuit or a legal problem. The conventional, reactive approaches to the law do not allow managers to make best use of the law to gain competitive advantage.

Given drawbacks with conventional approaches to the law, a new approach is necessary to maximize the use of law to gain competitive advantage. This new approach, based on *Proactive Law*, is embedded in the Manager's Legal Plan™, which involves the following four-step process:

Step One: Understand the law.

Step Two: Know how to cope with legal problems and learn from them.

Step Three: Develop business strategies and solutions to prevent future problems.

Step Four: Climb to the balcony to see the big picture and become more proactive.

The Manager's Legal Plan™ is about changing the belief that "the law" relates only to legal problems or someone threatening to sue. It helps you reframe legal concerns and find new business opportunities. The chapters that follow will provide specific examples of how this plan can be used to achieve sustainable competitive advantage.

Notes

1 PricewaterhouseCoopers 2009. *12th Annual Global CEO Survey. Redefining Success—Future Proof Plans* [Online]. Available at: http://www.pwc.ch/user_content/editor/files/publ_corp/pwc_12th_annual_global_ceo_survey_e.pdf [accessed: August 1, 2010].

2 Figure 3.1.2.1 in PricewaterhouseCoopers 2009, 24.

3 PricewaterhouseCoopers 2009, 10.

4 PricewaterhouseCoopers 2009, 24.

5 Cavenagh, T.D. 2000. *Business Dispute Resolution*. Cincinnati, OH: West Legal Studies in Business, 84.

6 Siedel, G.J. 2000. Six forces and the legal environment of business: The relative value of business law among business school core courses. *American Business Law Journal*, 37(4), 727.

7 Shell, G.R. 2004. *Make the Rules or Your Rivals Will*. New York, NY: Crown Business, 9. See also Bird, R.C. 2008–2009. Pathways of legal strategy. *Stanford Journal of Law, Business & Finance*, 14(1). Also available at: http://www.allbusiness.com/company-activities-management/company-strategy/13483188-1.html [accessed: August 1, 2010]. Bird proposes that there are five pathways that firms pursue when interacting with their legal environment, arguing that some firms treat laws as just a nuisance to be ignored, while others implement prevention programs to avoid litigation. Only a few firms, according to Bird, apply a genuine legal strategy to capture value in the marketplace.

8 Siedel 2000, 728.

9 Porter, M. 2004. *Competitive Advantage: Creating and Sustaining Superior Performance*. New York, NY: First Free Press Export Edition, 3.

10 Porter 2004, 3.

11 Dyer, J.H. 1996. Specialized supplier networks as a source of competitive advantage: Evidence from the auto industry. *Strategic Management Journal,* 17(4), 271–92.; Dyer, J.H. and Singh, H. 1998. The relational view: Cooperative strategy and sources of interorganizational competitive advantage. *Academy of Management Review*, 23(4), 660–79.

12 Gasparino, C. 2001. Merrill is paying in wake of analysts' call on tech stock. *Wall Street Journal*, July 20, C1.

13 *Judas Priest v. Second Judicial District* [1988] 760 P.2d 137.

14 1989. No, California, there is no Santa. *Economist*, May 13, 33.

15 See http://www.cisg.law.pace.edu.

16 In July 2010 the European Commission published a Green Paper outlining seven kinds of new systems the EU could adopt. The options range from the publishing of suggested model contracts to an EU-wide law replacing all national contract laws. See Green Paper from the Commission on policy options for progress towards a European Contract Law for consumers and businesses, http://ec.europa.eu/justice_home/news/consulting_public/0052/consultation_questionaire_en.pdf [accessed: August 1, 2010].

17 See http://webh01.ua.ac.be/storme/PECLre.html and http://frontpage.cbs.dk/law/commission_on_european_contract_law [accessed: August 1, 2010].

18 The Rome I Regulation, which applies to contracts concluded after December 17, 2009, replaced the Convention on the Law Applicable to Contractual Obligations (Rome Convention). See http://eur-lex.europa.eu/LexUriServ/LexUriServ.do?uri=OJ:L:2008:177:0006:0016:EN:PDF [accessed: August 1, 2010].

19 Ebeling, A. 2000. Sue everywhere. *Forbes*, October 16, 128.

20 See http://europa.eu/legislation_summaries/consumers/consumer_safety/l32012_en.htm [accessed: August 1, 2010].

21 Further examples of the convergence of laws include competition (or antitrust) laws and laws against sexual harassment. Many laws, such as laws protecting employees or commercial representatives, contain mandatory provisions that have extraterritorial reach. Some laws, such as EU competition rules, apply to non-EU companies acting inside the EU and even when acting outside the EU, when their conduct has an impact on EU trade.

22 Patrick, M.J. 1993. E-mail data is a ticking time bomb. *National Law Journal*, December 20, 14.

23 2001. Are efforts to extend patent and copyright laws good for business or good for society? *Knowledge@Wharton*, June 20 [Online]. Available at: http://knowledge.wharton.upenn.edu/article.cfm?articleid=378 [accessed: August 1, 2010].

24 Dictionary definitions of the word *proactive* highlight two key elements: an *anticipatory* element, involving acting in advance of a future situation, such as "acting in anticipation of future problems, needs, or changes" (proactive. 2009a. *Merriam-Webster Online* Dictionary [Online]. Available at: http://www.merriam-webster.com/dictionary/proactive [accessed: August 1, 2010]), and an element of *taking control* and *causing change*, for example: "controlling a situation by causing something to happen rather than waiting to respond to it after it happens" (proactive. 2009b. *WordNet® 3.0*. Princeton University [Online]. Available at: http://wordnetweb.princeton.edu/perl/webwn?s=proactive [accessed: August 1, 2010]).

25 See, for example Brown, L.M. 1950. *Preventive Law.* New York, NY: Prentice-Hall, Inc., 3. Also published under the title of *Manual of Preventive Law*, New York, NY: Prentice-Hall, Inc., 1950.

See also Brown, L.M. 1955. *How to Negotiate a Successful Contract*. Englewood Cliffs, NJ: Prentice-Hall, Inc.; Brown, L.M. 1972. *Planning by Lawyers: An Introductory Course in the Practice of Preventive Law*. Fourth Temporary Edition. University of Southern California Law Center; and Brown, L.M. 1986. *Lawyering through Life. The Origin of Preventive Law*. Littleton, CO: Fred B. Rothman & Co.

26 Brown 1950, 3. Louis M. Brown's legacy is carried on through the Louis M. Brown Program in Preventive Law and the National Center for Preventive Law (NCPL) at the California Western School of Law in San Diego. The NCPL is dedicated to preventing legal risks from becoming legal problems and acts as a clearinghouse for information and as a network for those interested in the theory of Preventive Law, or how it applies to particular areas of practice or the courts. See http://www.preventivelawyer.org.

27 For Proactive Contracting and related resources, see Chapter 6. In recent years, legal scholars in the US and Europe have explored the role of law as a positive force within companies. At the time when the Proactive Law movement developed in Europe, the focus in the US has been on law as a source of competitive advantage. For an overview of the history of these parallel developments and their intersections, see Siedel, G.J. and Haapio, H. 2010 (in press). Using Proactive Law for competitive advantage. *American Business Law Journal*, 47(4), Winter, Special Issue "Law as a Source of Strategic Advantage." Available as Working Paper at: http://ssrn.com/abstract=1664561. The Special Issue of the *American Business Law Journal* in which this article is published contains several articles illustrating ways in which the law can create value and strategic advantage.

28 The proactive approach to law builds on the preventive focus of Louis M. Brown and Edward A. Dauer and the work of Thomas D. Barton, who added a new emphasis on legal problem solving, the environments in which problems arise, and the need for lawyers to think preventively and proactively. See Barton, T.D. 2009. *Preventive Law and Problem Solving. Lawyering for the Future.* Lake Mary, FL: Vandeplas Publishing. In the fall of 2000, a group of practitioners and academics gathered at California Western School of Law to discuss the traditions and new directions of Preventive Law. For the early steps of building a bridge between the US and Nordic approaches, see, for example, Rudanko, M. 2000. *Preventive Law and International Trade*. Preventive Law Symposium, San Diego, CA, November 10–11, 2000, National Center for Preventive Law, California Western School of Law [Online]. Available at: http://www.preventivelawyer.org/main/default.asp?pid=essays/rudanko.htm [accessed: August 1, 2010].

29 See http://www.proactivelaw.org. Among the publications following conferences organized by the Nordic School are three English language books, Wahlgren, P. and Magnusson Sjöberg, C. (eds) 2006. *A Proactive Approach*. Scandinavian Studies in Law, Volume 49. Stockholm: Stockholm Institute for Scandinavian Law; Nystén-Haarala, S. (ed.) 2008. *Corporate Contracting Capabilities. Conference Proceedings and Other Writings*. Joensuu, University of Joensuu Publications in Law, No 21; and Haapio, H. (ed.) 2008. *A Proactive Approach to Contracting and Law*. Turku: International Association for Contract and Commercial Management & Turku University of Applied Sciences. Some of the early work of the Nordic School is available in Finnish or Swedish only. These include two books edited by Soile Pohjonen: *Ennakoiva sopiminen—liiketoimien suunnittelu, toteuttaminen ja riskien hallinta*. [Proactive Contracting—Planning, Implementing and Managing Risk in Business Transactions.] Helsinki: WSOY Lakitieto, 2002, and *Ex ante—ennakoiva oikeus*. [Ex ante—Proactive Law] Helsinki: Talentum Media Oy, 2005.

30 European Economic and Social Committee (EESC) 2009. Opinion of the European Economic and Social Committee on "The proactive law approach: a further step towards better regulation at EU level", 2009/C 175/05. *Official Journal of the European Union* C175, vol. 52, July 28, 26 [Online]. Available at: http://eur-lex.europa.eu/LexUriServ/LexUriServ.do?uri=OJ:C:2009:175:0026:0033:

EN:PDF [accessed: August 1, 2010]. Available in all official EU languages. The Section for the Single Market, Production and Consumption, under the leadership of Mr Jorge Pegado Liz, was responsible for preparing EESC's work on the topic, and author Helena Haapio acted as Expert in this work.

31 Dauer, E.A. 1988. Corporate legal health: Preventive Law dictates going to root causes to prevent claims from arising. *Preventive Law Reporter*, September.

32 Shell 2004, 20.

33 Weick, K.E. 1995. *Sensemaking in Organizations*. Thousand Oaks, CA: Sage, 54–5.

34 Weick 1995, 55.

35 Shell 2004, 19.

36 Benjamin W. Heineman Jr., 1994. *ACCA Docket*, Fall, 26.

37 American Corporate Counsel Association, 2001. *In-House Counsel for the 21st Century*. September 7 [Online]. Available at: http://www2.acc.com/Surveys/CEO/ [accessed: January 31, 2010].

38 Russo, J.E. and Schoemaker, P.J.H. 1990. *Decision Traps*. New York, NY: Fireside, Chapters 3 and 4.

39 Ury, W. 1993. *Getting Past No*. New York, NY: Bantam Books, 38.

40 Shell 2004, 22.

41 Shell 2004, 9.

CHAPTER 2 Meet Your Customer Needs: Move from Product Liability to Product Innovation

Chapter 1 explored the increasing importance of law in a global economy. The chapter also described a four-step process, the Manager's Legal Plan™, that enables you to use the law to seize competitive advantage for your company. This and the next four chapters apply this process to several critically important business issues that affect important stakeholders in your company. This chapter looks at your customers, key stakeholders without whom you could not be in business.

There are many aspects to your relationship with your customers and your ability to meet (or exceed) their needs. As stated in Chapter 1, creating value for your customers—and, in many cases, co-creating value with them—is central to your ability to seize competitive advantage. The importance of value creation is obvious and has received considerable management attention. In Chapter 6, we will look at ways in which you can use your contracts and contracting processes to define and shape your customer relationships for competitive advantage. This chapter will focus instead on a less likely source of competitive advantage relating to customers: product liability. In following the Manager's Legal Plan™, the chapter will show how product liability concerns can be reframed as opportunities to meet customer needs through new product development (NPD).

The Impact of Product Liability

Product liability is an especially controversial topic because its impact spreads beyond companies to consumers and society.

IMPACT OF PRODUCT LIABILITY ON COMPANIES

Product liability as we know it today is the result of changes in the law over at least four decades. These changes have left in their wake the bankruptcy of a large number of companies, including many industrial giants such as Johns Manville Corporation, A. H. Robins Co., and Dow Corning Corp. In addition to Johns Manville Corporation, several other companies have declared bankruptcy as a result of asbestos claims, including Owens Corning, Babcock and Wilcox, and Armstrong World Industries.

Product liability is often front-page news, as companies manufacturing tires, breast implants, tobacco, and a wide variety of other products face lawsuits where claims can exceed a hundred billion dollars. Less well publicized is the impact of product liability on smaller companies that are forced out of business because they cannot compete effectively while paying high product liability insurance premiums. Few people know about Havir Manufacturing, a small punch press manufacturer that was based in St. Paul, Minnesota. Havir was doing fine until, in one year, its product liability insurance premium jumped 1,900 percent, which equaled 10 percent of the company's sales. The company could not afford to stay in business. As a result, the company auctioned off its equipment and laid off its workers.[1]

For companies that survive, product liability costs can be oppressive. Acmat Corporation, which was in the asbestos removal business, saw its insurance premium jump in one year from $300,000 to $10 million, while its coverage dropped from $10 million to $6 million. The firm bought the insurance, which was essential to enable it to bid on public jobs.[2]

Product liability has an impact on companies outside the US as well. Companies that export products to the US have learned to face liability—and increasing insurance premiums—just like their US counterparts. Some have been unable to purchase coverage for US exports and have decided to withdraw from such exports.

However, as discussed later in this chapter, US-style product liability law has also moved to other parts of the world. For example, Europe's movement towards strict liability (as opposed to one based on fault) began in the 1970s,[3] and in 1985 the European Economic Community (EEC) adopted the Product Liability Directive,[4] which the Member States were required to implement by July 30, 1988. This Directive is part of a broader system involving, for instance, product safety laws and standards, workplace safety laws, and consumer protection laws, which all have an impact on both companies and consumers. As a result, the European system is committed more to *regulation* than to *litigation* as a means of promoting product safety.[5]

IMPACT OF PRODUCT LIABILITY ON CONSUMERS

From a consumer perspective, product liability is seen as a necessary form of protection to force companies to act responsibly in manufacturing and selling products. This consumer perspective causes managers to wear two hats. In your role as *manager*, you are concerned about the impact of product liability on your company. But as a *consumer*, you want safe products for yourself, your family, and friends.

The two hats are illustrated by a case in Texas. A 42-year-old attorney who specialized in defending companies in product liability cases went hunting with two judges and his 16-year-old son. After the hunt, the son entered the car holding a high-powered Remington® rifle. One of the judges suggested that he unload the gun. The son released the safety catch, which was necessary to unload the rifle. The gun fired, wounding the father and leaving him paralyzed from the waist down. The father proceeded to sue Remington, claiming that it should not be necessary to release the safety catch to unload a rifle. The company settled by paying him $6.8 million.[6]

IMPACT OF PRODUCT LIABILITY ON SOCIETY

Beyond the impact of product liability on individual companies and consumers is the concern that product liability might inhibit innovation and NPD. For example, on the basis of responses from CEOs of 264 companies, a Conference Board study concluded that 47 percent had discontinued product lines and 39 percent had decided not to introduce new products because of product liability. Over 40 percent of the CEOs indicated that product liability has had a major impact on their ability to compete.[7]

An article in the *Economist* refers to product liability as an innovation tax that "dissuades companies from selling their wares in America, prompts them to withdraw safe and effective products, and may even stop research altogether."[8] The American law of products liability has also been described as a "high jackpot lottery" "where some plaintiffs (and their lawyers) have reaped huge rewards, but where the costs of complying with an uncertain, and, in some cases, biased law, have unfairly impacted most Americans."[9]

The innovation tax outside the US has historically been lower because of barriers to excessive litigation, such as the following:

- absence of contingent fees;
- loser pays winner's attorney fees;
- discouragement of massive discovery filings;
- lower damage judgments;
- absence of punitive damages;
- non-use of juries in civil cases;
- lower expectations of damages.[10]

These barriers resulted in a competitive disadvantage for US firms relative to manufacturers that did not export their products to the US. For example, Dow Chemical Corporation at one time estimated that it spent *100 times* as much on litigation costs in the US as opposed to Europe.[11]

However, as noted in Chapter 1, several features of US law are now being adopted in other countries, including contingency fees and class actions. This convergence of the law, coupled with the globalization of business, has resulted in headlines like this one from the *Financial Times*: "ABB on verge of collapse as shares reach record low." The article noted that ABB's problems stemmed from product liability losses.[12] As noted by Lord Peter Levene, Chairman of Lloyd's of London, in commenting on the impact of Korea's movement toward US-style product liability: "Happily, Korea has not developed a compensation culture like the one that is causing so much grief for businesses in the US. The fact remains, however, that in the increasingly globalized world, companies do not operate in a vacuum."[13]

Apply the Manager's Legal Plan™ to Product Liability

Product liability is clearly a controversial topic with broad impact. As a manager, you should keep in mind that product liability is not targeted only toward your company; the law applies to your competitors as well. The companies that best manage product liability risks will have a better opportunity to reduce costs and position themselves to develop superior products. The four-step Manager's Legal Plan™ introduced in Chapter 1 illustrates how you can compete effectively by minimizing product liability risk and how you can reframe product liability concerns as new business opportunities.

STEP ONE: UNDERSTAND THE LEGAL ELEMENTS OF PRODUCT LIABILITY

Your CEO has just called you with a message that will change your life for several months or years and perhaps have a permanent impact on your career: "One of our US customers has just filed a product liability lawsuit against us." A more chilling version of this message is: "Our customers have filed a product liability class action against the company."

Your first step—something that you will probably do instinctively—is to discuss the case with an attorney. During this conversation, you will want to proceed directly to the bottom-line questions: What is the customer's version of the story? How much does the customer claim in damages? How does the legal system work? What are our chances of winning the case? What would it take to settle? Do we have insurance coverage—and what does it take to benefit from it?

These are all important questions and, in a world where your time is limited, it is tempting to go no further in the conversation with your lawyer. To use the law to seize competitive advantage, however, you must dig deeper. Specifically, you should ask the lawyer to describe the legal basis for the customer's claim. The explanation does not have to be deeply theoretical or technical. The attorney should be able to describe the law in business terms rather than legal terms. Through an understanding of the law, you will have a foundation for proceeding to the next steps: reacting to and resolving the case, learning from it, developing business strategies and solutions to prevent future legal problems, and reframing the legal problem as a business opportunity for competitive advantage.

If you operate predominantly outside the US, the exercise of learning about the legal elements of product liability might take you in a different direction. For instance in Europe, the Product Liability Directive cannot be viewed in isolation from European versions of product and workplace safety laws, harmonized standards, and consumer protection laws—as well as contract, sales, and tort laws. The requirements set by these other laws and standards can have a greater impact on your products and operations in the European Union (EU) than the European product liability laws themselves.

Some requirements are highly technical—and constantly subject to change. For example, if you are involved in machine manufacturing or supply in the EU, you need to make sure that your product designers and other personnel are familiar and know how to comply with the existing requirements related to CE marking,[14] including the declaration of conformity, technical construction file, and the applicable standards. The Machinery Directive[15] further requires, for instance, that the manufacturer of machinery must ensure that a risk assessment is carried out in order to determine the health and safety requirements that apply to the machinery. The machinery must then be designed and constructed taking into account the results of the risk assessment.[16]

Beyond the details of regulation, in general terms "product liability" is an umbrella term that covers liability for damage or injuries caused by three main types of defects: design defects, manufacturing defects, and marketing defects.[17] A plaintiff in a product liability case might assert any one or any combination of these claims, depicted in Figure 2.1, in one case.

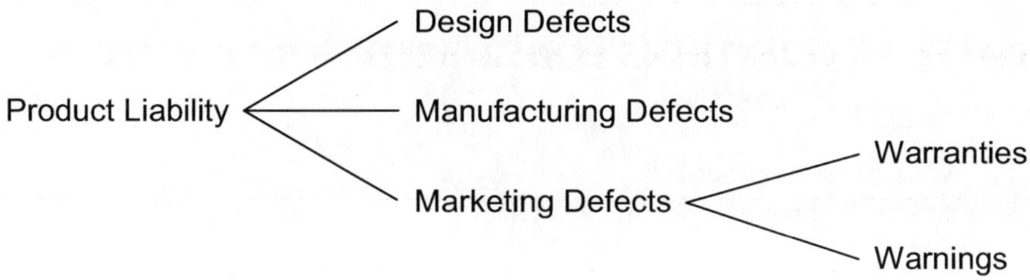

Figure 2.1 Causes of product liability

Design defects

Your company is responsible for damage or injuries resulting from defective product design. Your duties in designing a product are governed by reasonableness: Is the design reasonable given your customers' foreseeable uses of the product? Even in the US, courts recognize that requiring your company to develop a perfectly safe product is often unrealistic. For example, automakers have the ability to design cars that would virtually eliminate personal injuries in automobile accidents. But these cars would probably look like army tanks and would be inefficient (with mileage measured in gallons to the mile rather than miles to the gallon), unattractive, prohibitively expensive, and slow. In short, no one would buy them.

As a result, most courts have adopted a balancing test that considers, on one hand, the risks associated with a product and on the other the benefits (or utility) of the product. The test was summarized by the Supreme Court of Georgia in a case involving a nine-year-old child who died after eating rat poison.[18] The poison did not contain a bitter element that would deter consumption by humans or cause them to vomit if the poison were swallowed by mistake.

The court first noted that the case involved a design—rather than a manufacturing or marketing—defect. The court then observed that a risk-utility analysis represents the "overwhelming consensus" on the law of defective design: "This risk-utility analysis incorporates the concept of "reasonableness," that is, whether the manufacturer acted reasonably in choosing a particular product design, given the probability and seriousness of the risk posed by the design, the usefulness of the product in that condition, and the burden on the manufacturer to take the necessary steps to eliminate the risk."

After reviewing numerous sources, the court developed a list of general factors that are considered in a risk-utility analysis. These factors are presented in question format in Exhibit 2.1. Because these factors were not considered in the original trial (where the parents had prevailed), the Supreme Court of Georgia decided that a new trial was necessary.

EXHIBIT 2.1 QUESTIONS CONSIDERED IN RISK-UTILITY ANALYSIS[19]

1. How useful is the product?
2. Does the design create serious dangers?
3. Is injury likely?
4. Is the danger avoidable?
5. Does the customer have an ability to avoid the danger?
6. What is the state of the art (at time of manufacture)?
7. Can the danger be eliminated without impairing the utility of the product or making it prohibitively expensive?
8. Can the losses sustained by injured customers be spread through higher prices or insurance?
9. Are alternative designs feasible, taking into account cost and adverse effects of the alternative?
10. What are the benefits of the product—for example, appearance, attractiveness, usefulness for multiple purposes, and convenience?

Manufacturing defects

Manufacturers, like other defendants, are liable for carelessness (in legal terms, negligence) that results in injury to others. But over the last half of the twentieth century, American courts crafted an additional theory of liability—called strict liability—that makes it much easier for an injured consumer to win a case against a manufacturer. Under this theory, businesses that sell defective products that injure consumers are liable even though they exercise "all possible care" in preparing and selling the product. In other words, the consumer no longer has to prove that the manufacturer was negligent and the manufacturer can no longer successfully defend a lawsuit by asserting that it exercised all care humanly possible in producing the product.

Why would courts turn the business world upside down by fashioning this rule of strict liability? Within the business community there is a feeling that the law is based on the ability of businesses to pay damage awards because they have "deep pockets." Judges and legal scholars, however, claim that the law is designed to shift losses from one person (the injured consumer) to society in general. This loss-shifting occurs when manufacturers raise prices after incurring product liability costs. As one scholar observed: "[Strict liability] is not a 'deep pocket' theory but rather a 'risk-bearing economic' theory. The assumption is that the manufacturer can shift the costs of accidents to purchasers for use by charging higher prices for the costs of products."[20]

The cost-shifting aspect of product liability is illustrated by a case involving a high school student who was paralyzed after his spinal cord was severed while he was playing football. His lawsuit against the helmet manufacturer, Riddell, resulted in a judgment of $5.3 million. Riddell's insurance company proceeded to raise the company's annual product liability insurance premiums from $40,000 to $1.5 million. Riddell responded by raising the price of helmets over the next few years by 33 percent, virtually all of which was attributed to product liability costs.[21]

Football teams faced with higher helmet prices undoubtedly raised the price of tickets and advertising so that ultimately the cost fell on consumers. In other words, the cost of the accident was spread among a large number of consumers rather than falling entirely on the player and his family.

One problem with the legal theory in the real world of business is that many companies, unable to raise prices enough to reflect product liability costs, are forced out of business. At one time 20 companies manufactured football helmets, most of which have since been forced out of business.[22]

Another problem with the theory is that a hidden tax is imposed on consumers. According to an article in *Forbes*, this product liability tax "is levied on virtually everything we buy, sell, and use. This tax costs American companies, individuals and local governments at least $80 billion a year, and some estimate as much as $300 billion. It accounts for 30 percent of the price of a stepladder and for over 95 percent of the price of childhood vaccines."[23] Another source estimates that litigation adds 2.5 percent to the cost of a new product.[24] A friend of one of the authors who purchased a $75 football helmet for his son in junior high school reported that a sticker on the helmet noted that $25 of the price went toward product liability costs—a 50 percent tax!

The use of strict liability theory in product liability cases has spread to countries outside the US, although with variations. The products and damage covered, the limitation periods and other details differ from country to country, and so do the defenses available to defendants. These will be discussed in Step Two.

Marketing defects

While the details vary from one jurisdiction to another, generally speaking two types of marketing defects can lead to product liability. As depicted in Figure 2.2, liability can result either from express or implied warranties that you provide to your customers or from your failure to warn customers of hidden dangers associated with the product.[25]

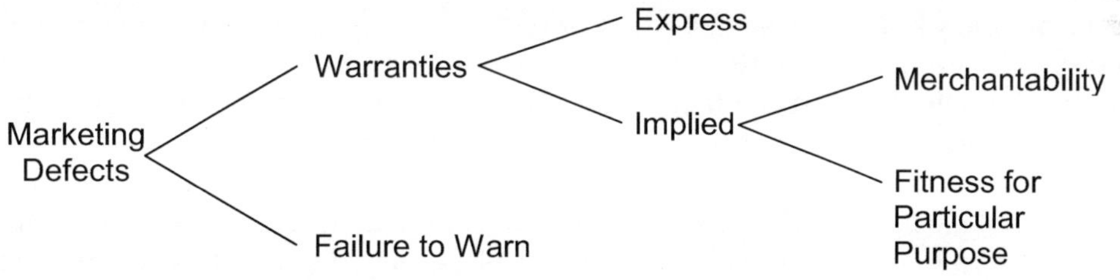

Figure 2.2 Marketing defects

Warranties. Your warranty liability is based on statements—called *express warranties*—that you make to consumers. When you state a fact, make a promise, or describe your product, you give express warranties. The information that you provide does not have to be distributed with the product and does not have to use the word *warranty* to create liability.

For example, an advertisement can create an express warranty. At one time cigarette companies emphasized the safety of smoking with advertisements like those in Exhibit 2.2.

The US Supreme Court has ruled that smokers can sue tobacco companies because, through these advertisements, cigarette companies gave express warranties that cigarettes are safe.[26]

EXHIBIT 2.2 TOBACCO ADVERTISEMENTS[27]

"PLAY SAFE Smoke Chesterfield"

"NOSE, THROAT, and Accessory Organs Not Adversely Affected by Smoking Chesterfields"

"[Chesterfields are] *entirely safe for the mouth*"

"CHESTERFIELD FIRST TO GIVE YOU SCIENTIFIC FACTS IN SUPPORT OF SMOKING"

"[L & M filters are] just what the doctor ordered"

Even when your company does not give express warranties, US law automatically gives purchasers two warranties, called *implied warranties*.[28] These warranties apply unless expressly excluded by contract. Chapter 6 will cover in more detail strategies that you can and cannot use through your contracts.

One of these implied warranties is the warranty of merchantability. With this warranty, your company promises to the purchaser that your products are of average quality and fit for ordinary purposes. For example, a customer sued Goodyear Tire & Rubber, claiming that the company sold faulty rubber hosing that was used to build heating systems in the floors of houses. According to an article in the *Wall Street Journal*, a jury decided that "Goodyear didn't breach its 'implied warranty of merchantability'." In other words, the hosing was of average quality and fit for ordinary purposes (in this case, fit for use in heating systems).[29]

The second implied warranty is the warranty of fitness for a particular purpose. Your company is assumed to give this warranty in situations where you know that the buyer needs your product for a particular purpose and that the buyer is relying on your skill and judgment in providing a product that will meet the buyer's needs.

Warnings and Failure to Warn. Your company has a legal duty to warn customers about dangers associated with foreseeable uses of your product and to provide instructions that explain how to use the product safely. The list of dangers includes product features that could lead to physical harm. In one case, a doctor replaced the heart valve of a patient named Bravman with a mechanical valve. The mechanical valve made a loud noise that, in some patients, could be heard in a quiet room from as far as 20 feet away. When Bravman sued the manufacturer, the court decided that there was no design defect (because the usefulness of the product outweighed the noise problems) or manufacturing defect.

However, the court determined that the manufacturer could be held liable for failing to warn the patient of the noise problem. There was evidence that the manufacturer knew that its mechanical valves were noisy. Other patients had complained and one had attempted suicide because of the noise. In this case, the patient alleged that he had lost sleep, become despondent, and been forced to take early retirement because of the noise. The court concluded that: "Unlike the purely psychological terror suffered by the protagonist in Edgar Allan Poe's *The Tell-Tale Heart*, Bravman's complaint, that his artificial heart valve creates excessive noise that prevents him from sleeping, among other things, is objectively verifiable."[30]

STEP TWO: KNOW HOW TO COPE WITH PRODUCT LIABILITY

As discussed in Chapter 1, the traditional reaction to legal problems like product liability lawsuits has been either flight or fight. For reasons discussed below, the flight option is no longer realistic in a global economy. The fight option includes two possibilities, fighting for product liability law reform and fighting a specific lawsuit, both of which will be explored later in the chapter.

Flight

Until the mid-1980s, when other countries began to adopt US-style strict liability, it was felt that US companies could escape the impact of product liability law by moving operations and sales to other countries. But this option was not feasible for companies that intended to market their products in the rich consumer market of the US, as they could not escape liability by arguing that their products were made in another country.

Increasingly, the option of moving operations is not feasible even for companies that intend to manufacture and market their product solely outside the US. As noted in Chapter 1, the law—like the economy—has become globalized and product liability has spread to Europe and Asia. Countries in the EU were the first to adopt US-style strict liability, and they were soon followed by countries in the Pacific Rim region, including Australia, China, the Philippines, and Japan.

In some cases, product liability law in other countries is harsher on companies and managers than the American version. In Vietnam, the product liability law provides that a manager who fails to meet quality standards "should be punished by up to one year of re-education."[31] In China, consumers filed more than 500,000 lawsuits annually during the three years following adoption of a new product law. According to a *Wall Street Journal* article: "Product liability, a concept practically unheard of here 20 years ago, has caught the attention of China's consumers—and they're applying it with a vengeance. For decades, the Chinese had little recourse when they were shocked, burned, or dismembered by shoddy state-produced goods. Now they can sue."[32] The same article notes a unique feature of Chinese law: newspaper articles can be introduced as evidence. Media campaigns result in headlines such as: "Is a Chinese Life Worth Less Than a Foreign Life?" and "A Needle in My Father's Heart."

Fight

Your product liability battles can take two forms. First, you can fight for reform of product liability law. Second, you can fight individual lawsuits filed against your company.

Fight for Law Reform. In the US, companies upset over the impact of product liability have pushed for reform of product liability law at the state and federal level. This fight has been successful to some extent at the state level, where laws have been enacted that place caps on certain types of damages, such as damages for pain and suffering and punitive damages. Other laws provide that if a product does not cause injury within a set time period, the manufacturer is not liable. However, supporters of law reform have been unsuccessful in achieving a return from strict liability to a fault-based system of liability.

Although attempts to reform product liability law may be laudable, reform efforts should not overshadow strategies to achieve competitive advantage within the legal system currently in place. After all, legal systems do not target your company alone; your competitors must play by the same rules. Law reform will simply move you and your competitors to a different field without creating a competitive advantage for your company.

Fight Individual Product Liability Lawsuits. As discussed earlier in the chapter, while the details and terminology may vary from country to country, it is likely that your customers will claim any or all of the three types of defects in their lawsuits against your company: design defects, manufacturing defects, and marketing defects. The strategy that you and your attorney will develop to defend a lawsuit will focus on these claims. Specifically, you will attempt to prove that there were no defects in your design, manufacture, and marketing of the product. For example, in a case in the US you might argue that the product was properly designed under the risk-utility analysis, the product was not defective when it left the manufacturing plant (a common argument in cases where customers alter products), and there were no marketing defects because the product did not violate the "merchantability" warranty (that is, it was of average quality).

Similar to US law, in the EU, the Product Liability Directive requires that the injured person proves the damage, the defect, and the causal relationship between defect and damage. The Directive also lists several defenses that companies can raise in product liability cases:[33] a producer is not liable if he proves (a) that he did not put the product into circulation; or (b) that, having regard to the circumstances, it is probable that the defect which caused the damage did not exist at the time when the product was put into circulation by him or that this defect came into being afterwards; or (c) that the product was neither manufactured by him for sale or any form of distribution for economic purpose nor manufactured or distributed by him in the course of his business; or (d) that the defect is due to compliance of the product with mandatory regulations issued by the public authorities; or (e) that the state of scientific and technical knowledge at the time when he put the product into circulation was not such as to enable the existence of the defect to be discovered;[34] or (f) in the case of a manufacturer of a component, that the defect is attributable to the design of the product in which the component has been fitted or to the instructions given by the manufacturer of the product.

A key issue at the heart of most product liability cases is whether the product was defective. For instance, in one case a company delivered a stack of produce to a grocery store. After a produce manager removed a box of bananas from the top of the stack, a 6-inch banana spider leaped from the stack onto the manager's hand and bit him. He later died of heart failure. His widow sued the company that sold the produce claiming that the bananas were defective. The court decided in favor of the company on the grounds that the product was not defective. The bananas "were edible and saleable. In these circumstances, neither the doctrine of strict liability nor breach of implied warranty of fitness applies."[35]

After winning a case like this, there is a tendency to breathe a sigh of relief and return to normal business activities. In a business world operating at Internet speed, there is little time to savor victory or reflect on its causes. But is this case really a victory for the company when all costs are considered? Beyond costs directly associated with the litigation, such as lawyers' and expert witness fees, there is the cost of management time spent on gathering documents, meetings with lawyers, and giving depositions. There are also opportunity costs associated with losing time that could be spent on business development. An even greater cost can be the loss in market share resulting from negative publicity that surrounds lawsuits. As a result it is important to exercise discipline after a victory (or loss) in court by moving to Step Three, the proactive search for business strategies and solutions that will minimize causes of product liability claims and, at the same time, reduce or prevent recurring product liability costs.

STEP THREE: DEVELOP BUSINESS STRATEGIES AND SOLUTIONS THAT MINIMIZE PRODUCT LIABILITY

The search for business strategies and solutions requires a long-term perspective on product liability and its impact on your company. The results of this search may vary by company, industry, or geographic territory, but there are three fundamental business approaches to minimizing the causes and consequences of product liability in a manner that will allow you to seize competitive advantage: a strategic approach, an organizational approach, and an operations approach. These approaches are depicted in Figure 2.3.

Figure 2.3 Business solutions for product liability

Strategic approach

The strategic approach focuses on this fundamental business question: Should you continue to make products that subject the company to potential liability? In answering this question, you may, for example, decide to drop certain products on the basis of your litigation experience and the size of damage awards. But through this knee-jerk analysis, you may lose significant business opportunities.

For a deeper strategic analysis, you should return to the legal elements of product liability discussed earlier. One of the key elements is strict liability, under which a company is liable when it sells a defective product even when the company is not negligent.

This rule is based on the theory that the company is simply an intermediary that adjusts prices and passes on the product liability costs to consumers. With this theory in mind, your strategic analysis should focus on whether your company can indeed pass on its product liability costs to consumers (as the theory predicts) or whether it must bear the costs because of an inability to raise prices. In other words, the analysis should focus on who ultimately pays, rather than on whether there is liability.[36]

To illustrate this analysis, let's assume that you work for a company in the industry that has incurred the highest product liability costs in the US—tobacco. Settlements and jury verdicts have pushed the product liability of the industry to billions of dollars. Faced with a portion of this liability, your company might easily be tempted to drop cigarettes as a product.

However, a deeper analysis would focus on whether this liability can be passed on to customers. For example, after tobacco companies agreed to a $206 billion settlement with 46 states in 1998, the companies raised their prices by 76 cents a pack, which allowed them to fund the settlement despite a 7 percent drop in cigarette consumption. As noted in a *Wall Street Journal* article: "Where does the [state settlement] money come from? Generally speaking, not the bottom line. Viewed from the consumer perspective, the settlements effectively transfer vast wealth from smokers to states and lawyers on both sides."[37] This analysis, by the way, is not to suggest that companies should manufacture and sell cigarettes, as there are other factors besides an economic analysis that should affect this decision.

Organizational approach

Once you make the strategic decision to continue a product line, you should review your organizational structure. This review brings into play the concept of limited liability companies. Under this concept, when you buy stock in a corporation, the most you can lose is your investment. If the company fails and declares bankruptcy, the creditors cannot seize your personal assets. In other words, the company represents a "corporate veil" that protects you from liability.

This concept also applies when one company (call it "parent") buys shares in another company ("subsidiary"). If subsidiary fails, parent is not liable for its debts. This creates an opportunity to isolate your product liability risks in a subsidiary. Your legal advisors will create the subsidiary as an independent corporation. Your company, the parent corporation, will typically own 100 percent of the subsidiary's stock. If, in the worst-case scenario, there are major product liability damage awards against the subsidiary, the parent company will lose its investment in the subsidiary but will not be liable beyond this investment.

There are exceptions to the principle of limited liability that are especially important to managers. A parent corporation that is directly involved with its subsidiary's product development risks direct liability. Another exception to the limited liability principle is especially common. If the parent corporation does not treat the subsidiary as an independent corporation, courts will "pierce the corporate veil" and hold the parent liable to the subsidiary's creditors. For example, several years ago world-class driver Mark Donohue was killed when a tire manufactured by Goodyear blew out during a race. When his estate sued Goodyear in the US, the company argued that, because the tire was manufactured by its British subsidiary, the lawsuit should be filed in England.

But the trial judge allowed the case to proceed against the parent company on the grounds that Goodyear dominated the subsidiary rather than treating it as an independent corporation. A comment on the case in *Forbes* observed, "One of the reasons companies set up subsidiaries, in fact, is to use the corporate form to limit legal liability. For the same reason that you can't sue GM shareholders if a Chevrolet's brakes fail, you can't sue Goodyear if a tire made by its subsidiary has a blowout. ... [But] companies get into trouble over the question of whether they have dominated subsidiaries to the extent that they are indistinguishable from the parent."[38]

Courts are also inclined to pierce the corporate veil when the subsidiary is inadequately capitalized, when the parent describes the subsidiary as a department or division (rather than as a corporation), when the subsidiary does not follow normal legal requirements such as holding regular board meetings, and when the parent uses the subsidiary's property as its own.[39] The message for managers is clear. Your legal advisors will be able to incorporate a subsidiary that can be used to manufacture products that carry significant product liability risks. But to be protected by the corporate veil that the advisors have created, you must allow the subsidiary to operate as an independent entity.

Operations approach

In addition to considering organizational structure, your decision to continue a product line should include a review of operations. While local law may require specific risk assessment and risk reduction methods to be used, the following basic steps will help you ensure that only safe products reach the customer. Your operations approach to minimizing product liability should relate to the three types of defects: design, manufacturing, and marketing. The importance of eliminating manufacturing defects is obvious and has already received considerable attention as a result of quality programs adopted by companies around the world. So has the importance of keeping adequate records, bearing in mind the working life of the product, the potential liability for product liability claims, and the possible need to identify suppliers of defective products. This chapter will focus instead on a process for reducing design and marketing defects, which are especially common forms of product liability. The review process has six key steps.

1. *Form a product review team.* In assembling product review teams, you may be inclined to invite participants with engineering backgrounds who understand product design. The risk is that engineers, while usually bright and logical, may be too focused on the product's intended purpose and may be uncomfortable thinking outside the box about how "real people" (that is, non-engineers) actually use products. For reasons discussed in the next section, your product review team should include representatives from functions throughout the company. You should also include potential customers on the team and invite them to describe how they might use your product. Depending on your product line and your markets, you will also want to include people with knowledge about specific regulations that set mandatory requirements for your products or operations and about any applicable safety or other standards, whether mandatory or not.
2. *Identify foreseeable uses.* You may recall from the earlier discussion of design and marketing defects that you must design the product and develop warnings based on the foreseeable ways in which customers use your product, rather than just on

the ways that you intend that they use the product. Thus the team should consider all possible ways that customers might use your product. For example, one of the authors has led simulations in which product review teams composed of experienced managers create a list of possible uses of a hairdryer. Within a matter of seconds, team members are able to think of uses similar to the list in Exhibit 2.3. Informal brainstorming should, of course, be supplemented with a review and analysis of claims relating to similar products.

EXHIBIT 2.3 FORESEEABLE USES OF A HAIRDRYER

People use hairdryers to:

- Dry clothes
- Start barbeques
- Shrink plastic
- Dry glue and paint
- Defrost refrigerators
- Thaw frozen pipes
- Dry pets
- Remove stickers
- Dry fingernail polish
- Dust
- Defrost locks

3. *Identify risks*. The team should identify risks associated with foreseeable uses. For instance, in reviewing the list in Exhibit 2.3, you might decide that there are risks associated with using the hairdryer to dry glue and paint but that using the hairdryer to defrost locks creates no danger.
4. *Redesign the product.* The team should determine whether the product can be redesigned to eliminate the risk. In considering design issues, the team should conduct a risk-utility analysis that focuses on the questions summarized in Exhibit 2.1.
5. *Develop warnings*. The team should develop warnings (and safety instructions) for the risks that cannot be eliminated through redesign. In product review team simulations, senior managers tend to skip discussion of redesign and move directly to the development of warnings once risks have been identified. This is a serious mistake because a court may not allow warnings as a defense if a safer design is available.

   For example, an individual suffered brain injury when a 16-inch Goodrich tire exploded as he attempted to mount it on a 16.5-inch rim. A prominent warning label attached to the tire contained warnings (see Exhibit 2.4) in red and yellow and also a drawing that depicted an exploding tire throwing a worker into the air. The injured individual had ignored all of the warnings. In a lawsuit against Goodyear, the Supreme Court of Texas affirmed a jury award of $5.5 million in damages. The court noted that "a product may be unreasonably dangerous because of a defect in manufacturing, design, or marketing." In this case, because there was evidence that the tire was defectively designed, the warning label did not excuse the design defect. As the court noted (quoting a legal authority): *"Warnings are not, however, a substitute for the provision of a reasonably safe design."* (The italics were added by the court for emphasis.)[40]

EXHIBIT 2.4 WARNING LABEL ATTACHED TO TIRE[41]

DANGER

NEVER MOUNT A 16" SIZE DIAMETER TIRE ON A 16.5" RIM. Mounting a 16" tire on a 16.5" rim can cause severe injury or death. While it is possible to pass a 16" diameter tire over the lip or flange of a 16.5" size diameter rim, it cannot position itself against the rim flange. If an attempt is made to seat the bead by inflating the tire, the tire bead will break with explosive force.

NEVER inflate a tire which is lying on the floor or other flat surface. Always use a tire mounting machine with a hold-down device or safety cage or bolt to vehicle axle.

NEVER inflate to seat beads without using an extension hose with gauge and clip-on chuck.

NEVER stand, lean, or reach over the assembly during inflation.

Failure to comply with these safety precautions can cause the bead to break and the assembly to burst with sufficient force to cause serious injury or death.

6. *Review warranties.*[42] The team should determine what, if any, warranties should accompany the product. Your company can avoid liability for express warranties simply by not giving them. In marketing your products you can also disclaim express warranties, although the disclaimer will not necessarily work if it conflicts with an express warranty. For example, a warranty from a US clothing manufacturer stated that the company would replace a product if it did not provide "one year of normal wear." Below this statement, in small type, was a disclaimer that the warranty would not apply if garments were "worn out." If tested in court, the one-year warranty should prevail over the disclaimer.

   In many cases you can also disclaim the warranties that are automatically provided by law—the implied warranties discussed earlier in this chapter. For example, to disclaim the implied warranty of merchantability under US law, the disclaimer must mention the word merchantability and, if in writing, must be conspicuous. The implied warranty of fitness for a particular purpose can be disclaimed through a conspicuous disclaimer that is in writing. For examples of disclaimers, simply visit your favorite web site. Chances are that you will find disclaimers similar to those found on the Amazon.com web site:

   TO THE FULL EXTENT PERMISSIBLE BY APPLICABLE LAW,
   AMAZON DISCLAIM [sic] ALL WARRANTIES, EXPRESS OR IMPLIED,
   INCLUDING, BUT NOT LIMITED TO, IMPLIED WARRANTIES
   OF MERCHANTABILITY AND FITNESS FOR A PARTICULAR PURPOSE.[43]

The six-step process can minimize, but not completely eliminate, product liability. You should, therefore, not only review your "outbound" warranties (that is, those given to customers), but also your "inbound" warranties (that is, those that are given to you by your suppliers). You should also review your contracts to ensure that you comply with (and pass on to your suppliers) requirements regarding functionality, performance, safety, labeling, compliance with certain standards, and so on. Contracts and the interplay of contracts with the law are covered in more detail in Chapter 6 where it is noted that in many cases, especially in business-to-business relationships, you can "make your own law" through your contracts.

You should also make sure that your product liability insurance covers you against damages awarded as a result of damage to property or personal injury caused by your products. Implementing the steps described above may help reduce your premiums.

This section has examined three business approaches—strategic, organizational, and operational—that you can use to seize competitive advantage by reducing or eliminating product liability risks and minimizing their consequences. You are now ready to climb to the balcony in an attempt to reframe product liability as a business opportunity rather than solely a legal issue. This attempt may enable you to use the law to achieve growth through NPD.

STEP FOUR: CLIMB TO THE BALCONY TO REFRAME PRODUCT LIABILITY AS A BUSINESS OPPORTUNITY

When you climb to the balcony to view product liability in perspective, the results may vary depending on your product line. But there is at least one perspective that should prove useful across product lines. This perspective relates to the six-step review process that was used above to reduce liability for defective design and to develop warnings for those design defects that cannot be eliminated.

In product review team simulations, managers often express hostility toward a feature of the law that allows customers to recover for injuries that result when they use products for purposes other than those intended by the manufacturer. Often the simulation brings to mind stories managers have heard or experiences they have had with their own customers' misuse of products. Some of these stories are urban myths (or, at least, they cannot be located in published case reports). These include stories of the cat that exploded when its owner attempted to dry it in the microwave and the woman who used contraceptive jelly on her toast every morning and still became pregnant.[44]

But other stories—sometimes drawn from the executives' own experience—are true. For example, a person driving a Ford® Pinto struck a horse. The horse flipped onto the roof above the windshield. The impact caused the roof to collapse, instantly killing the driver's wife. Ford Motor Company was held liable for a design defect because, among other reasons, "the accident and the manner of injury were not unforeseeable."[45]

When considering a case like this, there is a tendency to criticize judges who push the boundaries of foreseeability or customers who misuse products. While criticism may be justified in certain cases, by focusing on the legal aspects of product liability, you may overlook significant business opportunities. For example, let's return to the hairdryer example. You might consider most of the uses in Exhibit 2.3 to be examples of customer stupidity, as customers should not use hairdryers for purposes other than drying hair.

However, is this the attitude of a manager in a customer-focused, market-driven company? What are your customers trying to tell you when they use hairdryers for a wide variety of purposes? The common theme in the list is that customers need products that provide warm and/or moving air and consequently must use hairdryers for this purpose. Companies that move beyond a purely legal or risk minimization focus in their design review and use information from the process to develop new products will achieve competitive advantage. As legendary General Motors President Alfred Sloan once stated in a letter to shareholders: "To discuss Consumer Research as a functional activity would give an erroneous impression. In its broad implications it is more in the nature of an OPERATING PHILOSOPHY, which to be fully effective, must extend through all phases of the business ... [and] serve the customer in ways in which the customer wants to be served."[46]

"All phases of the business" includes the "law phase" of the business. In other words, law should be used not only to control costs and limit liability exposure but also to generate new product ideas and new value for customers. As a leading management consultant—a person who founded one of the top international consulting firms and has played key roles in the development of two others—once told one of the authors, the key to strategy is listening to customers. Listening to your customers through the legal information they provide extends beyond NPD. Once your product is on the market, it becomes important to listen to your customers through their complaints about your product, their warranty claims, and even their lawsuits against your company or your competitors. This form of data mining is especially useful in the continuing redesign of your products in order to maintain competitive advantage.

The listening process also extends to liability related to services that you provide with your products. For instance, at one time Domino's Pizza guaranteed pizza delivery within 30 minutes or customers would receive a discount. After several traffic accidents involving Domino's drivers the company faced public criticism and lawsuits.

If you were a Domino's executive, how would you respond to this problem? One response might be to require continuous training of your drivers. But it is likely that training would be costly and might not significantly reduce the number of accidents. Better screening of potential drivers would probably lead to the same result. Another approach would be to drop your 30-minute guarantee. But you might lose a significant marketing advantage, as well as the opportunity to provide the best service to your customers.

Domino's opted for the last approach, dropping the 30-minute guarantee. But in doing so, rather than complaining about the negative impact of the law on customer service, the company asked the question suggested by Alfred Sloan: What do our customers really want? The company discovered that, while customers want their pizza delivered as soon as possible, an important reason behind this desire for speedy delivery is that they want their pizza to be served hot. The solution? A new service-enhancing product—a bag that contains heating coils that keeps the pizza hot until delivery.

Chapter Summary

This chapter has applied the four-step Manager's Legal Plan™ for achieving competitive advantage to one of the most controversial and complex issues affecting you and your customers: product liability. It first examined the impact of product liability on your company, on consumers, and on society. The chapter then proceeded through the four steps of the Manager's Legal Plan™.

Step One: Understand the legal elements of product liability: While the details may vary from one jurisdiction to another, product liability often involves alleged damage caused by your product based on a combination of claims: design defect, which involves an analysis of your product's risk and utility; manufacturing defect, which today is based on the theory of strict liability; and marketing defect, which might arise from breach of warranty or failure to warn.

Step Two: Know how to cope with product liability: Of the two traditional response mechanisms that are embedded in our genetic code, flight or fight, flight is rarely possible because the theory of strict liability has spread worldwide. The product liability fight takes two forms. First, there is the fight for law reform, which has achieved modest success in some US states but does not provide competitive advantage to any one company. Second, the fight in individual cases will focus on defending against the claims summarized in Step One. At the most fundamental level, you must fight to prove that your product did not cause the damage or was not defective.

Step Three: Develop business strategies and solutions that minimize product liability: There is a tendency for managers to move on to other concerns when the product liability fight is over. But the key to using the law for competitive advantage is to move instead to this third step, which might minimize future claims by transforming the way you do business. This involves three approaches. First, the strategic approach uses the theory of strict liability to decide whether to add or drop product lines in certain markets. Second, the organizational approach focuses on the use of subsidiaries to isolate serious product liability risks. Third, the operational approach uses a design and marketing review process to identify foreseeable uses of your product, redesign the product, and develop appropriate warnings. Contract provisions and insurance are also important in allocating risk when liability cannot be completely eliminated.

Step Four: Climb to the balcony to reframe product liability as a business opportunity: This last step covers ways to use the law proactively. For instance, the design and marketing review process at Step Three not only minimizes liability but also generates growth through NPD. The process represents an important form of consumer research in any company that aspires to be market driven and focused on customer needs.

Notes

1 Wysocki, B. 1976. Manufacturers are hit with more lawsuits, rising insurance costs. *Wall Street Journal*, June 3, A1.

2 Andresky, J. 1985. A world without insurance? *Forbes*, July 15, 42.

3 Council of Europe 1977. *European Convention on Products Liability in Regard to Personal Injury and Death*. Strasbourg, January 1, 1977 [Online]. Available at: http://conventions.coe.int/treaty/en/Treaties/Html/091.htm [accessed: August 1, 2010].

4 Council Directive 85/374/EEC of 25 July 1985 on the approximation of the laws, regulations and administrative provisions of the Member States concerning liability for defective products. Official Journal L 210 of 07.08.1985. Available at: http://eur-lex.europa.eu/LexUriServ/LexUriServ.do?uri=CELEX:31985L0374:EN:HTML [accessed: August 1, 2010]. For a summary

and updates, see http://europa.eu/legislation_summaries/consumers/consumer_safety/l32012_en.htm [accessed: August 1, 2010].

5 Howells, G.G. 2000. The relationship between product liability and product safety—Understanding a necessary element in European product liability through a comparison with the US position. *Washburn Law Journal*, 39(3), 305–46 [Online]. Available at: http://www.washburnlaw.edu/wlj/39-3/articles/howells-geraint.pdf [accessed: August 1, 2010]. The Directives lay down essential safety requirements but leave the details to be fleshed out by European standards. "In contrast to products liability, which is viewed as a lawyer's paradise, standardization is an area of law largely uninhabited by legal practitioners." (Howells 2000, 308)

6 Geisel, J. 1978. Gun firm pays $6.8 million to attorney. *Business Insurance*, November 13, 12.

7 McGuire, E.P. 1988. *The Impact of Product Liability*. New York, NY: Conference Board, 6 and 8.

8 Tortuous reform, 1996. *Economist*, March 30, 20.

9 Presser, S.B. 2002. How should the law of products liability be harmonized? What Americans can learn from Europeans. *Global Liability Issues,* Vol. 2, February [Online]. Available at: http://www.manhattan-institute.org/html/gli_2.htm [accessed: August 1, 2010].

10 Presser 2002.

11 Presser 2002.

12 ABB on verge of collapse as shares reach record low, 2002. *Financial Times*, October 23, 1.

13 Garikipati, R. 2004. Korean firms must be vigilant of U.S. legal system. *Korea Herald,* June 18 [Online]. Available at: http://www.koreaherald.co.kr/service/print.asp?tpl=print&sname=Special&img=/img/pic/ico_spe_pic.gif&id=200406180041 [accessed: February 15, 2001].

14 CE is the abbreviation of "Conformité Européenne," French for "European Conformity." Regulation (EC) 765/2008 (http://eur-lex.europa.eu/LexUriServ/LexUriServ.do?uri=OJ:L:2008:218:0030:0047:EN:PDF [accessed: August 1, 2010]) lays down the general principles of the CE marking. The Regulation defines "CE marking" as a marking by which the manufacturer indicates that the product is in conformity with the applicable requirements set out in Community harmonization legislation providing for its affixing.

15 For the Machinery Directive 2006/42/EC, as revised, applicable from December 29, 2009, see http://ec.europa.eu/enterprise/mechan_equipment/machinery/revdir.htm. See also Frasier, I. (ed.) 2010. Guide to application of the Machinery Directive 2006/42/EC. 2nd Edition, June. European Commission, Enterprise and Industry [Online]. Available at: http://ec.europa.eu/enterprise/sectors/mechanical/files/machinery/guide_application_directive_2006-42-ec-2nd_edit_6-2010_en.pdf [accessed: August 1, 2010]. According to the Machinery Directive, machinery manufactured in conformity with a harmonized standard, the references of which have been published in the *Official Journal of the European Union,* shall be presumed to comply with the essential health and safety requirements covered by the standard. For the latest consolidated list of harmonized standards, see http://ec.europa.eu/enterprise/sectors/mechanical/documents/standardization/machinery/index_en.htm [accessed: August 1, 2010].

16 As regards performing risk assessments, the European Standard EN 1050:1997—*Safety of machinery. Principles for risk assessment* was superseded in 2007 by a new Standard, EN ISO 14121. See also Lovells, 2003. *Product Liability in the European Union. A Report for the European Commission.* February 2003, viii [Online]. Available at: http://ec.europa.eu/enterprise/regulation/goods/docs/liability/studies/lovells-study_en.pdf [accessed: August 1, 2010].

17 The discussion that follows uses the definition of a defect adopted in the US. In other jurisdictions, even when strict liability (liability without negligence) prevails, the terminology and the precise meaning of the term "defect" may differ. For instance, in the European Product Liability Directive, when considering whether a product is defective, the determining factor is lack of safety.

In accordance with Article 6 of the Directive: A product is defective when it does not provide the safety which a person is entitled to expect, taking all circumstances into account, including: the presentation of the product; the use to which it could reasonably be expected that the product would be put; and the time when the product was put into circulation. A product shall not be considered defective for the sole reason that a better product is subsequently put into circulation.

18 *Banks v. ICI* [1994] 450 S.E.2d 671.

19 *Banks v. ICI* [1994].

20 Keeton, W.P., Dobbs, D.B., Keeton, R.E. and Owen, D.G. 1984. *Prosser and Keeton on the Law of Torts*. St. Paul, MN: West, 693.

21 Edgerton, M. 1978. How one firm learned its lesson in liability cases. *Detroit Free Press*, March 19, D1.

22 Sports company tackles product liability reform by working with other companies, organizations, 1993. *Focus*, December, 2.

23 Bailey, R. 1988. Legal mayhem. *Forbes*, November 14, 97.

24 Abraham, S. 1997. American injustice: The case for legal reform. *Imprimis*, September, 2.

25 The discussion that follows uses the definition of a defect adopted in the US. See Note 17 above. Under some legal systems, instead of implied warranties, similar obligations are based on default rules related to liability for defects or liability for non-conformity (lack of conformity) of the goods.

26 *Cipollone v. Liggett Group, Inc.* [1992] 112 S. Ct. 2608.

27 *Cipollone v. Liggett Group, Inc.* US Court of Appeals (3rd Circuit) [1990].

28 While the details and language vary, obligations and liabilities similar to those created by implied warranties under US domestic law are part of most countries' laws. In addition to sales of goods acts and similar domestic sales laws they are also part of international law through the UN Convention on Contracts for the International Sale of Goods (CISG), which is discussed in Chapter 1. In the latter, instead of implied warranties, there are requirements as to the conformity of the goods and, if breached, remedies for non-conformity (lack of conformity) of the goods. See also Notes 17 and 25.

29 Aeppel, T. 2000. Goodyear wins round in suit over warranty. *Wall Street Journal*, February 8, B5.

30 *Bravman v. Baxter Healthcare Corporation* [1993] 984 F.2d 71.

31 MacIntosh, D. 1998. What is product liability? *International Business Lawyer*, February, 53.

32 Smith, G.S. 1997. Chinese discover product-liability suits. *Wall Street Journal*, November 13, B1.

33 For the European Product Liability Directive's provisions regarding the burden of proof and causality, see Article 4, and for its provisions on defenses to a claim, see Article 7. For differences in the implementation of the Directive, see Lovells 2003.

34 The Commission allowed EU Member States to decide whether to permit the development risk defense. Only Finland and Luxembourg have exercised the option to exclude this provision from the national laws implementing the Directive (Lovells 2003, 49–50).

35 *Anderson v. Associated Grocers, Inc.* [1974] 525 P.2d 284.

36 This also involves questions related to your company's product liability insurance—for instance, which products and geographical territories are covered, and the role of your suppliers and your contracts.

37 Geyelin, M. 2000. Yes, $145 billion deals tobacco a huge blow, but not a killing one. *Wall Street Journal*, July 17, A8.

38 Greene, R. 1984. Peeking beneath the corporate veil. *Forbes*, August 13, 58.

39 Powell, F.J. 1931. Parent and Subsidiary Corporations: Liability of a Parent Corporation for the Obligations of Its Subsidiary. Chicago: Callaghan and Company, Section 6 at 9.

40 *Uniroyal Goodrich Tire Co. v. Martinez* [1998] 977 S.W.2d 328.
41 *Uniroyal Goodrich Tire Co. v. Martinez* [1998].
42 For differences in concepts and terminology, see Notes 17, 25, and 28. Where implied warranties are not part of the applicable law, you should review other relevant terms of your contracts accordingly.
43 Conditions of Use. Amazon.com [Online]. Available at: http://www.amazon.com/gp/help/customer/display.html/ref=footer_cou?ie=UTF8&nodeId=508088 [accessed: August 1, 2010].
44 Postrel, V.I. 1997. The lessons of email deceit. *Forbes ASAP*, October 6, 24.
45 *Green v. Ford Motor Company* [1987] 742 P.2d 639.
46 Barksdale, H.C. (ed.) 1964. *Marketing in Progress*. Austin, TX: Holt, Rinehart and Winston, 199.

CHAPTER 3 Create Competitive Advantage through Your Talent Pool: Secure Access to Key Talent while Avoiding Employment Pitfalls

As noted in Chapter 1, access to, and retention of, key talent tops the list of the concerns faced by managers worldwide. So your ability to find and retain the best employees through attractive compensation and work-life balance programs while at the same time controlling employment costs is a critical element in achieving competitive advantage. But you do not need full-time employees in all areas where you need key talent. To reach maximum efficiency, you may decide to procure the services of outside providers and outsource some of your current internal services or processes. In some instances, you may be forced to reduce head count of your full-time staff. Regardless of whether you outsource or downsize your human resources, the law enters the picture. And in many contexts in our global economy, your human resource efforts will raise international and multi-jurisdictional issues.

Outsourcing is an especially popular tool to secure access to human resource competences while minimizing costs and focusing on core business. Functions that are being outsourced extend beyond call centers and information technology to functions such as engineering, procurement, facility management, and HR services. More recently, companies can also take advantage of the rapid growth of outsourced or offshored services such as contract review, legal, and finance functions. But are cost savings and efficiencies guaranteed?

A recent survey by the Society for Human Resource Management shows that outsourcing is the second most important trend affecting US workplaces.[1] According to a study by LogicaCMG, however, 36 percent of all major outsourcing deals that included redeployment or transfer of personnel, particularly those involving large companies in France, the UK, and Germany, ran into problems because organizations failed to understand the importance of the "social factor" (that is, the employees). In 15 percent of the companies surveyed, the result was termination or cancellation of a project.[2]

Despite the importance of this "social factor," employment issues are often overshadowed by other considerations. The company and the service provider sometimes work under the mistaken assumption that all company employees performing the functions to be outsourced can be terminated and replaced with presumably less-costly employees of the service provider, without liability to the company beyond severance costs. In many outsourcing contexts, especially those involving non-US countries, however, that is not the case. The clearest example is in the European Union (EU), where the so-called Acquired Rights Directive applies (a EU Directive that has been implemented into the local laws of each of the EU Member States).[3]

The key to successful outsourcing and/or downsizing your human resources is preparation. This chapter will show how the four-step Manager's Legal Plan™ enables you to secure access to key talent while avoiding employment pitfalls using examples from two quite different legal systems, the EU and the US. The chapter will focus primarily on outsourcing and on your ability to discharge employees even when outsourcing is not used.

Outsourcing, and employment issues generally, are not just about the law. You as the manager will need to cope with myriad other issues that are involved, including the psychological effects, performance losses, and disruptive effects often created by outsourcing and downsizing. You should combine your knowledge of the law with a practical approach to the management of people. The absence of complaints or lawsuits does not guarantee success—but it does establish a launch pad for reaching your business objectives and seizing competitive advantage.

Apply the Manager's Legal Plan™ to Secure Access to Key Talent while Avoiding Employment Pitfalls

Outsourcing can provide a company with an infusion of fresh perspectives, new competencies, and reduced employee costs. Yet in some contexts rumors of a possible outsourcing can bring anxiety and lost productivity to the workplace. Outsourcing can create some legal challenges as well, especially if your outsourcing involves foreign countries. So how do you as a manager proceed with an outsourcing decision? Applying the Manager's Legal Plan™ and proactively embracing outsourcing can give your company a competitive advantage by maximizing the benefits while reducing the negative by-products that outsourcing can produce.

In order to outsource—or to acquire and manage external or internal resources generally—you need contracts. You might already have a written employment contract or service contract yourself. To prevent misunderstandings and future problems, the first rule of thumb is to read the contract! Then learn about the law and whether it provides mandatory or additional (implied) provisions (as discussed in Chapter 6). As will be seen later, in some countries managers enjoy protections granted to employees while in others they do not. If you are interested in knowing whether and how your own position is protected in the areas discussed later in this chapter, you should talk with a competent advisor familiar with your jurisdiction and position before drawing conclusions or taking action. Knowing your own rights and responsibilities as a manager is a natural part of your legal plan.

STEP ONE: UNDERSTAND THE LAW (AND THAT IT IS NOT THE SAME EVERYWHERE)

In most states in America you can hire and fire employees at will. In most other countries, the typical approach is that employers must provide advance notice when employees are discharged and also must compensate employees who are fired without cause. In the EU, the termination of employees is usually subject to stringent notice, severance, and other requirements, and the law governing the treatment of employees is, in many instances, harmonized among the Member States.

When a business or a part of a business in an EU Member State is transferred, the employees—along with their rights, obligations, and employment benefits—are transferred to the new employer. In the US, in general, employees are in an at-will relationship, and no federal statute exists that would cause employees to transfer in connection with the transfer of business. As a result, unlike the EU approach, in a transfer of business or outsourcing situation in the US, either the new or the existing business owner can terminate the employee without notice or cause.[4] But the law of wrongful discharge in the US is complex and will be discussed later in this chapter. First, we will introduce the EU approach.

Understand European Union and Member State Laws

In the EU, an outsourcing transaction can trigger the transfer provisions of the Acquired Rights Directive, through which the EU has harmonized the laws of the various EU Member States.[5] This Directive, among other things, provides for the automatic transfer of the employment contracts of transferred employees from the transferor company to the transferee when an undertaking, business, or part of an undertaking or business is transferred.[6] When considering an outsourcing transaction within the EU, it is important to assess whether the planned transaction involves a transfer in the meaning of the Directive. This is particularly important as the transfer rules can be triggered at each stage of an outsourcing transaction—not only at the initial transfer stage, but also following the end of the outsourcing agreement and when there is a change of outsourcing supplier.[7]

Each EU Member State is responsible for incorporating the provisions of a Directive into its own laws, so there can be differences in how a Directive is implemented. The relevant Directive specifically permits Member States to pass laws that are more favorable to employees or to promote or permit collective agreements more favorable to employees. In England, for instance, a law called *Transfer of Undertakings (Protection of Employment)* (TUPE) applies to many business transfers and service provision changes, giving rights to employees in the companies affected. Under TUPE, any change in employment terms and conditions for a reason connected with the transfer is void (even if the employees agree to the change) unless it is for an "economic, technical or organizational reason entailing changes in the workforce" (that is, an ETO reason). With few exceptions, any dismissal for a reason connected with a TUPE transfer is automatically considered unfair.[8]

In a multi-jurisdictional outsourcing context, it is, therefore, vital to become acquainted with the rules of each relevant jurisdiction. In addition, one needs to take into account the collective bargaining agreements and individual contractual rights of impacted employees. Collective bargaining agreements are far more common in Europe than they are in the US.

By the automatic transfer of employment contracts (whether written or verbal contracts and whether part-time or full-time employees), EU law assures that the rights and obligations of transferred employees under their initial employment transfer with them. This usually means that *all* contractual benefits transfer, including holiday, car allowance, and other employment benefits. In addition to the automatic transfer of employment contracts, the Directive includes several key mandates that you must follow as you proceed with your outsourcing plan. For example, you may not terminate an employee solely due to the transfer; you must inform and consult with employees before and during the transfer; and an employee may object to the transfer.

In most cases within the EU Member States, even in an outsourcing situation you must have a justifiable reason before terminating an employee. While the details vary, an employee is typically entitled to statutory notice. For example, in England, the notice period is one week for the first two years of service and, after the first two years of service, an additional week's notice for each completed year of service up to a maximum of 12 weeks' notice.[9] In Sweden, the minimum statutory notice periods that apply when the employer terminates employment (entered into after January 1, 1997) increase step by step from one month if the employment has lasted less than two years to six months if the employment has lasted at least ten years.[10] Employers and employees can agree on longer contractual notice periods.

If an employer terminates an employee without notice or without a justified reason, the employee has a claim for wrongful dismissal. Employees can then recover a sum equivalent to that which they would have been paid during the notice period. Additional compensation will be due for unfair dismissal. For example, in England any dismissal for a reason connected with a TUPE transfer is automatically considered unfair, unless it is for an ETO reason. Employees with at least one year's service can claim unfair dismissal. Liability for any pre-transfer dismissals by the transferor passes to the transferee under TUPE, unless the dismissal was for an ETO reason.[11] The maximum compensatory award for unfair dismissal is currently £63,000.[12] However, for certain automatically unfair dismissals, there are no maximum limits.[13]

In some countries, employees are entitled to a statutory redundancy payment if made redundant after a certain minimum period of service. When available, the statutory redundancy payment is typically calculated based on the employee's length of service, age, and salary. In Italy, in all cases where an employment contract is terminated, the employer must pay the dismissed employee severance pay even if there is no redundancy but, instead, a resignation or just cause for dismissal. The amount payable can be quite high and may also include, for instance, payment in lieu of holidays not taken.[14]

The termination of management employees raises the same issues as the termination of other employees. Their dismissal must be based on proper grounds and they can be entitled to a severance payment provided for by statute, collective bargaining agreement, and their contract. The amount payable often depends on their length of service as well as on the period of notice given. The sums involved might be much larger than those in the case of non-managerial employees. In addition to their salary, managers often enjoy other forms of remuneration that must be taken into account. These can include golden parachutes (advantageous termination packages sometimes provided to managing directors and other senior level managers), bonuses, and stock options.

Understand US wrongful discharge law

Even though the law does not protect employees the way it does in the EU, wrongful discharge cases are especially common in the US. So much so that if you play a word association game with a manager in the US and say "wrongful discharge," a likely response is "high damage award." The fear of a headline damage award has caused many managers to focus on this area when evaluating their human resources.

One survey revealed that 55 percent of the companies surveyed had been sued by an employee over a recent 12-month period, and wrongful discharge was one of the two most frequent claims asserted in these cases.[15] (The other frequent claim was based on gender discrimination or sexual harassment.) In another survey, almost two out of three executives indicated that employees had sued them or had threatened suit on similar grounds in a one-year period.[16]

If your work involves the US, as a starting point you should be familiar with the basic concepts of law relating to wrongful discharge. The fundamental legal principle that governs this area is the employment-at-will rule. Under this rule, you can hire and fire employees at will in all states but Montana (which requires good cause for dismissals). This rule does not apply to employees governed by union collective bargaining agreements, but the overwhelming majority of employees in private industry do not belong to unions.

In recent years, US law has moved closer to the law in other countries as courts have developed three exceptions to the employment-at-will rule. First, the rule does not apply if the company has made statements to employees or in company documents that create contractual rights that override the rule. For instance, during negotiations with a company, a person who was later hired as director of marketing was told by a company officer that "if you are doing the job, you can be assured that you will not be discharged." When he was later discharged for no apparent reason, he sued the company—claiming that this oral statement prevented the company from firing him without cause. He recovered $300,000.[17]

Second, a company must act in good faith in dismissing employees. In one case, a company fired a salesperson who had worked for the company for 25 years. A jury decided that the termination, which took place the next business day after the salesperson had obtained a $5 million order, resulted from the company's desire to reduce the employee's bonus that would have been due as a result of the sale. An appellate court noted that the employee's contract was "a classic terminable at will employment contract ... [that] reserved to the parties an explicit power to terminate the contract without cause." But the court affirmed the jury decision because a company's decision to fire an employee must be made in good faith.[18]

Third, a dismissal may not violate public policy. For example, a nurse was hired as an at-will employee by a hospital. She went on a camping trip with her supervisor and employees of other hospitals. During the trip, members of the group staged a parody of the song "Moon River," which allegedly included their mooning the audience. The nurse refused to participate in this parody and in other activities that made her feel uncomfortable. Before the trip the nurse had received favorable performance evaluations. Shortly after the trip, her employment was terminated.

When the lower courts dismissed her lawsuit, the case was appealed to the Supreme Court of Arizona. The court held that "an employer may fire for good cause or for no cause. He may not fire for bad cause—that which violates public policy." Does refusal to participate in mooning violate public policy? The supreme court justices admitted, "We have little expertise in the techniques of mooning." But, citing the state indecent exposure law, the court concluded that "termination of employment for refusal to participate in public exposure of one's buttocks is a termination contrary to the policy of this state."[19]

In addition to these three exceptions, it is not unusual for an employee to allege defamation in connection with the discharge. For example, in one case an insurance salesperson named Larry was fired by his employer. When he was unable to find employment with other firms, he hired an investigator. Posing as a prospective employer, the investigator contacted the office manager of the firm where Larry had worked. The office manager told the investigator that Larry was "irrational, ruthless, and disliked by office personnel ... a classical sociopath ... a zero, a Jekyll and Hyde person who was lacking ... scruples." Because the statements were untrue, this conversation cost the employer $1.9 million in damages when Larry filed suit for defamation.[20] It is estimated that one-third of all defamation cases are brought by fired employees against their former managers.[21]

The combination of the exceptions to the employment-at-will rule and defamation law has produced a judicial lottery in the US where some employees win large damage awards and many win nothing. California is notorious for large awards in wrongful discharge cases. But large awards are not confined to California. A jury in Kentucky awarded two former Ashland Oil employees $70 million after the company wrongfully discharged them when they protested illegal foreign payments. The case was eventually settled for "only" $25 million.[22] And a Texas jury awarded a former energy company employee $124 million for a wrongful discharge after the employee refused to prepare documents that contained misleading information. The Texas case was also eventually settled for an estimated $25 million.[23]

STEP TWO: KNOW HOW TO COPE WITH LEGAL PROBLEMS AND LEARN FROM THEM

The discussion above shows that it is quite easy for your company to suffer a substantial financial loss if you do not understand the law. For obvious reasons, if you need to cut the number of employees or outsource some functions, it is important to plan ahead. While potential headcount reductions and cost savings may sound attractive, you should not proceed without understanding the law and, where necessary, without early engagement of competent advisors knowledgeable in the HR and legal questions that may arise in each of the jurisdictions involved.

Even if you follow notice and other requirements, you may receive objections, complaints, or threats of lawsuits from individuals on your staff. In consultation with your advisors, you will then need to decide on a case-by-case basis whether you will handle each complaint through flight (settlement) or fight (litigation).

In some cases, an amicable solution such as a mutual agreement about the expiration of the employment relationships can be desirable from both the company's and the employee's perspective, especially managerial employees. An agreed solution can allow a company to make a smooth transition to new management. Managers, in turn, may want to leave the company on good terms and maintain their reputations, while at the same time looking for ways to optimize severance and other payments from a tax perspective. So both parties may be willing and able to negotiate a settlement. To accomplish this, you may choose to explore mediation or other alternatives to litigation discussed in Chapter 7.

While the "flight" option of settlement might seem preferable to the "fight" option of litigation, both approaches may prove to be unfortunate. In the EU, for example, while you may be able to negotiate separation agreements with managers or other employees, you cannot escape mandatory protection that the law provides employees. As we will see under Step Three, the wisest course of action is often to avoid a complaint or lawsuit altogether.

Similarly, in the US, flight from wrongful discharge litigation to a company-friendly state is difficult. Although several states have not adopted all three exceptions to the employment-at-will rule—and a few (such as Georgia) have adopted none of them—legal trends indicate that these exceptions will eventually arrive in everyone's neighborhood. Flight outside the US is not realistic either because most countries provide automatic compensation when there is no cause for dismissal. Unlike the judicial lottery in the US, the laws in other countries make most discharged employees winners, even though the amounts might not be as large as they are in the US.

The wrongful discharge fight includes two possible options in the US. One option is to play the lottery by fighting individual claims. With this strategy, you may win most cases. As an attorney with the American Civil Liberties Union (ACLU) has noted: "The average employee who has been wrongfully terminated has as much chance of getting a jury trial as sprouting wings and flying to the moon."[24] But you also risk an occasional large damage award similar to those awarded by juries in California, Kentucky, and Texas.

The other option is to fight for law reform. Approximately half the states have enacted laws that protect employers from liability for defamation. These laws commonly create a presumption that a former employer who provides information to a prospective employer is acting in good faith. But this protection does not apply when the former employer knows that the information is false. Depending on state law, the former employer also may not be protected when providing information that is not related to job performance (such as lifestyle information) or when providing a reference that was not requested by a prospective employer.[25]

STEP THREE: DEVELOP BUSINESS STRATEGIES AND SOLUTIONS TO PREVENT FUTURE PROBLEMS

For some companies, a way to minimize employment-related problems is to hire fewer employees and acquire more talent from outside providers, such as subcontractors, specialized consulting firms, and other service providers. If your company is a start-up or is expanding into new markets, this may be a viable option—especially in geographies where employee protection goes very far and your long-term business presence is uncertain. For an established company with existing staff, the transition from becoming less of an employer and more of a user of subcontractors can be costly and time-consuming. When considering whether to terminate employees' contracts in connection with outsourcing or otherwise, it is important to keep in mind that US-style at-will employment is not recognized internationally, and employment termination is often subject to stringent notice and severance requirements, in addition to requirements to notify and consult with employee representatives.

Given the high financial risks associated with employment-related claims and litigation, you should take measures to minimize liability and negative surprises in connection with business reorganizations, such as downsizing or outsourcing. *Before* you proceed, you should conduct a proper due diligence to determine the rights of the employees affected.

When replacing employees with service provider personnel and/or discharging employees is involved, it is important to consult the laws of the relevant countries in deciding which employees' contracts to terminate and how to conduct the termination. You also need to take into account your employees' contractual rights. Awareness of the differences that exist in different countries and proper planning will take you a long way in preventing future problems and minimizing risk, including reputation risk.

Approaches for preventing potential legal problems in the European Union

Although there are common themes and principles in outsourcing transactions and downsizing efforts, you now know that the details of local law can vary considerably, even across the EU. Compliance with these laws takes time. For instance, when EU companies or subsidiaries are involved, knowing the requirements and conditions that apply in the relevant EU Member States will enable you to take preparatory steps to ensure that negative surprises are kept to a minimum during implementation. One important step in preventing complaints and lawsuits is to know when and how to communicate with your affected employees, informing them in a timely manner of the date, reasons, and consequences of the reorganization or transfer.

You can begin to devise a notification plan for your staff and appoint someone to carry out the notification requirements in due time. When you start planning early and in close consultation with your local advisors, you can also decide whose contract to terminate and make sure you fulfill the requirements in a timely manner and according to local laws, such as TUPE in England. You can ask your local advisors to provide you with the suggested timeframes for each action—and with suggested ways to describe the planned transactions in your company's internal and external communications.

Even in countries with mandatory employee protection, you still have ways to minimize legal risk. The drafting of employment or service contracts may offer one option, especially when setting the notice period and severance pay in a manager's employment agreement. In some countries, for example in Sweden, managing directors and certain other senior managers are often exempted from the applicability of the statute providing protection to employees. In Sweden, under the Swedish Employment Protection Act (EPA), neither the length of the notice period nor the amount of the severance pay is then regulated by law. Where the EPA does not apply, it is up to the parties to agree on severance issues. Under Swedish case law, however, an employee can only be exempted from the applicability of the EPA if that employee is entitled to a notice period of at least six months. The trend in Sweden has been that a managing director and other senior managers can receive up to 24 months' salary when given notice of termination, although the most common amount given is 12 months' salary. Employment agreements for such employees, on the other hand, often state a mutual notice period of six months and, if the employment is terminated by the company, a severance payment of six to 12 months' salary.[26]

Other precautions are also available, depending on the countries involved. For an internationally mobile workforce, you should consider offering jobs in other subsidiaries. In some contexts, you can negotiate severance agreements or mutual termination agreements.[27] You should always seek local advice on the optimal methods and their proper implementation.

Approaches for preventing potential liability related to wrongful discharge in the US

In the US, you should consider the following approaches for preventing potential liability related to wrongful discharge.

Review your hiring practices
First, review your hiring practices. Careful screening of prospective employees to eliminate those who are candidates for dismissal down the road is an obvious approach. Unfortunately, given the defamation risks associated with comments about an employee's performance, information is difficult to obtain from former employers.

Another hiring strategy is to increase the number of temporary employees. Companies have long used this strategy outside the US to avoid regulations that protect regular employees. In the US, temporary workers, informally called "permatemps," have become permanent fixtures at many companies.[28]

Document review and training
A second strategy is directed toward statements that might create an exception to the employment-at-will rule. Train and constantly remind managers that statements to staff like "as long as you do a good job, you'll have a job" create an inappropriate expectation that the company will fire employees only when there is good cause.

Also review company documents and delete language that might overturn the employment-at-will rule. For example, a few years ago one of the authors gave a presentation at a major utility company in Texas. In preparing the talk, he reviewed the company's recruiting brochure. A statement in the brochure caused concern. To paraphrase, it read: "After joining the company, you will first participate in an orientation program. You then will be assigned to a permanent position that is consistent with your career goals." The problem here is "permanent," a word that should be permanently avoided in all company documents. During the presentation he quoted the brochure. Immediately afterward, two human resource managers mentioned their concern about this language and asked for a copy of the brochure.

The following year the company invited him back for another presentation. In preparing for the return engagement, he noticed that the company had a new brochure and that the quoted statement had been "slightly" altered. Paraphrasing again, it now read: "At the end of the orientation program, an interesting career may be waiting for you." Clearly the company had understood the problem with the original brochure!

The third strategy is to attempt to reduce liability for defamatory statements by instructing your staff that they should not comment on the job performance of former employees. In fact, they should make no comments at all but should, instead, forward all inquiries to human resources. A human resources professional will then provide very limited information regarding the time of employment and title but will not discuss performance matters. This approach obviously causes problems for prospective employers trying to investigate someone's employment history. It also causes problems when you have dismissed someone for reasons unrelated to performance (for example, when you downsize your business) and want to say something positive to a prospective employer. Nevertheless, in a survey of Fortune 500 firms, all respondents said that they do not provide references.[29]

STEP FOUR: CLIMB TO THE BALCONY TO SEE THE BIG PICTURE AND BECOME MORE PROACTIVE

In the past, an organization's assets were measured in terms of land, buildings, and equipment. Then for a long time, the corporate mantra was that employees are the most valuable asset in any organization. While employees are still an important asset, in today's global, networked economy, management attention extends beyond employees to the entire talent pool, internal and external, and to what that talent pool accomplishes or co-creates together. Your ability to attract and retain the best talent and find the right balance between internal and external resources is crucial to your goal of achieving competitive advantage.

When you climb to the balcony you may see your employment and talent pool issues and your role in relation to them in a new light. If you find that you need to reorganize your business or replace some of your employees through outside service providers, you should not let employment law issues hinder your plans. Applying the Manager's Legal Plan™ and proactively embracing outsourcing can give your company a competitive advantage by maximizing the benefits while reducing the negative by-products that outsourcing can produce.

As you saw in the earlier steps of the Manager's Legal Plan™, your company can take action to increase the likelihood of a smooth transition. It is important to plan well ahead and make sure all of the employment implications are considered at the outset. Also remember that the treatment of employees in one deal could be different in different jurisdictions, and the business agreement will need to reflect that.[30]

If you work for a large multinational company, you may be under increasing pressure to deal with your employees on a global, rather than local, level. This may include implementing global employment policies that ensure that the same standards apply to all employees, regardless of geographical location. An important part of the process of adopting such policies is to consult with local counsel to ensure legal compliance in each jurisdiction in which the policies operate.[31]

Under the EU's Acquired Rights Directive the employees' terms and conditions pass to whomever inherits the employees. Because these terms and conditions can be difficult to change, you will need to consider the issues involved and have an understanding of the impact these issues can have on your plans. So addressing these issues at an early stage in policy and outsourcing planning is critical.

When you remove yourself from the legal fray and gain perspective, you may notice from the balcony that some of your company's current strategies are outdated or only address symptoms of a deeper problem. For instance, in the at-will legal environment of the US, you should ask yourself: What if we waived the at-will rights we have? What is the real cost of wrongful discharge litigation? Is it the potential damage award or is it the cost generated by the fear of litigation and damage awards? And are there sound business practices that can reduce potential awards?

The story of Lincoln Electric Company offers an example of a company that went to the balcony, saw the big picture, and did something many companies have not been willing to do: it waived the at-will rights it had under US employment law and, instead, offered guaranteed employment for all full-time workers who had been there at least three years. One might think that this would place Lincoln Electric at a competitive disadvantage. Not so. Despite having some of the highest-paid factory workers in the world, the company dominates the price-sensitive welding market. Fortune 500 executives regularly visit the company to learn its secret, and Lincoln has been a case study at Harvard Business School since 1947.[32] In his article "Pathways of legal strategy," Professor Robert C. Bird of the University of Connecticut uses Lincoln as an example of companies that leverage law to transform the organization and use legal resources for sustainable competitive advantage.[33] The company has not laid off employees in the US operations since 1948.[34]

According to the company, "[m]ore than 100 years ago, the founders of Lincoln Electric adopted a policy of absolute integrity—doing the right thing rather than what is expedient, popular or in vogue at the time. Today, that solid ethical heritage remains the foundation of Lincoln Electric's corporate governance practices as its officers and board of directors strategically manage the Company for growth."[35] According to John Stropki, Lincoln Electric's CEO, "I don't think of this as a social responsibility. I think my philosophy and that of my predecessors is that we can perform in an economically challenging environment, and we can spread that pain in a way that long term will better represent our shareholders' interests without crucifying our employee base, and we think it is good business, not bad business, to do that."[36]

The way Lincoln Electric has managed its business and used employment law goes against conventional wisdom in the US. For nearly a century, through good times and bad, Lincoln Electric management and employees have been able to sustain their unusual relationship. This has proved valuable in shaping company culture and how the company is perceived. It has created trust and loyalty—something that is not easy for competitors to copy.

The Lincoln Electric philosophy should be especially appealing to US companies because of the indirect costs associated with changes in the employment-at-will rule. The Rand Corporation conducted an in-depth empirical study that assessed the impact of the erosion of the rule. The study concluded that the indirect costs of the exceptions to the employment-at-will rule are a hundred times greater than the direct legal costs (such as jury awards) that receive the most attention from US managers. The indirect costs include keeping poor performers, making severance payments, and forcing managers to use complex and time-consuming processes before discharging anyone. In other words, the view from the balcony is that company costs in avoiding litigation far exceed actual litigation costs.[37]

The view from the balcony also provides a perspective on the typical US company's "no comment" approach to requests for information from prospective employers. This approach is fine as far as it goes, but it overlooks the fact that your conversations are not only with outsiders. For instance, what do you say when one of your staff asks you why an employee is no longer with the company? A "no comment" response might cause morale problems and unrest among your employees. But a comment that is untrue opens the door to a defamation lawsuit. For example, an employee who had worked for a company for 41 years was fired after the company accused him of stealing a $35 company telephone. The employee, who claimed that the telephone belonged to him, sued the company for defamation after it posted notices on company bulletin boards accusing him of theft. A jury awarded the employee $15.5 million in damages and the case was later settled.[38]

Even if you say nothing to outsiders or other employees, liability for defamation is still possible in some US states. For example, a trader on the Chicago Board of Trade worked for a brokerage firm for 12 years. In a case brought in a federal court in Illinois, the broker alleged that one afternoon, three of the firm's officials unexpectedly went to his office and, in plain view of other employees, interrogated him about his expense reports. They then escorted him from the office without allowing him to speak to his staff or take his belongings. He alleged that other brokerage firms would not discharge a high-level employee in this manner unless there had been a violation of the criminal law or a breach of ethics. When the firm asked the court to dismiss the case, the judge denied the request.[39]

Still another flaw with the "no comment" approach is the risk of liability for what you say to the discharged employee, even if no one else is present. For example, let's assume that you fire one of your employees, Frank, and you advise him privately that the reason for the discharge is that he is a sociopath, which is not true. Frank then applies for a job with another company. A manager from the company calls you and asks why Frank was fired. You refuse to comment, as required by company policy. The manager then asks Frank to explain why he left the company. Frank's choice is to lie about the reasons you gave, which is not an attractive alternative, or to explain that you told him that the reason for the discharge is that he is a sociopath.

After hearing Frank's explanation the manager (understandably) decides not to hire Frank. Frank then sues you for defamation. "Wait a minute," you say. "I did not defame Frank. He defamed himself by passing on the information." This is still defamation, according to courts in several states, because Frank had no choice. He was compelled to defame himself.

In summary, the conventional US "no comment" approach is flawed because it overlooks conversations with internal staff, actions that might be defamatory, and comments made privately to an employee.

Once you have reframed the legal concern (high litigation costs) as a business concern (the impact of keeping poor performers or giving them large severance packages or the impact of "no comment" policies on morale when staff members ask you why someone was fired), you should explore your business solutions. One solution that should immediately come to mind is a key feature of any quality program: manage by fact. In other words, tell the truth.

Two aspects of truth-telling are especially important in the context of wrongful termination. First, telling the truth and documenting your statements is critically important in the performance review process because your ability to show cause for dismissing a poor performer minimizes the exceptions to the employment-at-will rule. As a Human Resources director at a large energy company stated to one of the authors: "We are an at-will company, but we always try to show cause."

However, this is easier said than done. If you are a typical manager, it is difficult to be completely candid and honest when you sit down with an employee to review performance. For example, one company rates employees on a scale of one to ten, with ten as the highest rating. A study of the records at this company found that no supervisor gave employees a rating of lower than eight and the average score was nine.[40] In an environment where managers are not candid and honest, even poor performers will walk into court with performance reviews that indicate that their work has been "great." The solution: Use candid, fact-based statements when you conduct performance reviews.

Second, truth-telling is important in conversations about the performance of former employees because truth is a defense in a defamation action. As we have seen, the "no comment" approach that dominates US business today is only partially effective because it focuses on external communications while liability may extend to comments made within the company. The "no comment" approach also makes it difficult for your company to obtain information from other companies about prospective employees. By contrast, a truth-telling approach will protect a company across the board—whether the communication is with prospective employers, other employees within the firm, or the discharged employee.

Beyond its impact in wrongful termination cases, truth-telling is important in establishing trust within your company. In a world of flat, lean organizations and new forms of business alliances, trust is essential to competitive advantage. As noted in an article in the *Economist*, "The arguments in favour of trust seem overwhelming. Trust reduces the costs and delays associated with traditional monitoring systems and formal legal contracts. It enables companies to engage the hearts and minds of their employees, not just their passive compliance."[41] Replacing "no comment" policies with management by fact and truth-telling in your internal and external communication represents a major step toward creating an environment of trust.

In today's networked, global economy and *extended enterprises*, different participants in different countries bring different advantages to global competition. Some may bring natural resources, others may bring low-cost labor, yet others skilled research and development talent. The strongest competitive advantage your company possesses may well be its access to key talent, along with its capacity for innovation, creation of intangible assets, and ability to bring talent together. The Manager's Legal Plan™ should facilitate your ability to attract and retain the human resources you need to create and capture new value and strategic advantage.

Chapter Summary

Companies that have access to key talent while controlling their employment costs and avoiding employment pitfalls have a significant opportunity to seize competitive advantage. Many companies look towards outsourcing and subcontracting as a way to minimize costs, free up company resources, and focus on their core business. Sometimes it becomes necessary to terminate the employment of existing staff. In examining employment law concerns that can arise in these contexts and what can be done to avoid them, this chapter has applied the four-step Manager's Legal Plan™ using examples from two quite different legal systems—the EU and the US.

Step One: Understand the law (and that it is not the same everywhere): At-will employment, as it is known in the US, is not recognized internationally. In many countries outside the US, termination of employment contracts is subject to stringent notice and severance requirements, in addition to requirements to notify and consult with employee representatives. So the treatment of employees in one outsourcing deal can be different in different jurisdictions. In the US, changes in the employment-at-will rule have created the potential for large damage awards against companies. When working in the US, you need to understand the nature of these changes, especially the three exceptions to the rule.

Step Two: Know how to cope with legal problems and learn from them: By understanding the laws that apply, you are better equipped to choose whether to "fight or flight," litigate or settle. In some cases, from both the company and the employee's perspective, an amicable solution such as a mutual agreement about the expiration of the employment relationships can be optimal. In others, you may choose to litigate or fight for law reform.

Step Three: Develop business strategies and solutions to prevent future problems: In the EU, when an undertaking is transferred, its employees are transferred as well, along with the terms and conditions of their employment. By understanding the law in advance you will not be surprised by the fact that replacing your employees with service provider employees can become costly and time-consuming. In some instances, you can reach contractual agreement regarding notice period and severance pay and thereby prevent future problems. In the US, your steps to prevent problems may include greater use of temporary employees and careful review of company documents to ensure that they do not override the employment-at-will rule.

Step Four: Climb to the balcony to see the big picture and become more proactive: Do not let employment law issues hinder your business ventures. Obtain appropriate advice and then seek the most appropriate ways to attract and engage new talent and bring talent together to create and capture new value. When viewed from the balcony, the dominant solution to the US wrongful discharge problem can be to emphasize management by fact in the performance review process and in commenting on discharged employees. Management by fact, in turn, creates an environment of trust, which is important in gaining competitive advantage.

Notes

1 Schramm, J. 2006. *SHRM® Workplace Forecast.* The Society for Human Resource Management, June 10 [Online]. Available at: http://www.shrm.org/Research/FutureWorkplaceTrends/Documents/061606WorkplaceForecast.pdf [accessed: August 1, 2010].

2 Baker & McKenzie 2006. Employment pitfalls in international outsourcing transactions. *Outsourcing, Client Alert,* November 1 [Online]. Available at: http://www.bakernet.com/NR/rdonlyres/E138DC2E-5A94-41CA-A330-DC7159C6B433/0/USClientAlertOutsourcingNovember2006.pdf [accessed: August 1, 2010]. See also LogicaCMG 2006. *Ignore the social factor in outsourcing deals at your peril, finds new LogicaCMG study.* News, June 7 [Online]. Available at: http://www.logica.com/we-are-logica/media-centre/news/2006/ignore-the-social-factor-in-outsourcing-deals-at-your-peril-finds-new-logicacmg-study/ [accessed: August 1, 2010].

3 Baker & McKenzie 2006, 1–2.

4 Adler, K.A. and Semerdjian, S.A. 2009. United States, in *Outsourcing 2009.* PLC Cross-border Handbooks [Cd-Rom], Country Q&A. London, Practical Law Company/Legal and Commercial Publishing Ltd. However, US law might require companies to bargain with unions when operations are relocated. And the Worker Adjustment and Retraining Notification Act of 2002 (WARN) requires larger companies to provide advance notice to employees before mass layoffs (St. Antoine, T. 2006. Offshore outsourcing and worker rights. *Law Quadrangle Notes,* Spring, 69).

5 Council Directive 2001/23/EC of 12 March, 2001 on the approximation of the laws of the Member States relating to the safeguarding of employees' rights in the event of transfers of undertakings, businesses, or parts of undertakings or businesses. *Official Journal of the European Communities,* L82, 22 March, 2001, 16–20 [Online]. Available at: http://eur-lex.europa.eu/LexUriServ/LexUriServ.do?uri=OJ:L:2001:082:0016:0020:EN:PDF [accessed: August 1, 2010]. This Directive is sometimes also called the Acquired Rights Directive.

6 The Directive does not apply to all transactions; its targets are asset transfers, not share transfers, where the employment contracts before and after the acquisition remain with the same company. EU countries vary in their definition of the transfer of an undertaking. In case law, a broad interpretation has been given to what constitutes a transfer of an undertaking, which can be deemed to occur even if there is no direct contractual relationship between the parties. See Eversheds 2007. *HR Euronews—Protecting employee rights on the transfer of undertakings*. January 25 [Online]. Available at: https://www.eversheds.com/uk/home/articles/index1.page?ArticleID=templatedata%5CEversheds%5Carticles%5Cdata%5Cen%5CRedundancy_and_restructuring%5CHR_Euronews_Transfers_23Jan07 [accessed: August 1, 2010].

7 Peschek, R. and Taufner, M. 2009. Employment issues on transfers of economic entities in multi-jurisdictional outsourcing, in *Outsourcing 2009*. PLC Cross-border Handbooks [Cd-Rom], Cross-border chapters. London, Practical Law Company/Legal and Commercial Publishing Ltd. For instance, when certain services are outsourced by a company and that company decides to change service provider, this could result in an obligation of the new service provider to continue the employment relationship of the employees of the former provider. See Eversheds 2007 mentioned in the previous Note.

8 Brown, R., Lilley, A., Purton, T. and Wilson, A. 2009. UK (England and Wales), in *Outsourcing 2009*. PLC Cross-border Handbooks [Cd-Rom], Country Q&A. London, Practical Law Company/Legal and Commercial Publishing Ltd.

9 Morgan, V. 2008. Labour and employee benefits: UK (England and Wales), in *Labour and Employee Benefits 2008/09*. Volumes 1 and 2. PLC Cross-border Handbooks [Cd-Rom] Country Q&A, Labour and Employee Benefits Volume 1. London, Practical Law Company/Legal and Commercial Publishing Ltd.

10 Wallander, M. and Welander Wadström, J. 2008. Labour and employee benefits: Sweden, in *Labour and Employee Benefits 2008/09*. Volumes 1 and 2. PLC Cross-border Handbooks [Cd-Rom] Country Q&A, Labour and Employee Benefits Volume 1. Practical Law Company/Legal and Commercial Publishing Ltd.

11 Brown et al. 2009.

12 On August 1, 2010 the amounts were approximately 76,000 euro or 99,000 US dollars.

13 Morgan 2008.

14 Toffoletto, F. 2008. Labour and employee benefits: Italy, in *Labour and Employee Benefits 2008/09*. Volumes 1 and 2. PLC Cross-border Handbooks [Cd-Rom] Country Q&A, Labour and Employee Benefits Volume 1. London, Practical Law Company/Legal and Commercial Publishing Ltd.

15 Lewis, J. 2000. Workplace 2000. *Interchange*, Spring, 1–2.

16 Burns, J.A. 1996. Use and abuse of performance appraisals. *Employee Relations Law Journal*, 22, 167.

17 *Toussaint v. Blue Cross & Blue Shield* [1980] 292 N.W.2d 880.

18 *Fortune v. National Cash Register Company* [1977] 364 N.E.2d 125.

19 *Wagenseller v. Scottsdale Memorial Hospital* [1985] 710 P.2d 1025.

20 *Hill v. Buck* [1984] 678 S.W.2d 612.

21 Stricharchuk, G. 1986. Fired employees turn the reason for dismissal into a legal weapon. *Wall Street Journal*, October 20, 31.

22 Sella, M. 1989. More big bucks in jury verdicts. *ABA Journal*, July, 70.

23 Varchaver, N. 1993. Turmoil at Triton. *American Lawyer*, March, 56–8.

24 Samborn, R. 1991. At-will doctrine under fire. *National Law Journal*, October 14, 40.

25 Salgado, T.A. 1997. References given in good faith gain protection across country. *Executive Newsletter*, January, 6 and 8.

26 Nordblom Åhlberg, K and Pölönen, M. 2008. Sweden and Finland: Golden parachutes, in Severance negotiations: current international trends, by M. Pölönen et al. *2008,* in *Labour and Employee Benefits 2008/09*. Volumes 1 and 2. PLC Cross-border Handbooks [Cd-Rom] Cross-border chapters, Labour and Employee Benefits Volume 1. London, Practical Law Company/ Legal and Commercial Publishing Ltd.

27 See Pölönen et al. *2008*. Severance negotiations: current international trends, in *Labour and Employee Benefits 2008/09*. Volumes 1 and 2. PLC Cross-border Handbooks [Cd-Rom] Cross-border chapters, Labour and Employee Benefits Volume 1. London, Practical Law Company/Legal and Commercial Publishing Ltd.

28 Eisenberg, D. 1999. Rise of the permatemp. *Time*, July 12, 48. The use of permatemps can be risky because they might claim that, if they are doing the same work as regular employees, they should be entitled to regular benefits. Microsoft settled a class action based on a similar claim for $97 million—see Virgin, B. 2000. Microsoft settles "permatemp" suits. *Seattle Post-Intelligencer* (seattlepi.com) December 13 [Online]. Available at: http://www.seattlepi.com/business/micr13.shtml [accessed: August 1, 2010].

29 1993. Companies stop giving references, *Fresno Bee*, June 7, C4.

30 Baker & McKenzie 2006. See also Burden, K. 2009. *Redundancies and Outsourcing—Who Bears the Risk?* DLA Piper Publications, April 22 [Online]. Available at: http://www.dlapiper.com/global/publications/detail.aspx?pub=4209 [accessed: August 1, 2010].

31 Talibart, P. and Sinclair, E. 2008. International employment policies—issues arising from drafting and implementation, in *Labour and Employee Benefits 2008/09*. Volumes 1 and 2. PLC Cross-border Handbooks [Cd-Rom] Cross-border chapters, Labour and Employee Benefits Volume 1. London, Practical Law Company/Legal and Commercial Publishing Ltd.

32 Eisenberg, D., Sieger, M. and Greenwald, J. 2001. Lincoln Electric: Where people are never let go. *Time*, June 18 [Online]. Available at: http://www.time.com/time/magazine/article/0,9171,1000155,00.html [accessed: August 1, 2010].

33 Bird, R.C. 2008. Pathways of legal strategy. *Stanford Journal of Law, Business & Finance*, 14(1), Fall [Online]. Available at: http://www.allbusiness.com/company-activities-management/company-strategy/13483188-1.html [accessed: August 1, 2010].

34 Lincoln 2010a. *Current Openings/Lincoln Electric* [Online]. Available at: http://www.lincolnelectric.com/corporate/career/openings.asp [accessed: August 1, 2010].

35 Lincoln 2010b. *Corporate Governance/Lincoln Electric* [Online]. Available at: http://www.lincolnelectric.com/corporate/about/governance.asp [accessed: August 1, 2010].

36 Koller, F. 2009. *How Old-Fashioned Values Drive a Twenty-First Century Corporation: Lessons from Lincoln Electric's Unique Guaranteed Employment Program—Excerpt From the Preface* [Online]. Available at: http://www.frankkoller.com/the-book-excerpt/ [accessed: August 1, 2010].

37 Dertouzos, J.N. and Karoly, L.A. 1992. *Labor Market Responses to Employer Liability*. Santa Monica, CA: Rand, xi–xiv.

38 Libel/Slander Litigation. Susman Godfrey L.L.P. [Online]. Available at: http://www.susmangodfrey.com/practice/libel.html [accessed: September 10, 2001].

39 *Zechman v. Merrill Lynch* [1990] U.S., Dist. LEXIS 15949.

40 DuFresnes, E.J. 1994. Honest employee evaluations: Risk management for the 90s. *World Reports*, July–September, 43.

41 1995. Trust in me, *Economist*, December 16, 61.

CHAPTER 4 Use Regulation as a Source of Competitive Advantage: Transform Environmental Regulation into Value Creation

Three groups of stakeholders are especially important to the success of your company and your ability to create value for your shareholders. Chapters 2 and 3 focused on two of these groups in discussing how to meet customer needs and attract and retain key talent. The third key stakeholder, government, represents the interests of society at large when it imposes rules and regulations on business. This chapter examines environmental protection to show that even governmental regulation can create opportunities for competitive advantage.

The Impact of Environmental Regulation

Protection of the environment is an especially controversial and costly form of regulation. You wear two hats when the government regulates your company to protect the environment. One is the hat of a citizen concerned with degradation of the environment. We are all aware of general scientific studies that highlight threats to the environment.[1]

A specific example of the impact that business has on the environment is provided by James Womack and Daniel Jones in their book, *Lean Thinking*.[2] A teenager in England opens a can of cola, which takes a few minutes to drink, and then throws away the can. This simple act of consumption was preceded by many weeks of energy and other resource consumption in Australia, Norway, and England as bauxite ore was transformed into an aluminum can through purification, smelting, rolling mills, forming, painting, lacquering, and coating. The can was filled with a combination of elements that include sugar from beets raised in France, phosphorous from open pit mines in Idaho, and caffeine from a chemical manufacturer. Once filled, the cans were placed in cardboard cartons made of wood pulp from forests ranging from Siberia to British Columbia.[3]

Millions of production and transportation processes similar to the manufacture of a can of cola have a cumulative impact on the environment that affects both the natural and social systems on which business depends. As noted by one CEO, in referring to corporate social responsibility, "A healthy branch [business] cannot survive on a rotten trunk."[4]

Wearing your concerned citizen's hat, protection of the environment makes sense. But wearing your other hat, as a manager attempting to create shareholder value, you see environmental issues from a different perspective as you attempt to cope with a flood of environmental regulations. Huge amounts of money have been spent on environmental compliance over the past years, as the number of environmental rules and regulations at the local, national, and international levels has swelled. It is no wonder that environmental concerns dominate discussion of legal matters in company annual reports.

In some instances, environmental regulation raises serious doubts about whether regulators and authorities use common sense in writing and enforcing rules. Philip Howard, in his bestselling book *The Death of Common Sense,* mentions a 35-page Environmental Protection Agency (EPA) rule that required companies to install equipment that would filter benzene in waste pipes. Amoco complied with the rule at a cost of $31 million, but also pointed out to the EPA that the benzene pollution in the waste pipes was insignificant. When EPA officials visited the Amoco work site, they realized that a simple, inexpensive solution was possible. The rule was, to use Howard's words, "almost perfect in its failure. It maximized the cost to Amoco while minimizing the benefit to the public."[5]

Governments and regulators are starting to see the need for a change in terms of both policy and regulation. The European Union (EU) adopted an integrated energy and climate change policy in December 2008, including ambitious targets for 2020. It hopes to set Europe on the right track toward a sustainable future with a low-carbon, energy-efficient economy by:

- cutting greenhouse gases by 20 percent (30 percent if international agreement is reached);
- reducing energy consumption by 20 percent through increased energy efficiency;
- meeting 20 percent of our energy needs from renewable sources.[6]

In recent years, many governments and regulators have set up *Regulatory Reform* agendas and initiated *Better Regulation* schemes that extend to environmental regulation and beyond. In the EU, the European Commission is committed to developing a better regulatory environment for business that is simple, understandable, effective, and enforceable.[7] In addition to the Commission, the European Parliament and the European Economic and Social Committee (EESC) have long promoted and argued for *better regulation, simplification,* and *communication* as main policy objectives. Their main steps towards this goal are summarized in the recent Opinion of the EESC on the Proactive Law approach,[8] where the EESC develops a framework for avoiding over-detailed and unnecessary regulation. In its Opinion, the EESC refers to the work of *the Nordic School of Proactive Law*[9] and emphasizes that the Proactive Law approach is an important step towards better regulation at the EU level. The EESC recommends that the Commission, the Council, and the European Parliament adopt the proactive approach when planning, drawing up, revising, and implementing Community law and encourages Member States also to do so wherever appropriate.[10]

In the UK, the new way of thinking is demonstrated by the UK Department for Business, Innovation and Skills (BIS), a new ministerial department of the Government created in the summer of 2009. According to the Better Regulation Executive (BRE), "In the current economic climate, businesses must remain competitive. We are committed to ensuring that Government does not create unnecessary burdens on business, and removes existing ones where possible, whilst delivering key social and environmental protections. We are on track to achieve our target to reduce the burdens faced by business by 25% by 2010. But we need your help."[11]

Apply the Manager's Legal Plan™ to Environmental Regulation

Given recent developments, it may be tempting to focus your energy on fighting for saner rules or on minimizing the costs of compliance. While these measures may be necessary, they are not sufficient for you to gain advantage over your competitors. The four steps of the Manager's Legal Plan™ will help clarify opportunities for value creation that arise when environmental regulation is viewed as more than a cost of doing business.

STEP ONE: UNDERSTAND THE LEGAL FRAMEWORK OF ENVIRONMENTAL REGULATION

The first step in the Manager's Legal Plan™ is to understand the fundamental legal structure of environmental regulation.[12] Although this area of the law is complex, technical, and laden with more acronyms than you may ever care to master, keeping the big picture in mind when you deal with specific environmental matters should help you seize competitive advantage.

While the following road map of environmental law focuses on EU-level and US environmental protection, other countries and local governments also have their own environmental laws that parallel or complement EU and US law.[13]

EU environmental policy: polluter pays

The EU has formulated a long-term strategy to dovetail the policies for economically, socially and environmentally sustainable development, its goal being sustainable improvement of the well-being and standard of living of current and future generations. This strategy provides an EU-wide policy framework to deliver sustainable development—that is, to meet the needs of the present without compromising the ability of future generations to meet their own needs.[14]

In Europe, each country used to have its own laws and liability regimes that covered damage to persons and property. These laws seldom covered damage to the wider environment. Some national public law provisions allowed public authorities to pursue polluters in cases of water or soil pollution, but the authorities usually had a wide margin of discretion whether to act against the polluter. Article 174 of the EU Treaty, which became effective in 1993, states that EU policy on the environment "shall be based on the precautionary principle and on the principles that preventive action should be taken, that environmental damage should as a priority be rectified at source and that the polluter should pay."[15]

Based on the "polluter pays" principle, the Environmental Liability Directive (ELD)[16] establishes a common framework for liability with a view to preventing and remedying damage to animals, plants, natural habitats and water resources, and damage affecting the land. The principle of liability applies to environmental damage and imminent threat of damage resulting from occupational activities, where it is possible to establish a causal link between the damage and the activity in question.

The ELD distinguishes between two complementary situations, each one governed by a different liability scheme: occupational activities specifically mentioned in the Directive and other occupational activities. The first liability scheme applies mainly to agricultural or industrial activities requiring a license under the Directive on integrated pollution prevention and control,[17] activities that discharge heavy metals into water or the air, installations producing dangerous chemical substances, waste management activities (including landfills and incinerators), and activities concerning genetically modified organisms and micro-organisms. Under this first scheme, an operator may be held responsible even when not at fault. The second liability scheme applies to all occupational activities other than those listed in the Directive, but only where there is damage, or imminent threat of damage, to species or natural habitats protected by Community legislation. In this case, the operator will be held liable only if he is at fault or negligent.[18]

All but three EU Member States have adopted the ELD. However, the ELD gives significant discretion to the Member States, who can decide whether to use optional defenses (and other optional choices) and whether to develop stricter measures than prescribed by the Directive.[19]

European examples: REACH and the Emissions Trading Scheme

In addition to the ELD, the EU has taken many other steps toward protecting the environment. One of the most recent steps is modernizing European chemicals legislation and establishing REACH,[20] a single integrated system for the registration, evaluation, and authorization of chemicals. Its objective is to improve the protection of human health and the environment while maintaining competitiveness and strengthening the spirit of innovation in Europe's chemicals industry. The European Chemicals Agency (ECHA), located in Helsinki, will manage the registration, evaluation, authorization, and restriction processes for chemical substances to ensure consistency across the EU. According to the ECHA website, these REACH processes are designed to provide additional information on chemicals to ensure their safe use, and to ensure competitiveness of the European industry.[21]

A cornerstone of EU climate change policies is the EU's Emissions Trading Scheme (ETS) launched in 2005. The ETS, also known as the scheme for greenhouse gas emission allowance trading, was established by Directive 2003/87/EC.[22] EU governments have set limits on how much CO_2 power plants and energy-intensive factories are allowed to emit each year, accounting for almost half of the EU's total CO_2 emissions. The ETS gives financial incentives to reduce emissions by establishing a market-based trading system. Plants that emit less CO_2 than their limits can sell their unused emission quotas to other companies that have emissions higher than their allowances. Companies that exceed their emission limits and do not cover them with emission rights bought from others must pay hefty penalties.[23]

The EU ETS is already a key driver of international carbon trading and provides a solid foundation for a global carbon market. Currently, over 160 countries, representing over 90 percent of the global population, can engage in the emerging carbon market either through emissions trading schemes or through the Kyoto Protocol's project-based mechanisms.[24]

US National Environmental Policy and the Environmental Protection Agency

Anglo-American environmental law is very old, with origins going back at least to medieval England, where laws established the seasons when soft coal could be burned. But a comprehensive set of US environmental laws did not emerge until the last third of the twentieth century, when people began to recognize the threat to the environment. The year 1970 brought two landmark events, the signing into law of the National Environmental Policy Act (NEPA) and the creation of EPA.

NEPA declares that it is US policy "to create and maintain conditions under which man and nature can exist in productive harmony, and fulfill the social, economic, and other requirements of present and future generations of Americans." One tool for accomplishing this goal is a requirement that federal agencies must prepare an environmental impact statement (EIS) in every recommendation for legislation and whenever engaged in a major federal action that significantly impacts environmental quality. The EIS provides an assessment of likely environmental impacts of alternative courses of action.

While NEPA articulates national policy, the act applies only to activities of federal agencies. The EPA has a greater direct impact on business. This agency assists the government and private business in halting environmental deterioration, creates environmental regulations, and monitors industry for violation of federal law. The EPA has a variety of enforcement options, ranging from informal responses (such as a warning letter) to referral to the Department of Justice for criminal prosecution. The following four categories of federal environmental laws are especially important to business.[25]

Water pollution

Although legislation governing US waterways goes back to the late 1800s, the centerpiece of water pollution laws is the Clean Water Act. This act is designed to restore the "chemical, physical, and biological integrity of the Nation's waters." The act requires states to set water quality standards for various uses of water (such as drinking, recreation, and fishing), controls municipal sewage systems, and authorizes the EPA to protect marshes and other wetlands. The act also establishes strict standards for private industry's discharge of pollutants into waterways and sewage systems. Under the National Pollutant Discharge Elimination System (NPDES), you must obtain a permit if you want to discharge pollutants from a "point source" (for example, a pipe). Disposal of materials into the ocean requires an EPA permit under a separate law.

A second notable law relating to water quality is the Safe Drinking Water Act. This act establishes national standards for drinking water. The law also authorizes the EPA to regulate the injection of solid wastes into deep wells—for instance, through leakage from underground storage tanks.

Air pollution

The Clean Air Act is the key legislation directed toward air pollution. Under this act, the EPA sets National Ambient Air Quality Standards (NAAQS) that limit ambient (that is, circulating) pollution. These standards are implemented by the states, which are required to develop state implementation plans (SIPs) that represent a collection of regulations that states use to control pollution.

In 1990 Congress added almost 800 pages of amendments to the Clean Air Act (which was originally 50 pages long). These amendments established a permit system modeled after the Clean Water Act. Your permit describes the type and amount of pollutants that you are releasing and the steps that you are taking to measure and reduce pollution. The 1990 amendments also include market-based approaches to pollution control, including pollution allowances that you can buy and sell.[26]

Waste disposal

Two major federal laws are directed toward industrial dumping of hazardous wastes. First, the Resource Conservation and Recovery Act (RCRA) adopts a "cradle-to-grave" philosophy whereby the EPA has the power to govern the creation, storage, transport, treatment, and disposal of hazardous waste. If your company generates hazardous waste, you must obtain a permit (called a *manifest*) to store the waste at your site or ship it to an EPA-approved facility. If you own or operate a site, you must prove that you can pay for damage resulting from site operation. Even after the site is closed to further dumping, you must set aside funds to monitor and maintain the site safely. Under RCRA, the EPA also regulates your underground storage tanks.

The second law, the Comprehensive Environmental Response, Compensation, and Liability Act (CERCLA, also known as "Superfund"), gives the EPA emergency powers to respond to environmental dangers from hazardous waste disposal. The EPA can order immediate removal of wastes that represent an imminent danger (for instance, from a train wreck or oil spill) and can carry out "planned removals" when the danger is substantial. Under CERCLA, the EPA will prod you to clean up sites that you have abandoned. If you refuse, the government will clean up the site and will then assess damages of up to triple the clean-up costs. Amendments to CERCLA (called the Superfund Amendment and Reauthorization Act or SARA) protect innocent landowners who make an "appropriate inquiry" into the prior uses of real estate that they purchase.

Chemical hazards

The Toxic Substances Control Act controls the manufacture, processing, commercial distribution, use, and disposal of chemicals that pose unreasonable environmental risks. Under this law, the EPA tracks and screens the 75,000 industrial chemicals that are produced or imported into the US.[27] You must notify the EPA 90 days before manufacturing or importing a new chemical. The EPA may require you to label your products in a certain way, keep records on your manufacturing or disposal processes, and document adverse reactions to people exposed to your chemicals. The EPA may ban substances that are especially hazardous.

Another law, the Emergency Planning and Community Right to Know Act, was enacted following a disaster in Bhopal, India, where over 2,000 people died after chemicals escaped from a Union Carbide factory. This law is designed to help local communities protect the public from chemical hazards. For example, you must file information with state and local authorities about the chemicals that you use.[28]

Approximately 35,000 chemical pesticides are used in the US to eliminate insects, fungi, and rodents. Two major laws, the Federal Insecticide, Fungicide, and Rodenticide Act and the Federal Food, Drug, and Cosmetic Act, are designed to regulate these chemicals. The EPA has the right to determine whether individual pesticides balance effectiveness against safety and can ban the use of a pesticide that has an unreasonable effect on the environment. To enable the EPA to perform this function, you must provide the agency with a wealth of data about the pesticides that you manufacture, including the way they work and their side effects.

STEP TWO: KNOW HOW TO COPE WITH ENVIRONMENTAL REGULATION

With the big picture perspective of environmental regulation in mind, the next step is to explore traditional flight-or-fight opportunities.

Flight

Flight in this case could mean moving your business operations to another country. At one time it might have been possible for you to find other countries where environmental regulation was more lax than in your home country. Today, however, there is remarkable similarity in the laws as they appear on the books.

For example, at one time companies opened plants in the People's Republic of China because a combination of substandard environmental regulations and lax enforcement resulted in lower operational costs. But in recent years, China has upgraded both its environmental laws and enforcement. For instance, you are subject to up to ten years in prison for committing an environmental crime. These new laws prompted a major US company to close a plant in Jiangsu Province after concluding that it could not operate the plant at a profit because of a new environmental law.[29]

In many countries environmental regulation may even be more stringent than in your home country. New forms of regulation focus on products rather than pollution caused by the manufacturing process. For example, several countries have "take-back" laws that require you to take back product packaging so that it can be reused or recycled outside the public waste disposal system.[30] According to a study of 17 industrialized countries, the leaders in reducing pollution include Germany, the Netherlands, Sweden, Japan, and the United Kingdom.[31]

Fight

The traditional alternative to flight, fighting environmental regulation, takes place both before and after environmental laws and regulations are enacted (see Figure 4.1). Before a new environmental law is enacted, you have the opportunity to contribute to the public policy process by making your views known to the appropriate government body.

Much of EU law takes the form of Directives that set out general rules and objectives but leave Member States the choice as to how to attain them. In transposing Directives into national law, governments sometimes involve regional and local authorities (where laws occasionally are "gold plated" with the addition of requirements or procedures that are not required by the Directive). So your fight might take place at the EU, Member State, or local level.

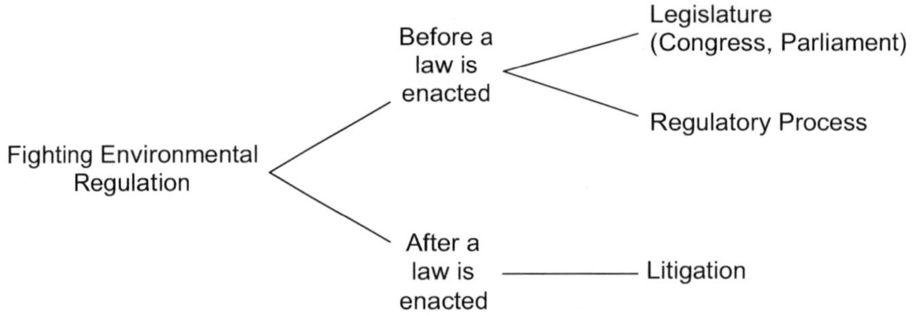

Figure 4.1 Fighting environmental regulation

Once a law has been enacted in the US, Congress authorizes agencies like the EPA to create regulations that fill in the details about how the law works. An agency will first publish a proposed regulation in the *Federal Register,* which will give you the opportunity to review it and provide comments. After considering your comments, and possibly revising the regulation, the EPA issues a final rule, which is then published in the Code of Federal Regulations.[32]

After a new law or regulation goes into effect, the fight often continues through the court system, especially in the US. A legendary case illustrates a fight before and after a final rule was adopted. Companies that produced peanut butter challenged a proposed government regulation specifying that peanut butter had to contain at least 95 percent peanut content. When this regulation was proposed in 1959, some manufacturers were producing peanut butter that contained 20–25 percent hydrogenated oils (lard). The manufacturers fought the proposed rule because a higher peanut content would increase their costs. Through a combination of tactics that included public hearings and appeals in the court system, the regulation was delayed for 12 years and, in the meantime, lowered to 90 percent peanut content.[33]

The peanut butter case was touted as a victory for manufacturers, who were able to continue manufacturing cheaper peanut butter during the 12-year regulatory process and who eventually obtained a 5 percent reduction in the proposed peanut content. Before investing significant resources in industry activities like this, however, you should carefully analyze the costs and the benefits from a competitive advantage perspective. From a cost perspective, are your expenditures benefiting other companies that are not participating in the battle (the "free riders" described in Chapter 1)? And on the benefit side, will your battle for or against a regulation give you competitive advantage vis-à-vis your competitors in the industry or will the battle, instead, improve the playing field for everyone without affecting your own competitive posture?

Even when it is clear that an environmental issue has a direct impact on your company, the cost of the fight may not be worth the benefit. For example, what would you do if someone produced a document about your company that you felt misrepresented the truth? McDonald's faced this question after London Greenpeace published a leaflet that accused McDonald's of a number of injustices, including destruction of rain forests. McDonald's identified five individuals who were responsible for the leaflet. Three of the five apologized and McDonald's decided to sue the other two, an unemployed single parent and a former gardener who had a part-time job in a pub.

Eleven years after the leaflet was published, McDonald's secured a "victory" with a judgment of approximately $98,000 against the two, although the trial judge also ruled that parts of the leaflet were true. The trial was the longest in English history and generated 40,000 documents. The two defendants were ineligible for legal aid (which is not available in libel suits in England) and defended the case without lawyers, creating a David versus Goliath scenario and considerable negative publicity for McDonald's. The trial cost McDonald's an estimated $16 million, even before the two defendants took their case to the European Court of Human Rights. In the words of one commentator: "Clearly the verdict will be enjoyed without much relish."[34]

When an agency action has a direct impact on your company or on you as an individual, the decision regarding whether to fight is easier. For instance, a supervisor who worked for a railroad in the US was charged with violating the Clean Water Act. The railroad had hired a contracting company to work on a project that involved using a backhoe to load rock onto railroad cars. An oil pipeline ran next to the railroad tracks where this work was performed. Parts of the pipeline had been covered before (but not after) the supervisor took over responsibility for the project. A backhoe operator accidentally hit the unprotected pipeline, causing an estimated 1,000–5,000 gallons of oil to flow into a river. The supervisor was charged with negligence in violating the Clean Water Act and was sentenced to six months in prison, six months in a halfway house, and six months of supervised release. Despite a fight that went all the way to the Supreme Court, the conviction was upheld on appeal.[35]

As these cases illustrate, there may be high stakes in a fight involving environmental matters. As a result, the search for business solutions, Step Three, becomes important.

STEP THREE: DEVELOP BUSINESS STRATEGIES AND SOLUTIONS TO ADDRESS ENVIRONMENTAL REGULATION

As with the traditional fight described in Step Two, there are both "before" and "after" business strategies to address environmental concerns. Two strategies are useful before environmental laws and regulations are adopted, while three strategies address concerns that arise after regulations become effective. See Figure 4.2.

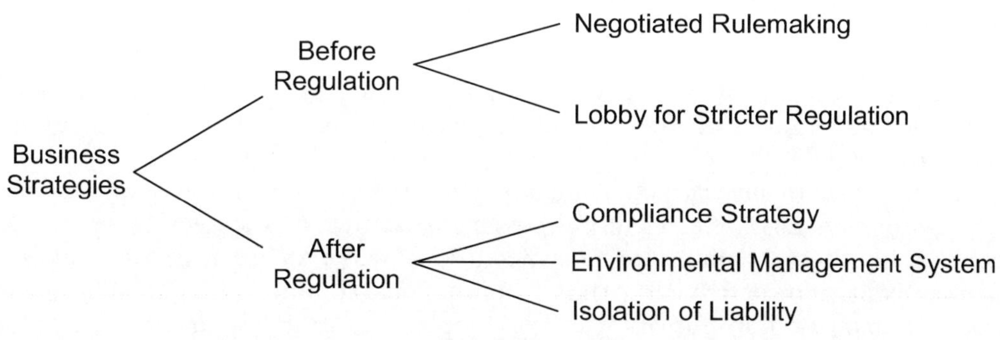

Figure 4.2 Business strategies for addressing environmental regulations

Before adoption of laws and regulations

Two strategies that are effective before the adoption of environmental laws and regulations are negotiated rulemaking and lobbying for stronger regulation.

Use Negotiated Rulemaking. As described earlier, the traditional approach to environmental rulemaking in the US involves notice from the EPA regarding a new rule and response from private parties in the form of comments. This process is slow and adversarial, and frequently leads to litigation. To surmount these problems, a negotiated rulemaking process (dubbed regulatory negotiation or *reg-neg*) has been developed. Under this process, regulators meet with private parties in an attempt to find shared interests and to reach consensus *before* a rule is even proposed.[36] Congress endorsed this process in 1990 with the enactment of the Negotiated Rulemaking Act.

For example, the EPA used the negotiated rulemaking process in establishing a rule relating to emission standards for ovens that process coal into coke. In January 1992, the EPA created a committee consisting of representatives from the EPA, environmental groups, the steel industry, states, and unions. Meeting every two to three weeks for four months, the committee drafted a proposed rule that was published in December 1992. The final rule, which was adopted 14 months later, has not been challenged in court.[37]

Argue for Stronger Environmental Laws. A second approach, which global companies use, is to argue for stronger environmental regulation in developing countries where they do business. For instance, the head of environmental affairs for a major corporation once told one of the authors that he had recently traveled to several less developed countries with a group of executives who held similar positions at other global firms. The purpose of the trip was to convince government officials in these countries to adopt and enforce stricter environmental laws.

This approach may seem counterintuitive, but there is a compelling logic that drives the push for higher standards. In the wake of increasing uniformity of environmental regulations worldwide, global companies often adopt global environmental standards that apply even in countries where environmental regulation is relatively weak. These high standards result in additional costs that make it difficult for global companies to compete with local firms. Strengthening local environmental law levels the playing field by forcing local companies to incur the same environmental expenses as the multinationals.[38]

After adoption of laws and regulations

Three strategies are effective after environmental laws and regulations have been adopted: compliance, adoption of an environmental management system (EMS), and isolation of liability within a subsidiary.

Comply with Environmental Law. The compliance strategy is obvious: attempt to comply with environmental law as efficiently as possible. This strategy is sometimes described as a reactive approach, in contrast to an avoidance mentality. An article in the *Academy of Management Executive* describes the shift: "Multinational corporations (MNCs) have gone through a dramatic transformation in their approaches to environmental protection, from 1) avoiding compliance with regulatory controls during the 1960s to 2) reacting to regulatory requirements and attempting to minimize the costs of compliance."[39]

As a result of the compliance mentality "the vast majority of hard investment in cleaner and safer processes is mandated by law." The scope of this investment is significant, amounting to almost 20 percent of total capital expenditures and up to 10 percent of sales in some industries.[40] Clearly the companies that can best control this expense will have a competitive advantage.

Perhaps the most important compliance tool is an environmental audit. As the name implies, this audit is conducted to determine whether you are in compliance with environmental regulations. As a corporate attorney observed, "The audit is perhaps the best mechanism for helping management to understand and identify environmental compliance issues. It is, therefore, a management tool. .... [An] audit will enable the company to identify, correct, and prevent the recurrence of violations, thereby avoiding liabilities."[41]

Create an Environmental Management System. An EMS is defined by the EPA as "a systematic approach to ensuring that environmental activities are well managed in any organization. ... An EMS is not fundamentally a compliance system. An EMS focuses on management systems. However, an effective EMS can be an important part of a compliance system, and can reasonably be expected to ensure and improve environmental compliance."[42]

There are many EMS models, the best known of which is ISO 14001. ISO, the International Organization for Standardization, is a Switzerland-based organization of national standards institutes. ISO finalized ISO 14001 in 1996. The most recent version of ISO 14001 was released in 2004. Companies that meet the ISO standard can "self-declare" their compliance to customers or can apply for neutral-party certification.[43] Although certification of conformity to the standard is not a requirement of ISO 14001, at the end of 2007, at least 154,572 certificates had been issued in 148 countries and economies.[44]

Compliance with ISO 14001 is voluntary and an EMS should be viewed primarily as a management system. However, there are many potential benefits, including better access to capital, lower insurance premiums, and improved efficiency, supply chain relationships, regulatory relationships, and public image.[45]

While ISO 14001 is an important standard, other EMS models are also in use. In 2000, the governments of Canada, Mexico, and the US published a list of ten elements that are compatible with many of these models, including ISO 14001.[46] These elements provide you with a checklist for reviewing your EMS:

1. An environmental policy that is well documented and clearly communicated.
2. Communication of legal requirements and voluntary undertakings to employees and others who might affect your ability to meet these standards.
3. Environmental objectives and targets, including a timeline.
4. A structure, resources, and assignment of responsibilities to meet your objectives and targets.
5. Operational controls to meet your objectives and targets.
6. Procedures for preventing or correcting occurrences that might affect your ability to achieve your objectives and targets.
7. Appropriate training to achieve your objectives and targets.
8. Integration of the EMS into your overall planning and decision-making processes.
9. Maintenance of appropriate documentation.
10. Continuous evaluation and improvement.

Isolate Environmental Liability. The "Organizational Approach" section of Chapter 2 describes the principle of limited liability as it applies to corporate shareholders. Under this principle, a parent corporation is not liable for the debts of its subsidiaries unless the parent is directly involved in the specific activity that created the liability or unless the parent does something (such as exercising a great degree of control over the subsidiary) that leads a court to pierce the corporate veil that normally protects the parent from liability.

These principles apply in the environmental arena. For instance, the US claimed that a parent corporation, CPC, was responsible under CERCLA for the costs of cleaning up environmental damage caused by its subsidiary, Ott Chemical, which was bankrupt. In reviewing this case (and sending it back to the trial court for further proceedings), the Supreme Court determined that CERCLA did not change general principles of corporate law. In the words of the Court, CPC would not be liable for the damage caused by Ott Chemical "unless the corporate veil may be pierced ... [or unless CPC] actively participated in, and exercised control over, the operations of the facility itself."[47]

The clear message from this decision is that it is possible for you to protect your parent corporation from environmental liability created by your subsidiaries through the principle of limited liability.

STEP FOUR: CLIMB TO THE BALCONY AND REFRAME ENVIRONMENTAL REGULATIONS AS A BUSINESS OPPORTUNITY

Step Three (the search for business strategies to address environmental regulation) is necessary for all companies but not sufficient to gain competitive advantage. The fundamental limitation of Step Three is that these strategies relate to compliance with environmental regulations and these regulations, in turn, concentrate on end-of-pipe controls. Focusing on these regulations may cause you to overlook significant opportunities to move ahead of your competitors. When you climb to the balcony for a broader perspective, you should ask this fundamental business question: Forgetting about legal requirements, does a green strategy create opportunities to lower costs and to increase revenue?

As noted in an article in the *Academy of Management Executive,* multinational corporations have decided that the answer to this question is yes, as they have progressed from avoiding compliance to reacting to environmental regulations in an attempt to minimize compliance costs to trying to turn environmental problems into opportunities.[48] For instance, "3M management pledged to go beyond government regulations, in part by developing environmental management plans that merge environmental goals with business strategy."[49]

There are four linked approaches to consider as you attempt to move from a reactive to a proactive posture. In considering these approaches, the economic context of your decisions and actions is especially important. As Harvard Professor Forest Reinhardt has wisely observed, instead of asking whether it pays to be green, you should ask what circumstances might make it pay: "A business's behavior with respect to the environment, like any other aspect of strategy or management, should be considered in the light of the basic economic situation of the business: the structure of the industry in which it competes, its own position within that industry, and its internal organizational capabilities."[50]

Make a commitment to sustainable development

The first of the four approaches is perhaps the most important. Your company should move from a compliance mentality to a strategy of commitment to sustainable development. *Sustainable development* is defined by the World Commission on Environment and Development as "that which meets the needs of the present without compromising the ability of future generations to meet their own needs."[51] By committing to this strategy, you may encourage your employees to think creatively about new products and processes while at the same time developing pride in your company.

Because investors are increasingly interested in acquiring stock in companies committed to sustainable development, Dow Jones has developed sustainability indexes. For example, the Dow Jones Sustainability World Index, which was launched in 1999, "covers the top 10% of the biggest 2,500 companies in the Dow Jones Global Total Stock Market Index in terms of economic, environmental and social criteria."[52] The web sites of these companies are a goldmine of information about best practices in sustainable development.

Some companies have gone beyond a commitment to a sustainable environment by making stewardship of the environment a core business purpose. Often these are smaller firms like Patagonia, which has a goal of restoring nature while providing high-performance gear.[53] Patagonia pledges 1 percent of sales or 10 percent of pre-tax profits, whichever is higher, to grassroots environmental groups.[54] But some larger companies also come close to making environmental stewardship a core purpose. For instance, DuPont's 2015 Sustainability Goals include doubling its investment in R&D programs with direct, quantifiable environmental benefits for its customers and consumers along with its value chains. By 2015, DuPont's goal is to grow its annual revenues by at least $2 billion from products that create energy efficiency and/or significant greenhouse gas emissions reductions for its customers. Further, by 2015, DuPont's goal is to nearly double its revenues from non-depletable resources to at least $8 billion.[55]

Select a framework for strategy implementation

Once you have made a commitment to a sustainable environment, you should select a framework for considering the specific actions that are presented in the next section. This framework should enable you to be a cost leader in your industry, to produce products and services that are unique, to win more business, and to become a sought-after business partner. Your framework might be based on one of the following three state-of-the-art models, or you might develop your own framework to meet your particular goals.

World Business Council for Sustainable Development (WBCSD). In 1991, the then Business Council for Sustainable Development coined a word to describe sustainable development from a business perspective: *eco-efficiency*. The WBCSD defines this word as "creating more goods and services with ever less use of resources, waste and pollution."[56] The objective of eco-efficiency is to increase the value of your products and services while at the same time reducing your business's consumption of resources and impact on nature. The WBCSD implementation framework addresses four areas:[57]

- Re-engineer your processes to reduce resource consumption, pollution and costs, while avoiding risks.
- Cooperate with other companies to add value to your byproducts.
- Redesign your products and find new ways to meet customer needs.
- Rethink your markets and re-shape demand and supply completely.

Two WBCSD programs—Eco-Efficiency Metrics & Reporting and the European Eco-Efficiency Initiative (EEEI)—have shaped our thinking on eco-efficiency. The EEEI is a program that the WBCSD conducts jointly with European Partners for the Environment (EPE) in Brussels, supported by the European Commission.

World Resources Institute (WRI). According to the WRI business value model, there are several reasons why companies adopt sustainable development strategies. These reasons include reducing costs and liabilities, and increasing customer loyalty and market position (by adding environmental benefits to products while at the same time outperforming competitors in meeting customer needs).[58]

The WRI framework includes three ideas:

- Do more with fewer resources—for example, by using knowledge and technology to reduce your use of materials.
- Improve your bottom line from nature—for instance, by using natural processes to reduce waste, as discussed later in this chapter under process redesign.
- Build connections with the community in which you operate, which may enable you to develop trust and identify emerging markets.[59]

Natural Capitalism. Amory Lovins and L. Hunter Lovins of the Rocky Mountain Institute and Paul Hawken, the founder of the retailer Smith and Hawken, have developed an approach they call "natural capitalism" for improving the environment, profits, and competitiveness. Writing in the *Harvard Business Review* (in an article that should be required reading for any manager seriously concerned about the environment),[60] they discuss the four inter-related changes in business practice that express the intent of natural capitalism:

- Increase the productivity of natural resources through design and technology.
- Shift to production models that are based on nature's designs, so that output is either "returned harmlessly to the ecosystem as a nutrient, like compost, or becomes an input for manufacturing another product."[61]
- Move to a business model that is based on a flow of services rather than the sale of goods.
- Recognize that the ecosystem underlies your business success by reinvesting in natural capital.

Select specific actions for meeting your commitment to a sustainable development strategy

Once you have selected or developed a framework for thinking about specific options, it is time to consider possible actions that will enable you to pursue your sustainable development goals. The experiences of other companies, such as those described here, provide a menu of best practices. These practices are organized using common themes drawn from the three frameworks just described. Fundamentally, the frameworks have an overarching "R and R" focus on redesign and reinvestment in the environment. See Figure 4.3.

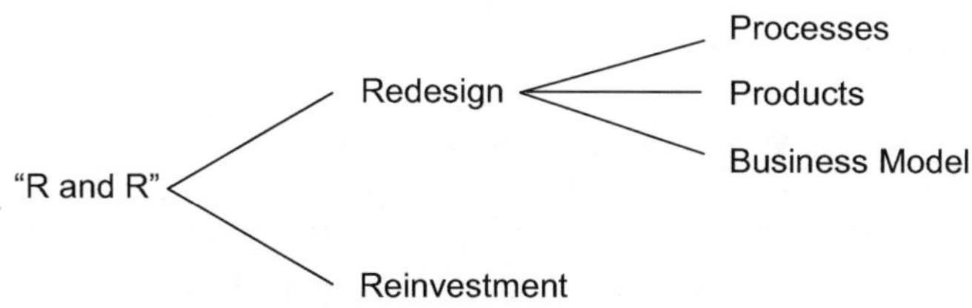

Figure 4.3 Menu of best practices

Redesign Your Processes. Three types of process redesign have received considerable attention. The first type focuses on minimizing and preventing waste (as opposed to coping with it via end-of-pipeline controls). For example, over a four-year period General Dynamics eliminated close to 40 million pounds of hazardous waste discharge, and in three years Chevron reduced its hazardous waste by 60 percent, which saved the company over $10 million in disposal costs.[62] According to a study, beyond direct savings, manufacturing performance improved in plants that increased their investment in pollution prevention; performance declined in plants that stressed pollution control instead.[63] Results from another study suggest that the companies most successful in reducing toxic chemical emissions (as measured by an EPA database) outperform other companies in returns on sales and assets.[64]

The second type of process redesign emphasizes lean manufacturing. Lean manufacturing is based on four elements of "lean thinking" described in the book of that title by James Womack and Daniel Jones: "the *continuous flow* of value, as *defined* by the customer, at the *pull* of the customer, in search of *perfection.*"[65] (The emphasis is in the original quotation.) Sometimes old-fashioned common sense will enable you to achieve leaner manufacturing, once your sustainable environment goals are in place. Advocates of natural capitalism cite the example of Interface Corporation, the world's largest commercial carpet company. Through two simple design changes in the system used to manufacture carpets at a factory in Shanghai, the company reduced its power requirements by 92 percent.[66]

The third type of process redesign emphasizes our role within the natural world. This form of process redesign requires an understanding of the distinction between "biological nutrients," which are returned to biological systems, and "technical nutrients," which are returned to the production cycle. An example of a biological nutrient is upholstery fabric developed for Design Tex that, when removed from an old chair, decomposes naturally on a compost pile. Technical nutrients are illustrated by Interface Corporation's design of a carpet that can be completely recycled (as opposed to more typical recycling that reduces the quality of material as it is reused). A customer who wants to replace the carpet will return it (the "technical nutrient") and the company will then provide a new one in the customer's choice of color.[67]

Redesign Your Products. Product redesign encompasses three principles. The first principle is that product design is increasingly important to gaining competitive advantage. For example, after DuPont's agricultural division developed a new type of biodegradable herbicide that allowed a dramatic reduction in herbicides per acre, DuPont rose from seventh to second in the industry.[68]

The second principle of product redesign is to consider a product's entire life cycle. The life cycle includes everything from the acquisition of raw materials through the customer's use and disposal of the product.[69] As noted earlier, this concept is already embedded in the law of several countries that require companies to take back product packaging so that it can be recycled without impact on the public waste disposal system. Many companies are not waiting for these laws to be enacted in their own countries before adopting take-back policies. For instance, by recycling over 1.5 million wooden reels, Sonoco has saved over a half-million trees.[70]

The third principle is value creation. A focus on life cycle will not be sufficient to create competitive advantage unless your environmentally redesigned products create value for your customers. For example, horizontal axis washing machines are environmentally friendly in that they need less detergent and less water than vertical axis machines. And they are also popular with customers because they clean clothes better, are smaller, and can be raised off the floor. An insecticide developed by SC Johnson brings benefits to the environment (because it uses half the volatile organic compound of competing products) and to the customer (because it smells better, won't ignite, and leaves less residue).[71]

Value creation for your customers often translates into value creation for your shareholders. For instance, the SC Johnson insecticide saves the company $2 million each year in manufacturing costs. And semiconductor firms have shown that reducing product size can increase profits. As noted by the CEO of DuPont: "Those firms make ever smaller products, but because they deliver more benefits they make bigger profits overall." A case in point is a DuPont product, polyester films. New films are half as thick as before but, because they are stronger, they sell at a price that is almost six times greater than the thicker film.[72]

Redesign Your Business Model. Redesigning your business model creates exciting and far-reaching opportunities for seizing competitive advantage. Your redesign process should focus on two basic questions. First, what business are you in? Second, are new forms of alliances possible with your suppliers and customers?

Answering the first question requires a hard look at customer needs. If you manufacture carpets, for example, you might understandably consider yourself in the business of selling carpets. But your customers do not necessarily want to buy carpets. Instead, they may simply want a floor surface that is functional, warm, attractive, and comfortable. If you focus on these needs, fundamental changes in your business model may come to mind that can significantly improve the environment.

For instance, Interface Corporation, the carpet manufacturing company mentioned previously, developed in the mid-1990's a new business model called Evergreen Lease™, in which its customers lease rather than purchase carpeting.[73] This program is designed to meet customer needs while enabling them to avoid large capital expenditures. The program covers the complete life cycle of the product, from initial installation through periodic rejuvenation to reclamation for recycling. Replacing only the worn parts of carpeting reduces material consumption by an estimated 80 percent and energy savings "from not producing a whole new carpet is in itself enough to produce all the carpeting that the new business model requires."[74]

Twelve years into its sustainability journey, Interface launched InterfaceRAISE™, a corporate consulting resource that aims to further amplify Interface's efforts to educate others seeking to implement the necessary steps for becoming sustainable. In piloting the InterfaceRAISE™ concept with leaders at Wal-Mart, General Mills, Sara Lee, and NASA, the company is fulfilling its mission to "lead others forward through the power of its influence," sharing best practices and tailoring its own tools for successful application in numerous other industries.[75] In the company's words: "Today, Interface is more than a carpet company. It has become a corporate sustainability benchmark and mentor for other global companies which know they must view their operations through a new lens to compete in today's world."[76]

Beyond leasing, there may be other opportunities to change your business model from a product to a service orientation. In some cases, you might be able to add an environmentally related service to your product line. For example, Kodak Environmental Services helps customers with regulatory compliance and recycling. In addition to benefits to the environment, services like these generate customer loyalty and make it difficult for your customers to switch to your competitors.[77]

Your search for a new business model might lead to a more fundamental change if you decide to sell a service instead of a product. For instance, suppose that you are in the business of selling paint to automotive companies. In analyzing your customers' real needs, you determine that, strictly speaking, they aren't interested in buying paint but that they do need painted cars. The solution? You operate their paint shop, getting paid for each car painted rather than for each gallon of paint sold. The environmental benefit? With this new model, your incentives shift to a search for ways to reduce expended paint. Within two years of DuPont taking over operation of a Ford Paint shop in the United Kingdom, the company was able to save around 8 percent in material costs, and its UK market share in this business jumped from 25 percent to 75 percent.[78]

The second question that you should ask in redesigning your business model is whether new forms of alliances are possible with your suppliers and customers. A fundamental business goal of such alliances is to make the value chain as efficient as possible by eliminating unnecessary transactions. This goal serves environmental purposes as well by reducing resource needs.[79] Alliances also allow for other environmental benefits. Because one company's waste can be another company's raw material or power source, new industrial parks match companies that can use one another's waste. Some companies have even developed markets for waste. Anheuser-Busch, for instance, sells waste from its breweries as fertilizer.[80]

Alliances are not limited to the value chain. Dow Chemical, for instance, has entered into an unusual collaboration with environmental activists. Working with the Natural Resources Defense Council, Dow asked five of its critics to review the company's business needs and processes in an attempt to find ways to cut waste. As a result, "Dow is on track to cut production of a list of toxic chemicals selected by the environmentalists by 37 percent and to reduce the release of the chemicals into the air or water by 43 percent."[81]

Environmental regulation may even create new business opportunities for you. Depending on your industry and location, if you are successful in your emission reduction efforts, you may be able to sell your unused quotas to others. Companies, governments and other entities may buy your quotas or offsets in order to comply with caps on the total amount they are allowed to emit.

Let's take the example of carbon offsets. Demand for carbon offsets around the world has led to a large and growing carbon market. Players in the carbon market include businesses, governments, financial institutions, non-profit organizations, and individuals that develop, broker, buy, sell, and trade carbon offsets. It has been estimated that in 2008 there were over $460 million (Canadian dollars) worth of transactions in the voluntary carbon market.[82]

For example, wind energy companies often sell carbon offsets. The wind energy company benefits because the carbon offsets it sells make such projects more economically viable. The buyers of the offsets benefit because they can claim that their purchase resulted in new non-polluting energy, which they can use to mitigate their own greenhouse gas emissions. The buyers may also save money as it may be less expensive for them to purchase offsets than to eliminate their own emissions. Other types of offsets available for sale on the market include those resulting from energy efficiency projects, methane capture from landfills or livestock, and destruction of potent greenhouse gases.[83]

Reinvestment in the Environment. Reinvestment in the environment is based on the fundamental business principle that you must reinvest earnings in your capital and the recognition that the natural environment represents an important form of business capital. Companies that invest in nature's capital are gaining new forms of competitive advantage. For example, companies in the wood products industry have learned that certification by the Forest Stewardship Council can lead to extra profits, while customer concerns about clear-cutting practices can lead to a significant loss of business.[84]

A new form of entrepreneur, dubbed the "enviro-capitalist," is taking reinvestment one step further by using business techniques to preserve the environment. For instance, a paper company must wait 30 years for its investment in a forest to mature. In the past, during this time period a company received no profits and incurred various costs, including litter, off-road traffic, and other by-products of increasing public use of forests. Enter Tom Bourland, a wildlife manager and entrepreneur for International Paper. Bourland developed a fee-based recreation program that meets the needs of people who are interested in a wilderness experience while also producing a profit for the company.[85]

Implement the actions you select

After selecting possible actions, it is time to focus on implementation. Under the philosophy that "what gets measured gets done," accounting and reporting are especially important activities in measuring your implementation progress and establishing credibility. Full cost accounting (FCA), also known as environmental accounting and true cost accounting, is an important management tool because it identifies all the costs associated with a product or process. With FCA, the costs assigned to a painting process might include not only direct costs, like paint and equipment, but also indirect costs such as waste disposal, regulatory paperwork, insurance costs, and other items that are usually considered "overhead." For example, several employees of a control valve manufacturer, concerned about hazardous waste produced by conventional coatings, proposed alternative coatings using traditional accounting. Their proposal was rejected because it did not improve profitability. They then did a FCA that included waste costs. With this approach, management was able to see the positive impact and supported the proposal.[86]

Among other decision-making tools for internal management use are the eco-efficiency indicators developed by the WBCSD. Eco-efficiency ratios are calculated through the use of an equation that divides the value of a product or service by its influence on the environment. The WBCSD has developed a number of practical guides that offer companies advice on how to select, use, and report on eco-efficiency indicators, thereby helping them to measure their progress toward sustainability.[87]

The Coalition for Environmentally Responsible Economies (CERES) has also been active in addressing sustainability challenges such as global climate change. Its mission is to integrate sustainability into capital markets for the health of the planet and its people. CERES has launched the Global Reporting Initiative (GRI), now the de-facto international standard used by over 1,300 companies for corporate reporting on environmental, social and economic performance.[88]

Chapter Summary

The government represents a key stakeholder in your business success. As this chapter on environmental protection illustrates, the Manager's Legal Plan™ creates opportunities for competitive advantage even when you are confronted with ubiquitous and expensive regulation.

Step One: Understand the legal framework of environmental regulation: This chapter provides an overview of environmental laws and regulations in the EU and the US and the policies behind them. This step also shows that while in the past, legislation tended to react to past failures, there are signs of a new, more proactive approach to law, even on the side of lawmakers.

Step Two: Know how to cope with environmental regulation: Flight is no longer a realistic response because environmental laws have become uniform across countries. Fighting environmental regulation takes place before laws or regulations are enacted or afterward, through litigation. In considering a fight at either stage, you must determine whether your firm would bear more than its share of costs (thus benefiting free riders in your industry) and whether winning a regulatory battle on behalf of your industry will provide any real competitive advantage for your firm.

Step Three: Develop business strategies and solutions to address environmental regulation: Two approaches used by companies before a new law or regulation is adopted are negotiated rulemaking and intensive lobbying for stricter environmental regulations in countries where enforcement has historically been lax. After adoption of environmental laws and regulations, compliance becomes the dominant strategy. The environmental audit, a key compliance tool, can reduce or even eliminate legal penalties. Beyond an audit, an EMS can produce business and legal benefits. And through the use of parent-subsidiary structures, you can isolate environmental risks and protect the parent corporation from devastating losses.

Step Four: Climb to the balcony to reframe environmental regulations as a business opportunity: You can use four key approaches to achieve competitive advantage:

1. Move from a compliance mentality to a sustainable development strategy.
2. Develop a framework for selecting the specific actions that will enable you to achieve your strategic goals. This chapter includes three leading frameworks based on eco-efficiency, business value, and natural capitalism models.

3. Select from among four types of actions: redesign of processes, products, and business models, and reinvestment in the environment. *Process redesign* includes pollution prevention, lean manufacturing, and the use of biological or technical nutrients. *Product redesign* focuses on the entire life cycle of your products and the value they bring to customers. *Business model redesign* emphasizes an understanding of your customers' underlying needs and possibilities for alliances. It also involves new opportunities such as sales of unused emission quotas or offsets. *Reinvestment in the environment* includes new forms of entrepreneurship developed by so-called enviro-capitalists.
4. Implement your chosen actions, using management tools such as FCA and eco-efficiency indicators.

Notes

1 Gladwin, T.N. 1999. A call for sustainable development. *Financial Times*, December 13, supplement, 2–4.

2 Womack, J.P. and Jones, D.T. 1997. *Lean Thinking*. London: Touchstone.

3 This example from *Lean Thinking* is described in Chapter 3 of Hawken, P., Lovins, A. and Lovins, L.H. 2000. *Natural Capitalism: Creating the Next Industrial Revolution*. Boston: Little, Brown and Co, 49–50.

4 This quotation has been attributed to J. Irwin Miller, former CEO of Cummins, Inc.

5 Howard, P.K. 1994. *The Death of Common Sense*. New York, NY: Warner Books, 7.

6 European Commission 2010a. *Climate Action—EU Action against Climate Change,* updated: June 7 [Online]. Available at: http://ec.europa.eu/climateaction/eu_action/index_en.htm [accessed: August 1, 2010].

7 European Commission 2010b. *Better regulation—Enterprise and Industry* [Online]. Available at: http://ec.europa.eu/enterprise/policies/better-regulation/index_en.htm [accessed: August 1, 2010].

8 European Economic and Social Committee (EESC) 2009. Opinion of the European Economic and Social Committee on "The proactive law approach: a further step towards better regulation at EU level," 2009/C 175/05. *Official Journal of the European Union*, C175, 52, 28 July, 26 [Online]. Available at: http://eur-lex.europa.eu/LexUriServ/LexUriServ.do?uri=OJ:C:2009:175:0026:0033:EN:PDF [accessed: August 1, 2010]. Available in all official EU languages. The Section for the Single Market, Production and Consumption, under the leadership of Mr Jorge Pegado Liz, was responsible for preparing EESC's work on the topic, and author Helena Haapio acted as Expert in this work.

9 See http://www.proactivelaw.org and Chapter 1.

10 European Economic and Social Committee (EESC) 2009. Sections 2.8, 3.8, and 5.2.

11 UK Better Regulation Executive (BRE) 2010. *Simpler for Business* ... [Online]. Available at: http://www.betterregulation.gov.uk/private/ [accessed: January 31, 2010].

12 This section has been adapted in part from Lieberman, J.K. and Siedel, G.J. 1992. *Business Law and the Legal Environment*. 3rd Edition. Orlando, FL: Harcourt Brace Jovanovich, 724–31. The US Environmental Protection Agency (EPA) web site, http://www.epa.gov, includes a section titled "Laws and Regulations" at: http://www.epa.gov/lawsregs/ [accessed: August 1, 2010].

13 If you are interested in British law, you can visit the NetRegs web site, http://www.netregs.gov.uk, which provides free environmental guidance for businesses in the UK. Their approach is very

business-friendly: "We will help you to understand what you need to do to comply with environmental law and protect the environment. We may even help you to save money by showing you ways to use your resources more efficiently."

14 European Union (EU) 2009a. *Strategy for Sustainable Development*, updated: December 18 [Online]. Available at: http://europa.eu/legislation_summaries/environment/sustainable_development/l28117_en.htm [accessed: August 1, 2010].

15 European Union (EU) 2007. *Questions and Answers Environmental Liability Directive*. MEMO/07/157, April 27 [Online]. Available at: http://europa.eu/rapid/pressReleasesAction.do?reference=MEMO/07/157&format=HTML&aged=1&language=EN&guiLanguage=en [accessed: August 1, 2010].

16 *Directive 2004/35/EC of the European Parliament and of the Council of 21 April 2004 on environmental liability with regard to the prevention and remedying of environmental damage* [Online]. Available at: http://eur-lex.europa.eu/LexUriServ/LexUriServ.do?uri=CELEX:32004L0035:EN:HTML [accessed: August 1, 2010].

17 *Directive 2008/1/EC of the European Parliament and of the Council of 15 January 2008 concerning integrated pollution prevention and control* [Online]. Available at: http://eur-lex.europa.eu/smartapi/cgi/sga_doc?smartapi!celexplus!prod!DocNumber&lg=en&type_doc=Directive&an_doc=2004&nu_doc=35 [accessed: August 1, 2010].

18 Summaries of EU Legislation. *Environmental Liability—Directive*. http://europa.eu/legislation_summaries/enterprise/interaction_with_other_policies/l28120_en.htm [accessed: August 1, 2010].

19 European Commission 2010b. Environmental Liability. Introduction, updated: April 21 [Online]. Available at: http://ec.europa.eu/environment/legal/liability/index.htm [accessed: August 1, 2010].

20 *Regulation (EC) No 1907/2006 of the European Parliament and of the Council of 18 December 2006 concerning the Registration, Evaluation, Authorisation and Restriction of Chemicals (REACH)*. See also European Union (EU) 2009b. *Regulatory Framework for the Management of Chemicals (REACH), European Chemicals Agency*, updated: June 13 [Online]. Available at: http://europa.eu/legislation_summaries/internal_market/single_market_for_goods/chemical_products/l21282_en.htm [accessed: August 1, 2010].

21 European Chemicals Agency (ECHA) 2010. *ECHA website* [Online]. Available at: http://echa.europa.eu/home_en.asp [accessed: August 1, 2010].

22 *Directive 2003/87/EC of the European Parliament and of the Council of 13 October 2003 establishing a scheme for greenhouse gas emission allowance trading within the Community and amending Council Directive 96/61/EC.*

23 European Commission 2010c. *Environment—Climate Change—What the EU Is Doing* [Online]. Available at: http://ec.europa.eu/environment/climat/campaign/actions/whatiseudoing_en.htm [accessed: August 1, 2010].

24 Commission of the European Communities (CEC) 2006. *Communication from the Commission to the Council, the European Parliament, the European Economic and Social Committee and the Committee of the Regions. Building A Global Carbon Market. Report pursuant to Article 30 of Directive 2003/87/EC*. Brussels, November 13, 2006. COM(2006)676 final [Online]. Available at: http://ec.europa.eu/environment/climat/emission/pdf/com2006_676final_en.pdf [accessed: August 1, 2010].

25 Among other major environmental laws are the Endangered Species Act, which protects endangered plants and animals; the Oil Pollution Act, which strengthens the EPA's ability to respond to and prevent oil spills; and the Pollution Prevention Act, which changes US law from a focus on "smokestack" regulation to prevention of pollution at the point of origin.

26 US Environmental Protection Agency (EPA) 2008. *The Plain English Guide to the Clean Air Act* [Online]. Available at: http://www.epa.gov/air/caa/peg/ [accessed: August 1, 2010].
27 US Environmental Protection Agency (EPA) 2010a. *Summary of the Toxic Substances Control Act,* updated: March 4 [Online]. Available at: http://www.epa.gov/regulations/laws/tsca.html [accessed: August 1, 2010].
28 Siedel, G.J. 1993. *Real Estate Law.* 3rd Edition. St. Paul, MN: West, 433.
29 Tao, J. 2000. Environmental liability of foreign invested enterprises in the People's Republic of China. *International Business Lawyer,* July/August, 314.
30 Hayes, D.J. and King, J.E. 1994. Nations take stricter action on environment. *National Law Journal,* February 7, 32.
31 Anderson, C.L. and Kagan, R.A. 2000. Adversarial legalism and transaction costs: The industrial-flight hypothesis revisited. *International Review of Law and Economics,* 20(1), 6.
32 US Environmental Protection Agency (EPA) 2010c. *Basic Information.* Laws & Regulations, updated: March 4 [Online]. Available at: http://www.epa.gov/regulations/basic/index.html [accessed: August 1, 2010].
33 Siedel, G.J. (ed.) 1976. *The Lawyer and Business.* St. Paul, MN: West, 97–100 (reprinted from Goulden, J.C. 1972. *The Superlawyers.* New York, NY: Weybright and Talley).
34 Graffy, C. 1997. Big Mac bites back. *ABA Journal,* August, 22; *McLibel Two Take UK Government to Euro-court* 2000. Press Release, September 20 [Online]. Available at: http://www.mcspotlight.org/media/press/releases/msc200900.html [accessed: August 1, 2010]. According to a press release issued by the Registrar on February 15, 2005 (Chamber Judgment—*Steel and Morris v. The United Kingdom*), the European Court of Human Rights held unanimously that there had been a violation of Articles 6 (right to a fair trial) and Article 10 (freedom of expression) of the Convention on Human Rights and awarded a judgment of 35,000 euros to the applicants for non-pecuniary damage, and 47,311.17 euros for costs and expenses. McDonald's was not a defendant in this appeal. See http://cmiskp.echr.coe.int/tkp197/view.asp?action=html&documentId=801399&portal=hbkm&source=externalbydocnumber&table=F69A27FD8FB86142BF01C1166DEA398649 [accessed: August 1, 2010].
35 *U.S. v. Hanousek* [1998] 176 F.3d 1116.
36 Goldberg, S.B., Sander, F.E.A. and Rogers, N.H. 1999. *Dispute Resolution: Negotiation, Mediation, and Other Processes.* New York, NY: Aspen Law & Business, 501–2.
37 Ashford, N.A. and Caldart, C.C. 2007. *Negotiated Regulation, Implementation And Compliance In The United States* [Online]. Available at: http://hdl.handle.net/1721.1/41848 / http://web.mit.edu/ctpid/www/tl/docs/NegReg_CrociHandbook.doc [accessed: August 1, 2010].
38 "Business advantages accrue to the companies that take the right steps to ... manage how worldwide environmental issues affect them." Robinson, S.N., Earle, R. III, and McLean, R.A.N. 1994. Transnational corporations and global environment policy. *Prism,* First Quarter, 57.
39 Berry, M.A. and Rondinelli, D.A. 1998. Proactive corporate environmental management: A new industrial revolution. *Academy of Management Executive,* 12(2), 41.
40 Arnold, M.B. and Day, R.M. 1998. *The Next Bottom Line: Making Sustainable Development Tangible.* Washington, DC: World Resources Institute, 22–3.
41 Carey, H.M. Jr. 1987. Environmental auditing: One lawyer's perspective. *ACCA Docket,* Winter, 17.
42 US Environmental Protection Agency (EPA) and US Department of Energy 1998. *Environmental Management Systems Primer for Federal Facilities.* Washington, DC: EPA and US Department of Energy, 1, 22.
43 Begley, R. 1996. Is ISO 14000 worth it? *Journal of Business Strategy,* September–October, 53.

44 ISO 2009. *Environmental Management—The ISO 14000 Family of International Standards* [Online, International Organization for Standardization]. Available at: http://www.iso.org/iso/theiso14000family_2009.pdf [accessed: August 1, 2010].

45 Minnesota Pollution Control Agency 2009. *Frequently Asked Questions about Environmental Management Systems*, updated: June 26 [Online]. Available at: http://www.pca.state.mn.us/programs/ems-faq.html [accessed: August 1, 2010].

46 Commission for Environmental Cooperation (CEC) 2000. *Improving Environmental Performance and Compliance: 10 Elements of Effective Environmental Management Systems* [Online]. Available at: http://www.epa.gov/compliance/resources/policies/incentives/ems/cecguidedoc.pdf [accessed: August 1, 2010].

47 *U.S. v. Bestfoods* [1998] 118 S. Ct. 1876. The company referred to in the text as CPC later changed its name to Bestfoods.

48 Berry and Rondinelli 1998, 41.

49 Bringer, R.P. and Zosel, T. 1998. Environmental pollution control: Making pollution prevention a corporate priority, in *Encyclopaedia of Occupational Health and Safety*. Volume 2, 4th Edition, edited by J.M. Stellman. Geneva: Intenational Labour Organization, 54.32.

50 Reinhardt, F.L. 1998. Environmental product differentiation: Implications for corporate strategy. *California Management Review*, 40(4), 44.

51 Gladwin 1999, 3.

52 Dow Jones Sustainability Indexes 2009. SAM Indexes GmbH [Online]. Available at: http://www.sustainability-index.com/07_htmle/indexes/overview.html [accessed: August 1, 2010].

53 Arnold and Day 1998, 2.

54 Patagonia 2010. *Patagonia Grants—At Least One Percent of Sales or 10 Percent of Pre-Tax Profits—Whichever is More* [Online]. Available at: http://www.patagonia.com/web/eu/patagonia.go?assetid=2927 [accessed: August 1, 2010].

55 DuPont 2010. *2015 Marketplace Goals* [Online]. Available at: http://www2.dupont.com/Sustainability/en_US/Marketplace_Goals/index.html [accessed: August 1, 2010].

56 World Business Council for Sustainable Development (WBCSD) 2000. *Eco-efficiency: Creating More Value with Less Impact* [Online]. Available at: http://www.wbcsd.org/web/publications/eco_efficiency_creating_more_value.pdf [accessed: August 1, 2010].

57 World Business Council for Sustainable Development (WBCSD) 2000, 5.

58 Arnold and Day 1998, 19–39.

59 Arnold and Day 1998, 7–18.

60 Lovins, A.B., Lovins, L.H. and Hawken, P. 1999. A road map for natural capitalism. *Harvard Business Review*, May–June, 145–58.

61 Lovins et al. 1999, 146.

62 Berry and Rondinelli 1998, 42.

63 Klassen, R.D. 1999. The impact of environmental technologies on manufacturing performance. *Academy of Management Journal*, 42(6), 613.

64 Arnold and Day 1998, 27.

65 Hawken et al. 2000, 127.

66 Lovins et al. 1999, 148.

67 McDonough, W. and Braungart, M. 1998. The next industrial revolution. *Atlantic Monthly*, October, 88–90.

68 Carey, J. 1997. When green begets green. *Business Week*, November 10, 102.

69 For resources related to EPA, "Environmentally Preferable Purchasing," see, for instance http://www.epa.gov/epp [accessed: August 1, 2010].

70 Sonoco, 2007. *Changing the Way World Sees Packaging. The Business of Sustainable Packaging Leadership*. Packaging Strategies Sustainable Packaging Forum, Pittsburgh, PA, September 26, 2007 [Online]. Available at: http://www.sonoco.com/NR/rdonlyres/EB1A3F4C-F332-4737-A47B-9B5735E1AB1A/0/sus_slides_pkg_leadership.pdf [accessed: August 1, 2010].

71 Arnold and Day 1998, 29, 31.

72 1999. DuPont's punt. *Economist*, October 2, 76.

73 Interface, Inc. 2010. Evergreen Lease™. Selling carpet without selling carpet—Evergreen Lease is born. *Interface Global Innovations in Products, Process & Culture* [Online]. Available at: http://www.interfaceglobal.com/Innovations/1995-Evergreen.aspx [accessed: August 1, 2010].

74 Lovins et al. 1999, 154.

75 Interface, Inc. 2006. *Interface Launches Sustainability Consulting Practice*. GreenBiz.com News, September 24 [Online]. Available at: http://www.greenbiz.com/news/2006/09/24/interface-launches-sustainability-consulting-practice [accessed: August 1, 2010]. InterfaceRAISE, which is a wholly owned subsidiary of Interface, Inc., is committed to the goal of sustainability and doing business in ways that minimize the impact on the environment while enhancing shareholder value.

76 InterfaceRAISE, LLC 2007. *InterfaceRAISE & Wal-Mart: Mentoring the World's Largest Retailer* [Online]. Available at: http://www.interfaceraise.com/pdf/Wal-MartCaseStudy.pdf [accessed: February 5, 2010].

77 Arnold and Day 1998, 30.

78 Arnold and Day 1998, 12.

79 Arnold and Day 1998, 48.

80 Heal, G. 2000. Environmental disaster: Not all bad news. *Financial Times*, October 30, supplement, 13.

81 1999. Profitability meets the environment, *Dividend*, Fall, 17.

82 David Suzuki Foundation 2010a. *Purchasing Carbon Offsets. A Guide for Canadian Consumers, Businesses and Organizations* [Online]. Available at: http://www.davidsuzuki.org/publications/reports/2009/purchasing-carbon-offsets/index.php [accessed: August 1, 2010].

83 David Suzuki Foundation 2010b *Carbon offsets*. Climate change basics [Online]. Available at: http://www.davidsuzuki.org/issues/climate-change/science/climate-change-basics/carbon-offsets/index.php [accessed: August 1, 2010].

84 Lovins et al. 1999, 155.

85 Dunn, G. 1998. Enviro-capitalists. *Religion and Liberty*, 8(3) May–June [Online]. Available at: http://www.acton.org/publications/randl/rl_review_275.php [accessed: August 1, 2010].

86 1997. Full cost accounting: What's the whole story?, in *Small Business Waste Reduction Guide*. Revised December 1997. University of Wisconsin-Extension Madison, Wisconsin Center for Environment and Energy & Small Business Development Center [Online]. Available at: http://www.uwex.edu/ces/ag/sus/sbdc/pdftocdt/s2_5.pdf [accessed: August 1, 2010]. See also EPA 1995. *An Introduction to Environmental Accounting as a Business Management Tool: Key Concepts and Terms*. United States Environmental Protection Agency, Office of Pollution Prevention and Toxics. EPA 742-R-95-001. June 1995 [Online]. Available at: http://www.epa.gov/oppt/library/pubs/archive/acct-archive/pubs/busmgt.pdf [accessed: August 1, 2010].

87 Verfaillie, H.A. and Bidwell, R. 2000. *Measuring Eco-Efficiency: A Guide to Reporting Company Performance*. World Business Council for Sustainable Development (WBCSD) [Online]. Available at: http://www.wbcsd.org/web/publications/measuring_eco_efficiency.pdf [accessed: August 1, 2010]. The results of a special one-year pilot program by 24 companies are also documented in this report.

88 Coalition for Environmentally Responsible Economies (CERES) 2010. *About Us* [Online]. Available at: http://www.ceres.org/Page.aspx?pid=415 [accessed: August 1, 2010].

CHAPTER 5 Sustain Ongoing Success through Innovation, Intangible Assets, and Intellectual Property Rights: Leverage Collaboration to Create Value through Intellectual Property

The Impact of Innovation and Intangible Assets on Your Business

To stay in business, you must develop new solutions, business models, and revenue streams at a growing speed. Even if you are ahead of your competition right now, you must move ahead. Even if you are moving ahead, your speed must be faster than the speed of other companies' advances to avoid being left behind. You need to innovate to ensure that your company continues to provide value in the future. You need to reinvent your products, services, and business models.

The Internet and new technologies have made cross-border collaboration and transactions possible for companies of all sizes. They have also made audiovisual production and distribution systems available to practically everyone. This environment facilitates both user-driven innovation and potentially more disruptive innovation than many established companies are willing to pursue. In the open-source model, innovation comes from hundreds of thousands of people. Their creativity and innovation are enabled by YouTube® or Google Videos™, where anyone can upload a three-minute movie. Anyone can create a new business on eBay™. Technology enables the transition from innovative nations to nations of innovators. How businesses seek new ideas may determine which thrive and which survive. Because the line between leader and also-ran is razor thin, companies must innovate faster, operate leaner, and think globally just to survive.[1] "It is not the strongest species that survive, nor the most intelligent, but the ones most responsive to change."[2]

At the outset, we need to clarify that this chapter is about innovation, rather than inventions. You need not be an inventor to become an innovator. The traditional image of an inventor is that of a solitary genius in a laboratory. That image does not fit innovators. Innovators can, but do not need to, work in laboratories. Innovators not only create, but also apply their creations. When applied, their ideas can generate new innovations that in turn give rise to new products and services, new ways of doing business, and even new markets and industries. Because innovation is increasingly collaborative in today's economy, customers and users play a key role as innovation co-creators.[3]

C.K. Prahalad and Venkat Ramaswamy, both then Professors at the University of Michigan's Ross School of Business, introduced the concept of co-creation to the wider business community in their 2000 *Harvard Business Review* article and later in their book *The Future of Competition*.[4] The authors argue that the future of competition is being shaped by changes in the meaning of value, the roles of the consumer and the company, and the nature of their interactions—changes that are profoundly altering the value creation process. Rather than being embedded in the products and services created by companies and delivered to customers, the authors conclude, value is being created jointly by the consumer and the company. According to the authors, value is now centered in the experiences of consumers, and value cannot be unilaterally determined by the company. Further, value may be influenced not just by one firm but by a network of firms acting together to create an experience network, with the market serving as a forum for co-creation experiences.[5]

So you need access to a pool of talent and innovative ideas, and you need to know how to discover, co-create, and extract new value using them. To sustain your competitive advantage and thrive long term, you must also know how to protect your valuable ideas. This is where intellectual property (IP) enters the picture.

The Changing Landscape of Intellectual Property

In today's global economy, knowledge assets and related intangibles have overtaken manufacturing assets to account for the lion's share of market valuation. This is particularly true for technology companies. According to Horatio Gutierrez, Vice President and General Counsel, Intellectual Property & Licensing Group of Microsoft, "We're moving toward a global economy where the true strategic asset is IP."[6]

Even manufacturing-oriented members of the technology community say that IP is now, or is fast becoming, their primary source of value-creation. For example, according to an executive from Apple, famous for its Mac® and its iPods®, "Our core competence and market valuation doesn't come from manufacturing iPods. The value we bring to the marketplace and the world is the ability to keep dreaming up seminal ideas, like iPods." According to an executive at Qualcomm, "The manufacturing cost and the materials cost, that's an ever-diminishing percentage of the total value of any technology device." The real value today, "is the idea, the knowledge, the capability," and ultimately, "the relevant patents."[7]

The importance of IP extends beyond technology companies. All companies have a trade name and ideas, data, knowledge, and information that matter in their business. Most have a web address, domain names, logos, and brands to promote their goods and services and to distinguish themselves and their offerings from their competition. Many have software code, trademarks, and inventions. IP law is designed to protect these valuable assets. Different kinds of tools exist to protect different kinds of creative work. As we will see, some of them (but not all) require novelty. While some expire after a certain period, not all do. A trademark, for instance, can be an asset you own forever.

Savvy CEOs are attempting to unleash the hidden value represented by their IP. As Richard Homan, CEO of Xerox, put it, "My focus is on intellectual property. I'm convinced that the management of intellectual property is how value added is going to be created at Xerox. And not just here, either. Increasingly, companies that are good at managing IP will win. The ones that aren't will lose."[8] Given this sense of direction, attorneys, too, are developing a new mindset. According to Suzanne Harrison, co-author of the book *Edison in the Boardroom,* while attorneys must continue to "take the legal view and protect [intellectual assets], they should also be looking beyond that to find ways to use IP to generate revenue."[9] Xerox attorney Barry Smith puts it more bluntly when he describes his new job as thinking "about intellectual property as a moneymaker."[10]

The view of IP as a moneymaker or strategic asset is a rather recent phenomenon. For instance, in 1990, the 50 patent attorneys employed by Xerox "operated defensively. There was no special unit that ripped apart competitor's products to root out patent infringement. Nor were legal staff assigned to pursue infringers."[11] That approach is still dominant at many companies.[12] It has been estimated that companies use only 3 percent of their patents.[13] The rest sit on company shelves like "Rembrandts in the attic" (to echo the title of a book on the failure of companies to capitalize on their patents).[14]

Some go as far as stating that IP is now the *only* real source of sustainable competitive advantage. In their book *The Invisible Edge,*[15] IP strategists and former Boston Consulting Group partners Mark Blaxill and Ralph Eckardt argue that focusing on tangible operational priorities, like efficiency, cost-cutting, and best practices, cannot sustain a company's leadership if its most valuable asset—its IP—is not protected and developed. The authors call IP "the last legal monopoly" and note: "If we put aside the legalese and use plain business language, the power of IP is pretty simple. There are three components that determine a company's profits: sales volume, the selling price, and the cost of production—and IP is the main driver of all three." They advise business leaders to put IP at the center of strategy development and internalize IP's fundamental contribution to competitiveness and profitability. Ultimately, they argue, companies that understand and effectively manage IP will be the big winners.

This chapter explores the importance of innovation, intangible assets, and IP, not only to benefit your bottom line in the short term, but also to enable you to thrive in the future. The Manager's Legal Plan™ will be used to help you develop and execute a strategic plan that will yield sustainable competitive advantage over the long term. We focus especially on potential positive aspects and outcomes of collaboration between businesses. In this chapter, we cover intangible assets and IP. In the following Chapter 6, we cover contracts and contracting—the tools and processes that allow cooperation and collaborative advantage to happen.

Intangible Assets and Intellectual Property Defined

Let's say, for example, that you work for a typical manufacturing company. When you view your company assets from a big picture perspective, what do you see? If someone asked you this question in the 1980s, your response would have been "factories and equipment," which at that time represented most of a manufacturing firm's market value. Those assets currently account for less than a third of market value. Today, even at manufacturing firms, the most valuable asset is IP.[16] Your company's development, protection, and use of this key asset are critical to competitive advantage.

An asset can be defined as a source of future benefits. The concept of intangible assets (or intangible capital—or intangibles, for short) is generally used to describe a source of future benefits that does not have a physical embodiment. It has been estimated that 75 percent of a company's assets may be composed of intangible assets.[17] Intellectual property rights (IPR) constitute a central part of such company assets. From your point of view as a manager, skills and competence related to IP can thus play a significant role.

Different professions tend to use different language: accountants tend to speak of intangible assets, lawyers of IPR and strategists of intellectual capital. In this book, the term *intangibles* and *intangible assets* are used interchangeably. Both are understood to include IPR, which in turn include, among other rights, patents, trademarks, trade secrets, and copyrights.

In some instances, contracts—the topic of Chapter 6—are considered to be part of intangible assets. Whether or not you include them in the definition of intangible assets, you want to remember that contracts and IPR coexist and that you can combine them for maximum benefit for your company and for the network or *extended enterprise* in which your company participates.

From Competitive Advantage to Collaborative Advantage

Today's companies do not compete and win alone. Networks or chains of companies—*extended enterprises* or *business ecosystems*—do. A company that stands alone may fail alone. In research and development, collaboration between bright minds across nations, organizations, and professions can lead to results that would not be attained otherwise. This is true for both high-tech companies and more traditional companies. In complex projects, such as aerospace, power generation, or construction, multiple companies work together, each bringing their knowledge and skills to the endeavor that none of them could accomplish alone.

In *The New Age of Innovation,* C.K. Prahalad, named "the World's Most Influential Management Thinker" in 2007 by the *Times* of London, together with M.S. Krishnan, both then Professors at the University of Michigan, Ross School of Business, argued that the key to creating value and the future of every business depends on accessing a global network of resources to co-create unique experiences with customers, one at a time. According to them, "no single firm has the knowledge, skills, and resources it needs to co-create value with consumers. Every firm has to learn to access resources from multiple sources."[18]

In their book *Burning the Ships,* Marshall Phelps and David Kline confirm the view that "no company is any longer able to accumulate by itself all the technologies and business competencies needed for success."[19] The authors offer an insider's account of how Microsoft looked for and found a new collaborative direction. Marshall Phelps, Microsoft's corporate Vice President for IP Policy and Strategy, joined the company in 2003, after a 28-year career at IBM Corp., where he served as Vice President of IP and Licensing and built IBM's IP portfolio into a two-billion-dollar-a-year licensing program. Phelps' mission was not about making money from IP; it was to help reform company culture and transform Microsoft's relations with the industry to build and foster new, collaborative relationships: "How was Microsoft to survive and succeed in the emerging new era of 'open innovation,' where collaboration and cooperation between firms, rather than single-minded competitive warfare, would be the keystones of success?"[20]

Phelps and Kline list the many benefits of collaboration. Their list includes the fact that collaboration enables a company to more broadly and rapidly disseminate its technologies and products into the market through the cooperative efforts of others. Collaboration also provides the framework for pursuing joint product development work with other companies that can lead to greater success in the marketplace. Collaboration can facilitate entry into new markets, broaden freedom of action within a market, and provide access to needed outside technologies. And, of course, a company can generate revenue directly through patent licensing.[21]

So what is the role of IP in this new collaborative arena? Phelps and Kline talk about "IP-enabled collaboration." They see the collaborative use of IP as the "central driving engine" of what they call "virtual circles of innovation." In their view, the creation and utilization of IP is part of a virtuous circle in which R&D leads to the creation of IP, which leads to the licensing of that IP, which in turn leads to new R&D, more IP creation, and so on. This creates additional virtual circles in the innovation behavior of the firms that license that IP by enabling them to enhance their own R&D, leading to their own increased IP creation, downstream licensing opportunities, and so on. Finally, the authors argue, these virtuous circles cascade throughout the industry, leading to a wider adoption of the licensed technologies and additional innovation. Instead of tapping IP's *exclusivity* value—that is, using IP to block competitors from using the company's technology—the focus here is on leveraging IP's *inclusivity* value by using IP to build collaborative relationships that are needed to remain successful in the new open innovation world.

Henry Chesbrough, who runs the Center for Open Innovation at the University of California at Berkeley's Haas School of Business, and Andrew R. Garman, former Vice President at Lucent Technologies, in their 2009 *Harvard Business Review* article[22] encourage companies to move innovation from inside out and suggest open-innovation moves that provide a framework for getting the greatest value from a company's research initiatives. One of the moves they suggest is to make your IP work harder for you and others. According to the authors, many businesses recover 10 to 20 percent of their annual R&D spending in this way.

Managing alliances, partnerships, and other collaborative arrangements is now part of most managers' work. They must seek to secure *cooperative advantage* (or *collaborative advantage*)—not just advantage for their own company, but also for customers and allies in the *extended enterprise*. This involves a mindset that enables managers to leverage global resources and visualize and strengthen various actors' capabilities and interdependencies. These actors include their own employees, suppliers, customers, partners, scientists, and governments. The goal is to generate value for all stakeholders in the *extended enterprise*: customers, shareholders, employees, entrepreneurs, and collaborators. And collaborative advantage requires managers and employees to work well across organizational boundaries.

Your connections and interactions with your customers and business partners along with the outcomes of those connections and interactions create a crucial part of your company's intangible assets. In addition to developing access to a pool of talent, innovative ideas, and business networks, you will benefit greatly from the application of the Manager's Legal Plan™ in this context. The Plan will enable you to protect and exploit your intangible assets, avoid violating the rights of others, and secure a fair division of the benefits generated by your network. This begins with an understanding of the laws that apply and how the IP system works.

Apply the Manager's Legal Plan™ to Intangible Assets and Intellectual Property Rights

STEP ONE: UNDERSTAND THE LAW

Understanding the law in this area is important for two reasons: You need to know, first, how you can protect your own intangible assets, and, second, how you can avoid violating the rights of others.

The law gives you many options to protect your intangible assets. As in so many other areas, one size or solution does not fit all. So you need a basic understanding of your choices. In some instances, using a single tool may be enough for you to protect your innovations and exclude competitors (if that is your goal). In other instances, you may need to use several tools in combination that reinforce one another. While some IP tools will inevitably be more valuable to your business than others, failure to implement appropriate protection can prevent your company from fully realizing the benefits of its innovations. In the words of Mark Blaxill and Ralph Eckardt, "innovation without protection is philanthropy."[23]

To make informed choices, you need to understand the legal aspects of IP. You need to determine which tools and which areas of the law are relevant and useful for your business, and how you can best align your protection with your business goals. Then you need to find the right balance between developing and exercising your protection and voluntary sharing of your IPR.

How the intellectual property rights system works

The law gives innovative individuals and companies various forms of protection and exclusive rights that improve their opportunities to commercialize their ideas, products, and services. These are generally known as IPR. IP includes trade secrets, patents, copyrights, and trademarks.

IPR are generated by creative activity, often through research and development. The ins and outs of the legal protection, registration procedures, and remedies for infringement vary from country to country. It is surprising but true that even in today's global business world most IP rights are local. So if you want to protect your brands and inventions globally, you need to act locally in each country where you want to obtain that protection. Counter to common belief, there is no such thing as a world patent.

Your legal team and your patent or trademark experts can assist you. Most have networks that can provide information and assistance worldwide. To gain a strategic edge over your competitors and decide when to seek expert assistance, you need to understand the most common options to protect your IP. These are depicted in Figure 5.1.

Figure 5.1 Options to protect your intellectual property

As the name implies, a *trade secret* is a secret that is used by a company in its trade, such as a formula, device, manufacturing process, or customer list. Because trade secrets are not subject to legal registration, their protection is largely up to you and your employees. If you have information that has economic value as a result of its secrecy, you need to preserve its confidentiality. If you don't, or if your competitors discover the secret on their own—and no other protection exists—you will lose the competitive advantage you might otherwise have held. When kept secret, trade secrets can be protected for an indefinite time, the classic example being the Coca-Cola Company's secret formula.

The purpose of a *patent*, in general terms, is to protect how something works, or how it is made. In order for a patent application to be successful, the idea must have two characteristics: it must be novel, and it must be non-obvious. Patents are granted by a country—or by a group of countries, such as the European Patent Organisation. They are subject to the laws of the country in question, which vary from one place to another. Patent protection normally expires 20 years from the date the application was filed. Fees are payable in order to apply for and to maintain a patent, and filing a patent in a number of countries, including the relevant translations, and so on, can be quite expensive. Yet as we will see later, the licensing fees and other opportunities may be well worth the fees and effort.

While a patent is concerned with the function, operation, and manufacture of an item, a registered *design* applies to the appearance of a product or part of a product. The features include the lines, contours, colours, shape, and ornamentation of the item which give it a unique appearance. You can also register a design showing the ornamentation alone, for instance a pattern to go on a product. Your design must be novel at the time you apply, and the appearance of the product design must not be dictated by its technical function. A registered design typically lasts for five years and may be extended over four five-year periods up to a maximum of 25 years.

Copyright protects how ideas are presented in, for example, literary or artistic works. Copyright does *not* protect the ideas themselves. The period of protection is normally the lifetime of the creator plus 70 years. If you are the author or creator of an original literary, musical, or artistic work, you can obtain a copyright. It is important to understand that some basic assumptions differ between countries. For instance in the UK and many European countries, as long as the work is original, copyright protection is automatic;

there are no registration or other procedures to follow, and copyright exists whether or not it is asserted using the copyright © symbol or otherwise. The symbol (©) can still be used—and it is advisable to use it—to signify that the work is copyright protected. In some countries, but not all, if the work was undertaken in the course of employment, by law, the employer rather than the employee has the copyright.

Trademarks are normally words or figures (or combinations) used to identify and distinguish products. Service marks are used to identify services, and business names (trade names) are used to identify a company or business. These can in principle last forever, at least if they are used in commerce. Fees are normally required to keep registered trademarks and service marks in force.

You can also protect your business and your IP using *contracts*, including employment and service agreements and mechanisms such as properly crafted confidentiality undertakings and covenants not to compete. So there are various tools and practices for IPR protection. Your industry, location, markets, and operating environment will determine which types of protection are best suited for your company. Some of them do not work well together. For example, if you seek patent protection, you will usually need to disclose valuable information, the idea from the society's point of view being that you obtain protection in exchange. Because the reviewing agency might not grant the protection you were seeking when you made your disclosure, you might be better off choosing trade secret protection instead. Often a combination of IPR and contracts will best serve your needs.

When it comes to intellectual property rights, ownership matters!

According to Professors C.K. Prahalad and M.S. Krishnan, the co-authors of *The New Age of Innovation,* the nature of resources—financial, human, and technological—has transcended the firm and its legal boundaries. Today, the authors argue, when resources are global, the focus should be on *access* and *influence,* not *ownership* and *control.* "It is all about leveraging a global resource base."[24]

However, while the focus has changed, ownership is still important. For instance, if you wish to include a manuscript, an image, a photograph, or a sound recording in your own work, you need to identify the owner of copyright and obtain permission, where required. In working with inventions, you also need to understand who owns IPR to avoid major legal problems.

You should ask about ownership sooner rather than later to clarify the rights of your company, employees, service providers, and other contract partners. Paying for IP does not necessarily mean that you *own* the outcomes, ideas, and inventions generated during the process. For example, in some countries the employee or party who generated the discovery might be the owner if you do not agree to the contrary. While the basic assumptions differ across countries and contexts, you will want to establish a systematic approach by which you secure the rights you want and need. Sometimes you may not need ownership because the right to access IP and a limited license to use it is sufficient to meet your needs—and much more cost-effective.

The bottom line in respect of IPR is that ownership matters. Ownership provides the right to use, access, and influence. If someone else owns what you need, the owner can put you at a competitive disadvantage.

STEP TWO: KNOW HOW TO COPE WITH LEGAL PROBLEMS AND LEARN FROM THEM

When your company has secured IP rights protection, you must be prepared to defend your rights. Otherwise, you risk losing their value. So you need to be willing to consider bringing litigation against infringers. On the other hand, when defending your rights and commencing litigation, you need to be prepared to be counter-attacked—for instance, through a threat of invalidating your patent.

Your company may use intangibles and IPR defensively or aggressively. Either way, you will want your attorney to explain your and the other side's IPR, the legal landscape, and your alternatives. But your company's course of action is not solely for your legal team to decide because business considerations are often at stake.

If a lawsuit arises where you are accused of infringing someone else's rights, you can choose between "fight or flight," litigate or settle. You need to make the same decision if you encounter infringers. You may decide to approach them (or one of them) with a license offer. Or, if you want to create a reputation for strongly protecting and enforcing what you own, you may decide to sue. In working with your legal counsel, you can employ a more or less aggressive approach. A less aggressive approach to IP assertion would involve sending an alleged infringer a licensing offer, or filing a complaint first and then sending such an offer and beginning negotiations.

In making your "fight or flight" decisions, alternative dispute resolution (ADR) and decision tree analysis are especially useful. These tools are explained in detail in Chapter 7. Chapter 7 also includes examples of how a mini-trial (an ADR process) was used to settle a patent infringement case and how decision trees are used to make management decisions relating to copyright litigation.

Bitter patent battles are often fought on several fronts. An infringement claim in court often breeds a counter-claim in the same court. The same legal battle can also be taken to court in different countries. When one company claims infringement of its patent(s), the alleged infringer has many ways to attack the patent(s)—for example, by questioning the patent's novelty and non-obviousness. The alleged infringer can ask a government patent office to invalidate the patent. In the US, the party claiming infringement can file a complaint with the International Trade Commission (ITC), which has the power to ban imports of infringing products.

These tactics are often used by the parties to improve their negotiating positions. Frequently the best solution for both sides is to settle the case with a mutually acceptable cross-licensing deal, either with acceptable payment levels, or with an agreement that calls for no payments between the parties. Even though the patents or patent portfolios may not be precisely equal in value, this may be a win-win solution due to the strategic value of collaboration.

Because your approach will depend on many factors, including the size and strength of the possible infringer(s), you need to take care in making a decision to initiate litigation. A large defendant may be more capable of paying, but at the same time be less willing to agree to a significant settlement or enter into a licensing agreement. Protracted litigation with someone unwilling to settle becomes more expensive, delays any potential licensing revenue and potentially puts the fate of your company's prospective licensing royalties in the hands of a court or a jury.

Targeting a smaller infringer first may prove advantageous. Such targets may be less willing to engage in protracted litigation. Securing a number of licensing agreements with smaller infringers builds momentum, may be more effective in convincing others to enter into a licensing agreement, and generates revenue that can be used to offset litigation costs incurred against larger infringers. The downside is that a smaller defendant may decide not to enter into a licensing agreement due to lack of funds and initiating a lawsuit against a defendant that may be effectively judgment-proof would be fruitless. You need to take into account that in subsequent actions, any rulings adverse to you as the IP owner may limit the value and enforceability of your company's IP. On the other hand, securing a large judgment or settlement may make other infringers more likely to come voluntarily to the licensing table.[25]

According to Ronald Schutz, a leading US patent litigator, "winning a patent infringement case today is about objectives and risk management—it is as much a business decision as a legal one."[26] "The definition of a 'win,' or what constitutes success," he continues, "will depend on who the patent owner is and what the patent owner's objectives are. Practicing patent owners who are suing a competitor may have objectives ranging from putting their competitor out of business through an injunction to obtaining a cross-license to their competitor's patent portfolio. Nonpracticing patent owners who are also suing are probably only interested in money."[27]

The success of the aggressive strategy in the field of trademarks is illustrated by McNeil's courtroom battles related to TYLENOL®. McNeil Laboratories has actively filed suit to prevent companies from interfering with its trademark. For example, McNeil obtained a preliminary injunction that prevented American Home Products from launching EXTRANOL, a product that would have competed with its own new product, EXTRA-STRENGTH TYLENOL®. McNeil obtained an injunction that prevented Kroger from selling non-aspirin pain relievers named ACTENOL, SUPERNOL, and HYDENOL. And through settlement of litigation, the company forced a competitor to drop "nol" from a product initially called FEVERNOL.[28]

It is not surprising that "plaintiff" has been called the fifth "P" of marketing (joining product, price, promotion, and placement),[29] as the number of new IP cases has grown tremendously. Xerox, for example, has become so aggressive in pursuing infringers that a competitor has charged the company with moving "marketplace competition into the courtroom."[30]

While you need expert advice in addressing IPR concerns, you as the manager need to remain in charge because your response and actions will have an impact on your business and its reputation. Regardless of the approach you select, you will want to learn from your IPR experience so that you can develop business strategies and solutions that will protect your rights in the future.

STEP THREE: DEVELOP BUSINESS STRATEGIES AND SOLUTIONS TO PREVENT FUTURE PROBLEMS

Bill Gates is quoted as saying, "In this business, by the time you realize you're in trouble, it's too late to save yourself. Unless you're running scared all the time, you're gone."[31]

You do not want to infringe other companies' rights if you can avoid it. Nor do you want to encounter infringers unprepared. You can take precautions and protective steps. These can be quite simple steps and need not involve great expense.

Say you have launched a major advertising campaign for a new product or service with a new name in mind. Or you plan to register a new trademark or to apply for a patent for an invention. Obviously you want to determine whether the name you are hoping to use is already taken by someone else or whether using or selling your invention will violate someone else's existing rights. To do so, you can carry out a trademark search or a patent clearance investigation (sometimes also called a "freedom to operate" investigation). While such searches or investigations do not provide absolute certainty, they can prove quite valuable.

With the results, you can either abandon your plans early and cut your losses, or work around the existing rights ahead of time, saving the time and resources that could be tied up in a dispute.

The results can also help you gain confidence as to the possible success of your application, determine your organization's risk of infringement, and identify potential infringers.

You can carry out some simple searches yourself. But to complete a comprehensive and thorough search, you will want to engage a professional service company. Some service companies may charge a high fee for conducting a search that you can easily complete yourself for free. Before agreeing on a search, you should ask the service company to clarify what exactly their searches entail and how much they charge.

Aspects of IP are present in choices you as a manager and your employees make on a daily basis. Some of them may be routine—such as publishing your company materials on the Internet or copying materials from third parties' Internet publications. Even if you are not working in a technology company, you and your employees have access to the World Wide Web, and you may carry around a whole library (the Internet), games, radio, television, a camera, audiovisual content, and a positioning device, all in your mobile phone alone. Technology has made copying and distribution of digital material very easy and practically free of cost. You should make sure you and your employees have a basic understanding of whether the law allows such copying and distribution. You need to educate yourself and your personnel so that an inadvertent disclosure does not infringe the IPR of others—or result in loss of your valuable trade secret protection. As mentioned earlier, the country where you work may have laws regarding how to obtain the right to, for instance, an invention made by your employee. To prevent future problems and loss of rights, you should acquire, within the boundaries of the law, assignments of rights, non-disclosure agreements, and covenants not to compete.

With proper planning, your preventive measures, employee education, and IP portfolio (often combined with contractual protection) will help you to prevent claims and disputes or at least eliminate or reduce their potential impact. While your legal team and your patent or trademark experts can assist you here, you as the manager must marshal the required resources and remain in control. Keep in mind that one of your best prevention strategies and protections is your own IPR portfolio. If you are known for owning strong IPR, you are not an easy target.

STEP FOUR: CLIMB TO THE BALCONY TO SEE THE BIG PICTURE AND BECOME MORE PROACTIVE

Having taken Steps One, Two, and Three, you will have an understanding of the legal aspects of IP and intangible assets and how to cope with legal problems. You will also realize that IPR is not just about legal tools but also about marketing and management tools. Step Four is where you determine the status of your current intangibles and IPR and where you want to be. Your IPR offer tremendous financial opportunities that can be lost if you do not use them. So you should pay close attention to how your IP is protected, managed, and exploited.

With the big picture perspective provided by your view from the balcony you can see assets, strengths, and options, and perhaps also problems, that may have been invisible earlier. Your competitors may still think that IPR are something for IP experts and lawyers alone. According to a survey conducted by PricewaterhouseCoopers in 2007, over two-thirds of the executives today believe that IP management is too often treated merely as a legal issue—a belief particularly prevalent in North America and Asia-Pacific.[32] This is a tremendous opportunity for you to move ahead of your competition.

If you haven't done so already, you should start by creating an inventory of the IPR that your company currently owns. You will also want to ascertain your competitors' IPR. You may find, for example, that you are working in a patent jungle—or in a patent desert. When you know what the landscape looks like and where you stand, you can combine your business acumen with your knowledge about the law and start making choices and plans for the future.

In developing your protection, if you are working in a company manufacturing, selling, and servicing industrial equipment, you will probably want to focus on patents, trade secrets, trademarks, and service marks. If, instead, you work for a consumer electronics company, the kind of protection you want to focus on is more likely to include utility patents, design patents, and trademarks, especially product shape trademarks. In both cases, you are likely to be also interested in copyrights—and how to integrate the different IPR.

Often, integration is the area where you as the manager have a key role to play. You want to make sure that the different departments and functions of your company have organizational coordination and managerial leadership for optimum results.[33] Otherwise, your company's routine practices that impact your rights can lead to suboptimal outcomes. People in the new product development (NPD) process may appear to behave rationally from their own perspective. Their perspective, however, may preclude design right integration due to competing interests and goals in other areas of the company.[34] Overcoming this problem requires knowledge of both the legal and business aspects of IPR. Armed with this knowledge, your balcony perspective enables you to see how your current NPD process works, and take the lead in organizational coordination, leading to sustainable competitive advantage.

In their book *Burning the Ships*, Marshall Phelps and David Kline tell the story of the transformation of Microsoft. The authors describe how in the old days, IP was seen merely as a "rights" issue rather than business imperative. IP was left to the legal department to manage, and IP strategy was just a legal strategy—in short, the decision whether to litigate or license. Executive involvement was rare, and the IP organization, to the extent that one existed, was composed solely of lawyers and perhaps a few licensing executives.[35]

Today's open innovation environment, the author's argue, has complicated IP leadership enormously. Because IP must support the company's overall strategy, its management must start at the senior-levels of executive leadership and filter down into the activities of all business units and functional groups.

In the words of Bill Gates as quoted in the Phelps and Kline book: "the CEO has got to set a tone and lead by example. You've got to encourage groups that are doing well. And you've got to give negative feedback to groups that aren't thinking about IP enough. The leadership has to do that, because otherwise the domain of being a researcher or an engineer or a lawyer or a business development executive is going to limit their vision only to the immediate tasks they face. So the leader has to bootstrap IP awareness throughout the company. And then it gets inculcated and becomes part of the culture."[36]

In developing your IPR portfolio, you will also need to think about what is necessary to incentivize your employees to become innovators and "intrapreneurs." If your company has a tendency to require employees to turn over all their inventions to your company and you do not provide enough incentives, you may start losing to other companies that tie employees' compensation to the market value of their inventions, which in turn can result in much greater IP development with all the opportunities that follow. For example, Japanese patent law (unlike US law) requires companies to reward engineers for their patents, which results in a high number of patents. Of the top 20 companies to gain patent approvals in the US in 2008, half were Japanese and only seven were US companies.[37]

According to the survey conducted by PricewaterhouseCoopers in 2007,[38] the overwhelming majority of executives say IP management is vital to the success of their companies. Moreover, they say IP management will become even more important over the next several years. Nonetheless, more than 60 percent of executives feel that their companies could extract significantly more value from their IP by means of active IP management.

The survey suggests the desired strategy of creating tighter links between research, technology acquisition, and business objectives. Thinking beyond the boundaries of your company is also important. In the words of one executive from a large European telecommunications company: "Until recently, we tended to keep our patents in a drawer, collecting dust. Now we are beginning to realise they have value beyond what we might see in our own business, so we are marketing these to other companies. They are very valuable."[39] Close interaction here not only helps companies to develop portfolios of essential IP; it helps them to avoid costly litigation.[40] Equipped with a fresh view of intangible assets and IPR, you can see that dispute prevention and decisions related to IP disputes are not just about the law.

Taking a proactive approach, you can play a key role in marshalling legal, IP management, and other resources to develop, strengthen and exploit your IP portfolio and policy. By so doing, you and your team have an opportunity to turn your IP management and legal departments from cost centers to profit centers.[41]

With this mindset, options for creating value include licensing or selling IP and creating joint ventures with companies that can maximize the value of IP. The results have been dramatic at companies that have embraced an IP strategy. The leader in leveraging its IP is IBM, where annual patent royalties grew from $30 million in 1990 to almost $1 billion a decade later.[42] Underscoring the relationship between IP strategy and competitive advantage, attorney Victor Siber—one of the developers of IBM's

IP strategy—notes, "When a company makes a billion on licensing fees that money goes right to the bottom line—and it's usually money that comes from the competitors."[43]

Today, the success of many companies depends on their ability to position themselves in global networks where they can generate competitive and collaborative advantage over competing networks. To sustain their advantage, they need to innovate. Companies known for their ability to produce more added value and innovative ideas than others are the most attractive network partners. This helps to create a virtuous circle: networks of such companies in turn attract more of their kind and can recruit the best talent who create still more value and innovations. Becoming a member of choice in such networks is an important goal that you as a manager want to achieve for your company.

Chapter Summary

In today's business environment, IP has become a core strategic asset. When properly protected, your IPR can be your *most valuable* assets. You can use them for first-mover advantage, differentiation, premium prices, and for the exclusion of others. You can also sell or license them to others. While you want to protect, defend, and maximize your own rights, you also want to prevent infringement of the IPR of other companies. If another company claims that you have infringed their IP rights, you may be able to use your own rights to negotiate a creative settlement, as many infringement cases are settled by the parties giving each other cross-licenses.

A strong portfolio of IPR will enable you to use your rights offensively or defensively. Perhaps most important in today's and tomorrow's marketplace is your ability to choose to use your IPR to attract new partners or to release your IPR in exchange for open innovation. So your IP can serve as an entrance ticket to collaboration that would not otherwise be available. In order for you to rely on your IP you need to recognize, focus on, develop, and protect what distinguishes your company from others.

This chapter has applied the four-step Manager's Legal Plan™ for achieving and sustaining competitive and collaborative advantage through intangible assets and IPR. The chapter has shown that by understanding the law and marshalling required resources you can proactively develop, protect, and exploit your intangible assets and sustain ongoing success through them.

Step One: Understand the law: Determine which areas of the law are relevant and useful for your business and the parties you collaborate with and then learn to master the areas that matter. Make sure that you and your employees have a basic understanding of what the law allows you to do and where the limits are. Educate yourself and your personnel so inadvertent actions do not lead to your company infringing others' IPR—or losing your valuable trade secrets or other protection.

Step Two: Know how to cope with legal problems and learn from them: Your company may use intangibles defensively or aggressively. You can use your IPR for generating damage awards in infringement cases, but also as part of your defense and negotiation strategy if you are accused of infringing someone else's rights. The threat of taking legal action to invalidate a patent is a typical negotiation tactic that often leads to an amicable solution. A strong IPR portfolio gives you freedom to choose whether you want to "fight or flight," litigate or settle, and if you settle, what the terms will be. In the end, with proper protection in place, you may find a cross-licensing arrangement mutually advantageous. Whichever way the dispute is resolved, you as the manager will want to stay in charge—and use your experience (along with IPR cases in which other companies have been involved) to learn for the future.

Step Three: Develop business strategies and solutions to prevent future problems: Prevention of IPR disputes is better than cure. Simple precautions can go a long way, beginning from trademark searches and patent clearance investigations. Your personnel should receive training and support that will help them take the right steps to prevent unnecessary problems and to react to unwanted use of your IPR. When properly planned and used, your combination of protections will help you to prevent claims and disputes from arising or to eliminate or reduce their potential impact. Although your legal team and your patent or trademark experts can assist you here, you—as the manager—must remain in control. One of your best prevention strategies and protections is your own IPR portfolio because you are not an easy target if you are known for owning strong IPR.

Step Four: Climb to the balcony to see the big picture and become more proactive: Seen from the big picture perspective of the balcony, your intangibles offer tremendous opportunities, and your IPR become a core strategic asset. Yet they will not help you financially if you do not use them. After having determined the status of your current intangibles and where you want to be, you should focus on managing and enhancing the value of your IP. By working proactively with IP and legal experts, and integrating the different departments and functions that are involved, you can develop your IPR portfolio into a source of revenue. In fact, your IP may become your company's single most valuable wealth-creating asset. While in the old days, IP strategy may have been just a legal strategy and IP may have been left to the legal or IP department to manage, IP today deserves your managerial attention. A strong and protected portfolio of intangible assets can gain you an entrance ticket to collaboration that will enable you to constantly innovate, create, and capture new value, and sustain competitive and collaborative advantage.

Notes

1 van Opstal, D. 2009. *Science and Business: Moving Beyond Lab and Board Room*. Council on Competitiveness, July 1 [Online]. Available at: http://www.compete.org/images/uploads/File/PDF%20Files/Science_and_Business.pdf [accessed: August 1, 2010].

2 This quotation is often attributed to Charles Darwin, for instance as etched into the floor of California Academy of Sciences. Yet it was never written by Darwin, and its origins remain unclear. (*Six things Darwin never said—and one he did*, 2010. The Darwin Correspondence Project, University of Cambridge [Online]. Available at: http://www.darwinproject.ac.uk/six-things-darwin-never-said [accessed: August 1, 2010]).

3 Council on Competitiveness, 2004. *Innovate America. Thriving in a World of Challenge and Change.* National Innovation Initiative, Interim Report 7/23/04 [Online]. Available at: http://www.goalqpc.com/docs/reports/NIIInterimReport.pdf [accessed: August 1, 2010].

4 Prahalad, C.K. and Ramaswamy, V. 2000. Co-opting customer competence. *Harvard Business Review*, January–February, 79–87; and Prahalad, C.K. and Ramaswamy, V. 2004. *The Future of Competition. Co-Creating Unique Value with Customers*. Boston, MA: Harvard Business School Press.

5 Prahalad and Ramaswamy 2004, 137.

6 PricewaterhouseCoopers 2007. *Exploiting intellectual property in a complex world.* Technology executive connections, vol. 4 [Online]. Available at: http://www.pwc.com/en_GX/gx/technology/pdf/exploiting-intellectual-property.pdf [accessed: August 1, 2010], 9 and 11.
7 PricewaterhouseCoopers 2007, 11.
8 Rivette, K.G. and Kline, D. 2000a. Discovering new value in intellectual property. *Harvard Business Review*, January–February, 54.
9 The profit center 2001. *LD21*, Spring, 17. See also Davis, J.L. and Harrison, S.S. 2001. *Edison in the Boardroom: How Leading Companies Realize Value from Their Intellectual Assets.* New York, NY: Wiley.
10 Aman, C. 1999. The money of invention. *Corporate Counsel*, May, 46.
11 Aman 1999, 46.
12 Rivette and Kline 2000a, 56.
13 Moore, P.L. 2000. For sale: Great ideas, barely used. *Business Week*, April 3, 80.
14 Rivette, K.G. and Kline, D. 2000b. *Rembrandts in the Attic: Unlocking the Hidden Value of Patents.* Boston, MA: Harvard Business School Press.
15 Blaxill, M. and Eckardt, R. 2009. *The Invisible Edge: Taking Your Strategy to the Next Level Using Intellectual Property.* New York, NY: Portfolio (Penguin Group USA Inc.).
16 Rivette and Kline 2000a, 58.
17 2009. *The [Finnish] Government's Resolution on The Strategy Concerning Intellectual Property Rights*, March 26 [Online]. Available at: http://www.tem.fi/files/22788/vn_periaatepaatos_ipr_strategia_en.pdf [accessed: August 1, 2010], 1.
18 Prahalad, C.K. and Krishnan, M.S. 2008. *The New Age of Innovation. Driving Co-created Value through Global Networks.* New York, NY: McGraw-Hill, 1.
19 Phelps, M. and Kline, D. 2009. *Burning the Ships. Intellectual Property and the Transformation of Microsoft.* Hoboken, NJ: John Wiley & Sons, Inc., xix.
20 Phelps and Kline 2009, xx.
21 Phelps and Kline 2009, 46.
22 Chesbrough, H.W. and Garman, A.R. 2009. How open innovation can help you cope in lean times. *Harvard Business Review*, December, 68–76. The authors discuss outside-in and inside-out open innovation and strategic moves that can reduce research and development costs today without sacrificing tomorrow's growth.
23 Blaxill and Eckardt 2009, 123 and 136.
24 Prahalad and Krishnan 2008, 33.
25 Sullivan, J. 2005. Aggressive IP strategies open up new revenue streams. *Intellectual Asset Management Magazine,* October/November, 25–9 [Online]. Available at: http://www.bakerbotts.com/files/Publication/0f023c74-766b-44ad-a226-192f10c2caf1/Presentation/PublicationAttachment/5e39a585-8c86-4ebc-80ee-1d5f4fade71c/Aggressive%20IP%20Strategies,%20Sullivan.pdf [accessed: August 1, 2010]. See also Schutz, R.J. 2009. Patent Litigation: The Changing Economics of Risk and Return, in *From Assets to Profits. Competing for IP Value & Return,* edited by B. Berman. Hoboken, NJ: John Wiley & Sons, Inc.
26 Schutz 2009, 161.
27 Schutz 2009, 165.
28 Trademarks 1994. *Outside Counsel*, Summer, 2–3.
29 Kneale, D. 1982. Tylenol, the painkiller, gives rivals headaches in stores and in court. *Wall Street Journal*, September 2, 1.
30 Aman 1999, 38.
31 See, for example, BrainyMedia, 2010. *Bill Gates Quotes.* BrainyQuote [Online]. Available at: http://www.brainyquote.com/quotes/authors/b/bill_gates.html [accessed: August 1, 2010].

32 PricewaterhouseCoopers 2007, 5 and 21.

33 For the importance of developing corporate contracting capability in this connection, see Chapter 6 and Lee, N. 2008. From tangibles to intangibles—Contracting capability for intangible innovation, in *Corporate Contracting Capabilities. Conference Proceedings and Other Writings*, edited by S. Nystén-Haarala. University of Joensuu Publications in Law, No 21, 33–50 [Online]. Available at: http://ssrn.com/abstract=1350337 [accessed: August 1, 2010].

34 Orozco, D. 2009. Rational design rights ignorance. *American Business Law Journal*, Winter, 599.

35 Phelps and Kline 2009, 148.

36 Phelps and Kline 2009, 147.

37 Hall, K. 2009. Is Asia winning a race to patent ideas in the U.S.? *BusinessWeek*, Eye On Asia Blog, January 16 [Online]. Available at: http://www.businessweek.com/globalbiz/blog/eyeonasia/archives/2009/01/do_patent_talli.html [accessed: August 1, 2010].

38 PricewaterhouseCoopers 2007.

39 PricewaterhouseCoopers 2007, 13.

40 PricewaterhouseCoopers 2007, 5 and 21.

41 This topic is discussed in more detail in Chapter 7.

42 Rivette and Kline 2000a, 56.

43 Aman 1999, 44.

CHAPTER

6 Use Contracts to Improve Business and Prevent Problems: Be Proactive in Contracting to Achieve Competitive Advantage

In the earlier chapters we have discussed the positive aspects and outcomes of collaboration between businesses. In this chapter, we will cover contracts and contracting, the tools and processes that enable productive collaboration. This chapter focuses on the impact of contracts and contracting on your business and how your company and you, as a manager, can benefit from them.

For traditional thinkers, contracts are legal tools. They are about promises that the law will enforce. Contracts create (or amend) rights and responsibilities, and the law will provide remedies if contractual promises are broken. For today's managers, such a view is too limited and legalistic. This chapter will show that apart from being legal tools, contracts are management tools. For today's managers, contracts and contracting mean business, as they are important enablers for your business, bargains, deals, and relationships. As war is too important to be left to the generals alone, contracts and contracting are too important to be left to the lawyers alone.

The Impact of Contracts and Contracting on Your Business

Today's business takes place in an increasingly complex, global, and networked environment, where contracts play a key role. Major business decisions crystallize into a contract or agreement of some sort. Projects ranging from construction and equipment supply to IT acquisition and outsourcing all involve contracts, both on the sell-side and on the buy-side. Collaborative R&D, selling, procurement, finance, invoicing, change control, claims, and many other fields operate within the framework of contracts.

In collaborative ventures and large projects with multiple suppliers and subcontractors, the interfaces among the various providers must be managed well. Required actions must be taken at the right time and in the right place, by one's own organization and by the other parties. The required coordination, communication, and control can be built on and provided by contracts.

Contracts impact future rights, cash flows, costs, earnings, and risks. In supplier-buyer relationships, *everything*—schedules, deliveries, payments, rights, responsibilities, and remedies—revolves around the underlying contracts. The terms of those contracts have a tremendous impact on the outcome of transactions and relationships. These terms affect profitability, increase or decrease costs and liabilities, and play a major role in customer and supplier satisfaction. If contracts fail, business performance will suffer. A lot is at stake, including good-will and reputation. Expensive contractual disputes endanger relationships and consume time and resources that could otherwise be used for productive work.

In their book *The Invisible Edge*,[1] Mark Blaxill and Ralph Eckardt state that the key to competitive advantage is to own the distinctive parts of your business that create value. They argue that the only way to truly *own* your distinction is through intellectual property (IP). But owning your distinction and IP is not enough: you need contracts in order to create and capture value from what you own, whether tangible or intangible assets. Contracts can determine whether, when and for how long a business will make—or lose—money.

The fundamental purpose of commercial contracts today is to maximize value, not just from single transactions, but from long-term relationships. You need contracts to be able to do business and govern collaborative projects and relationships. Good-quality contracts clarify requirements, memorialize the parties' business deal, set the stage for successful delivery, and provide tools that help the parties get the relationship back on track when problems surface. Yet not all contracts work as planned.

If you are an experienced business manager, you may claim that you know your business and how it works. But how familiar are you with contracts in general and your contracts in particular? Do you know whether they share risk realistically or are sources of unlimited (and perhaps uninsured) risk and liability exposure? Are you confident about them and in control? If you are not in control of your contracts, then who is?

If you are not able to answer these questions, you are probably like most executives today, thinking that contracts are really not their business and that contract managers, lawyers, sourcing professionals, or "someone else" takes care of them. This approach is no longer acceptable. Today's managers cannot claim to manage and be in control of their business without knowing how contracts work—and even more importantly, how they can make contracts work to provide strategic advantage for their companies.

We therefore encourage you to become involved with and to take control of your contracts. By doing so, you may discover an entirely new set of tools to add to your managerial toolbox. With a little help from subject matter and contracts experts where needed, you may start to see and seize opportunities and strategic advantage others do not know exist.

In this chapter we will explain how you can use the Manager's Legal Plan™ to gain competitive advantage through contracting. Along the way, we will show how a company's contract portfolio may be subject to greater losses than one realizes—although we believe that the greatest risk in business is not taking any risks. When you understand contracts and contracting, you can use them to seize competitive advantage, encourage innovation, support sound risk taking and help balance risk with reward.

What Do We Mean by "Contracts" and "Contracting"?

When hearing the word "contract," many people tend to think solely of signed, formal documents. Traditional management literature seems to have a rather legalistic view of contracts also, with an emphasis on their legally binding function and their being subject to remedy in the courts. This viewpoint does not take into account the difference between contracts and contracting. What is the difference between the two? The former is an outcome, often (but not necessarily) a document recording that outcome, whereas the latter is a process. This chapter demonstrates why management should take an interest in both, along with their company's contracting policies and practices.

The word "contract" has two basic meanings: (1) an agreement (a bargain, a deal) and (2) the document representing the agreement (or attempting to represent it because documents are often not complete embodiments of an agreement). Contracts can take many forms and they can be created in many different ways. They may be signed documents or a chain of letters or electronic messages. Contracts may be formed, for instance, through an offer (bid, quotation) followed by a purchase order, or through a purchase order followed by an order confirmation. As we will see later in this chapter, the basic requirements of contracts are not the same throughout the world or in all contexts. In some cases, to be valid, contracts need to be in writing; in others, they do not. In some countries and contexts, the formation of a valid contract requires that each side provides something of value, *consideration*; in others, it does not.

"Contracting," too, has different meanings. Even if we set aside the meaning of the term in other contexts (such as contracting an illness or becoming infected), some people think in terms of procurement, others in terms of sales. For many, contracting is about making a *written* agreement. The vertical dashed line in the center of the following figure (Figure 6.1) depicts the moment when a contract is made and signed, often understood to be "contracting" in the narrow meaning of the word.

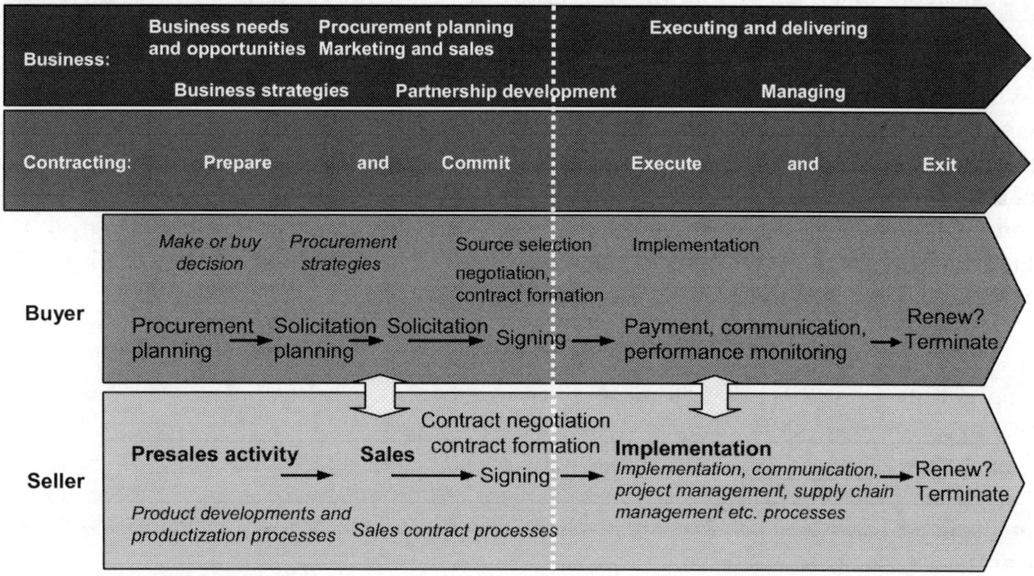

Figure 6.1 Contracting and business processes[2]

In today's complex, multilocational deals, contracting is rarely a craft activity conducted by an expert at a desk, producing a written document bearing the heading "contract." Preparing, negotiating, and signing documents are important steps in the contracting process, but there is more. Today's contracting is a process in which a wide range of people, functions, and technologies are involved: a collaborative venture that requires a knowledgeable and well-connected team.

The term "contracting" is used here to refer not only to *preparing* and *making* but also to *managing* and *implementing* contracts (or, as is often the case, a portfolio of contracts). For our purposes, it is useful to break down the contracting process into phases: 1) planning, solicitation, and bidding (pre-award); 2) negotiation and signing (award); and 3) implementation, performance, and administration (post-award). Figure 6.1 shows how the business and contracting processes of suppliers and buyers are intertwined and emphasizes the significance of implementation as part of the contracting process.

Proactive Contracting

Proactive Contracting (as that term is used here) is built on the use of contracts as Proactive Law tools. However, it is not predominantly about the law or lawyering. First and foremost, it is about the conscious use of contracts and contracting processes as management tools that guide and support the success of your business. It is about bringing businesses the certainty they require to prosper and providing them with the legal tools and support that enable them to reach their goals. Preventing legal problems is one among those goals—yet it is only secondary.

The goal of Proactive Contracting is to provide a framework for integrating legal foresight into the tangible practice of everyday business and to merge good contract, legal, project, quality and risk management practices with a proactive approach to law. As already stated in Chapter 1, the proactive approach differentiates two aspects of *proactivity*: the *promotive* dimension (promoting what is desirable—for instance, enabling the parties to align, articulate, and reach their goals and providing incentives for desired performance) and the *preventive* dimension (preventing what is not desirable—for instance, preventing misunderstandings and other unnecessary causes of disputes). For Proactive Contracting, promoting business success comes first and minimizing legal risk and preventing legal trouble second.[3]

Using contracts to reach these goals requires proper planning, negotiation, documentation, implementation, and operation. For the purposes of Proactive Contracting, contracts and contracting processes can be used to prepare for, guide, and manage: (1) performance (implementation toward successful relationships and trouble-free transactions); (2) risk and contingencies; and (3) dispute resolution. To benefit fully from the opportunities offered by contracts and contracting, the involvement of management is crucial on all three levels. It is so fundamental that, without it, Proactive Contracting fails.[4]

While the focus in this chapter is on the business arena, the proactive approach is not limited to business organizations. In recent years, the number of contracts has exploded in government organizations as well, and an increasing number of public managers find new challenges in forming contract-based relationships and setting the rules by which those relationships will operate in a high-tech, market-driven world.[5]

Proactive Contracting seeks to provide tools and methods that help in realistic risk allocation and in the prevention and prompt resolution of issues that can adversely impact relationships, so as to reduce the staggering burden of wasted time and money caused by conflict. Here, the goal of a contract is to provide a reliable platform and a good roadmap for the parties to follow in their ongoing relationship to reach their objectives and, at the same time, to minimize the potential for problems, differences of opinion, disputes, and litigation. These goals are related; a good roadmap not only documents the basic business understanding and enhances performance but also minimizes the potential for problems.

Apply the Manager's Legal Plan™ to Contracts and Contracting

STEP ONE: UNDERSTAND THE LAW

The type and content of your company's contracts depend on many contextual aspects of your business, industry, and activities; the nature of your relationships; your role and bargaining power; whether you deal with businesses, governments, or consumers; and so on. Companies often have their own specific policies, practices, and standards, including standard contracts and terms, which vary considerably in, say, financial services, power generation, paper and pulp production, information and communication technology, oil and gas, and construction. The applicable legal, market, and regulatory requirements vary also. The rules and principles of the applicable contract law and context-specific law, such as sales law, determine which promises will be enforced by the courts. Fortunately, in international trade, solutions to most of the legal difficulties raised by varying laws and jurisdictions can be provided through contracts.

So you will need contextual knowledge of both the laws that apply and the contracts that are currently entered into in your field. You will need a basic understanding of these before you can make informed choices as to the future policies and practices of your company. Equipped with this understanding you can "make your own laws" through your contracts, especially if you are dealing business-to-business.

Even though you may not be personally in charge of drafting, you will need to know how contracts are formed in your business under the legal system(s) where your business operates, especially if mandatory disclosure, form, or other requirements apply. The requirements related to contract formation and to the validity of contracts and their terms (often involving a discussion of standard terms and limitations of liability and whose terms prevail when the seller's and purchaser's forms contain differing terms) vary from one country to another. So you will need to be willing to learn some contract law basics. With this knowledge you will be able to achieve Contract Literacy, which is discussed in Step Three.

For instance, in many countries, the law does not require a formal written contract for a sale of goods or services. Bids, purchase (or change) orders, confirmations, memoranda, letters of intent, and the like, even e-mail messages and informal verbal conversations, can create (or change) contracts. In some jurisdictions, quotations (offers, bids) are binding upon the party making them, unless expressly otherwise stated; in others, the opposite is true. In some jurisdictions, offers can be terminated or withdrawn until accepted; in others, they cannot. You do not want your company to commit too early nor do you want to be disappointed by assuming a legally binding commitment or enforceability where it is lacking. You do not want to guess, for example, whether a letter of intent is binding. Once you know what you want you can present it to the other party and, if accepted, state it in your contract.

While it helps to know the rules of the game—say, those relating to contract formation—in one legal system, you should never assume that the same rules apply in another. If you want to give or receive a legally binding commitment, you need to learn about the law in the legal system involved. If in doubt, you should ask for competent legal advice *before* you make a decision.

While some quite fundamental principles differ from one country to another, there are a few basic truths about the interplay of contracts and the law that every manager should understand. One of them is the fact that some important parts of your contracts may be "invisible." You contract may contain "hidden" requirements, responsibilities, remedies, and risks—but also "hidden" rights and reliefs. Where the contract is silent, that is, where it does not specifically address the issue at hand, the default rules of the law enter the picture. These may be found in statutes, codes, principles, case law, and precedents, depending on the legal system. You do not want to encounter any of these rules unprepared after forming a contract.

In this context, there are some distinctions that should be considered when designing and interpreting contracts. These are context-dependent and include the distinction between *goods* as opposed to *services, results* as opposed to *resources, ownership* as opposed to *license to use* and other limited rights.[6] These distinctions will lead you to different default rules when, for example, a contract is breached and its contents—the terms on which the parties specifically agreed—do not provide guidance. The default rules will further determine how other gaps in your contract will be filled. In the following section, we will refer to these default rules and gap-fillers (along with other terms that the law may import into your contracts) as "invisible terms."

Beware of invisible terms: the law may write your contract for you!

Let's take the example of a straightforward contract for the sale and purchase of goods. When you want to determine your rights and responsibilities based on the contract, reading the document entitled "contract" (where one exists) rarely gives a full picture of your position. You may find relevant provisions in various places, including appendices (such as technical specifications, warranties, schedules, and so on), the purchase order and/or other documents that created the contract, and Standard Terms and Conditions. Many long-term supply agreements, distribution agreements, and other frame (or umbrella) agreements contain terms that have an impact on individual sales contracts made within their scope. If the different provisions and documents do not agree with one another, you need to determine their order of precedence.

In addition to what is specifically addressed and written into the contract, one needs to recognize what is *not* written but still becomes part of the deal: the invisible terms. These may be provided by mandatory laws, such as consumer protection laws, or by non-mandatory laws, such as sales laws. The latter may be called different names, such as Uniform Commercial Code, Sale of Goods Act or, in international dealings, Convention on Contracts for the International Sale of Goods (also known as the CISG, Vienna Convention and UNCITRAL Convention). In international sales and purchases of goods, the CISG often applies automatically, by default, absent contrary agreement. The CISG is now the "uniform international commercial code" or "international sales law" of more than 70 countries, which account for over three-quarters of all world trade.

Sales laws contain provisions related to, for example, requirements for the quality and fitness of the goods (implied warranties), examination, notices, and the buyer's and supplier's rights and obligations in case of defects or non-conformities. Even where no mention is made of warranty or liability, the supplier has obligations and liabilities regarding defects. For instance, the obligation to rectify a defect and pay damages can arise as a matter of law rather than as a matter of contractual agreement.

So if you don't specifically address something in your contract, courts may write your contract for you using the following sources:

1. Mandatory legal rules, where some exist.
2. Usage of trade and parties' established practices (course of performance or course of dealing).
3. Default rules: non-mandatory legal rules and principles (implied terms, implied warranties).

If a dispute arises, litigating lawyers, judges, and arbitrators are accustomed to determining which warranties, obligations, and liabilities are included and which are excluded in a contractual arrangement. They consider express terms, including provisions dealing with forum selection and choice of law, allocating responsibilities and risks (such as who bears the risk as regards the product's fitness for purpose) and excluding or limiting particular types of warranties, liabilities, and remedies. But they also pay close attention to regulatory requirements and mandatory laws, usage of trade and established practices, and default rules.

STEP TWO: KNOW HOW TO COPE WITH LEGAL PROBLEMS AND LEARN FROM THEM

Even if people know how contracts and laws may impact business dealings and risk, during negotiations they sometimes trust that they can "work things out later." When problems later arise, there is a hesitancy to refer to the contract. In some cases, this is understandable because the parties are concerned about preserving the business relationship. But ignoring the contract can be financially risky and in law, like medicine, prevention is often better than cure.

One important guideline to keep in mind is that a contract, once made, cannot be unilaterally amended. Before you make a contract, you make many choices—some of them perhaps unknowingly—that may later determine whether you will win or lose if a dispute arises. In the words of Louis M. Brown, "When you 'sign on the dotted line,' you obligate yourself; before you sign, you have a freedom of choice not available later."[7]

So you want to get your contractual choices right from the start. One of the choices you make is how you will resolve legal problems between you and your contracting partner. If you make no choice, you may have actually chosen litigation because the other party might not share your desire to avoid court processes. Once a dispute has arisen, it is more difficult to steer the dispute to mediation or arbitration. If you prefer these dispute resolution methods to litigation, your contract should provide for these processes in the first place. The contract should include a well-thought-out choice of law clause as well to prevent an unnecessary dispute over this question.

Once a dispute has developed, it is often difficult to get the participants to agree or even discuss rationally the optimum method for resolving the dispute. One party may want a quick resolution; the other party may prefer delay. One party may want to avoid publicity; the other party might prefer public exposure of the controversy. Whenever the parties are unable to agree on the method of dispute resolution, the only remaining dispute resolution system, by default, will be litigation.[8]

If you encounter a problem after entering into a contract, when considering "flight or fight"—for instance, whether to attempt to solve a delay in a delivery situation with your supplier amicably or let it escalate to a heated discussion, difference of opinion, conflict, or dispute—you need to determine your position and rights. Before exercising them, you need to weigh the possible short-term benefits of requiring strict compliance and compensation against the risks and costs of having to start a battle and potentially switch suppliers. If suppliers end up performing late, you refuse to pay them or deduct liquidated damages from your payment to them and a lawsuit arises, you might still "fight or flight"—that is, litigate the lawsuit or settle. Whichever way the situation is resolved, you will want to learn from it for future projects and contracts. There are many precedents in court cases related to contract failures that can also prove highly educational in this respect.

Yet it is not in your interest to develop case law based on disputes. Businesses do not succeed by winning disputes or court cases, or by blaming others and then claiming damages. Their reputation, their workplaces, and their ability to continue and prosper may have been destroyed long before they collect on any judgment.

While disputes might be an inevitable part of business, you should remember that they impact your future business and reputation. Management involvement in both the decision as to how disputes are to be resolved (for example, whether through courts or alternative dispute resolution (ADR)) and in the actual resolution of disputes, whether by business or legal procedures, is a decisive success factor.[9] Like contracts, contract disputes are part of your business—a part too important to be left to lawyers alone.

STEP THREE: DEVELOP BUSINESS STRATEGIES AND SOLUTIONS TO PREVENT FUTURE PROBLEMS

Proactive contracting techniques and dispute control processes exist that can help to prevent problems from occurring, and control problems and differences of opinion so that they don't escalate into disputes and legal action. At the same time, they can improve communications and create good relationships among the contracting parties, thus enhancing performance.[10]

Step Three emphasizes the importance of paying attention not only to your contract documents and processes but also to how they are managed, including how your contracts are planned, crafted, negotiated, signed, handed over to the project/delivery team, and implemented.

Conflict prevention and management

It has been known for years that the earlier a dispute or a potential dispute is addressed, the better the chances of a fair and prompt solution. Across the world, in the private and the public sector alike, emphasis has been put lately on the importance of forward planning, dispute avoidance, and dispute management. A number of institutions have developed conflict management procedures and taken advantage of ADR mechanisms when disputes arise. In a number of companies, the focus is shifting from ADR to Early Dispute Resolution (EDR), which is discussed in the next chapter.[11]

In Australia, a standard concerning the prevention, handling, and resolution of legal problems was introduced in 1999.[12] In the UK, the Office of Government Commerce (OGC), which supports the public sector in improving procurement and commercial activities, published its Dispute Resolution Guidance in 2002. The Introduction, very much in line with the proactive approach, states:

> *Contractual disputes are time consuming, expensive and unpleasant. They can destroy client/supplier relationships painstakingly built up over a period of time and can impact the supply chain. They can add substantially to the cost of the contract, as well as nullifying some or all of its benefits or advantages. They can also impact on the achievement of value for money. It is in everyone's interest to work at avoiding disputes in the first place. ... Inevitably, however, they do occur and when they do the importance of a fast, efficient and cost effective dispute resolution procedure cannot be overstated. ... In particular it is Government policy that litigation should usually be treated as the dispute resolution method of last resort.*[13]

So your contracts should contain provisions for the resolution of disputes. Yet conflict prevention and management is not restricted to dispute resolution clauses alone. One of the most powerful ways to prevent and control disputes between contracting parties is to rationally allocate risks by assigning each potential risk to the party who is best able to manage, control, or insure against the particular risk. Conversely, unrealistic shifting of risks to a party who is not equipped to handle the risk can increase costs, sow the seeds of disputes, create distrust and resentment, and establish adversarial relationships that can interfere with the success of the business enterprise.[14]

Managers need to pay close attention to the proper management of contract relationships so that agreements remain non-adversarial. If a problem or conflict arises, managers should remain in charge, even when a conflict develops into a legal dispute. If you work in a large corporation, Early Case Assessment (ECA) and other EDR processes are probably already built into your company's processes. If not, you should look into these and see how they could help you protect your business and its reputation.[15]

There are two basic categories of contract clauses that can reduce profits, increase risks of loss, and lead to disputes. First are contract clauses that are accepted knowingly, as legitimate trade-offs for obtaining a deal or commencing collaboration on mutually acceptable terms. Second are contract clauses that are accepted without people being aware of the risks that could have been avoided or mitigated through proper preparation. The latter are of special interest in Step Three.

While an element of risk exists in any transaction, when taking risks you want to know the level of risk so that you can balance the perils against the expected outcome. However, purchase price or fee, not risk, is often the yardstick used for policies related to individuals' authority to sign on behalf of a company. Adding to the challenges is the fact that the level of risk is not usually written into the documents themselves. People signing on behalf of your company may not always recognize that they are involved in contract making or risk taking; they just "do their jobs." In such cases, business deals, transactions, and contracts can evolve and result in people letting chances for profit or savings slip by or risks go unmanaged.

Contract Literacy: business knowledge every manager needs

As a prudent business manager, you want to be aware of your company's contractual rights and duties. And you do not want to be negatively surprised by "invisible" requirements, obligations, or liabilities you did not know existed. Today's business managers and organizations need Contract Literacy. This requires not only knowledge about the law, the subject matter of Step One, but also a basic understanding of the interplay of business, contracts, and the law—and becoming interested in and actively involved at the early stages of contracting.

When reading a contract, there are two principal aspects to Contract Literacy: being willing and able to understand, first, what the contract says (that is, what is specifically agreed) and, second (the often more demanding task), what the contract does *not* say but still becomes part of or affects the deal. These aspects are presented in Figure 6.2.

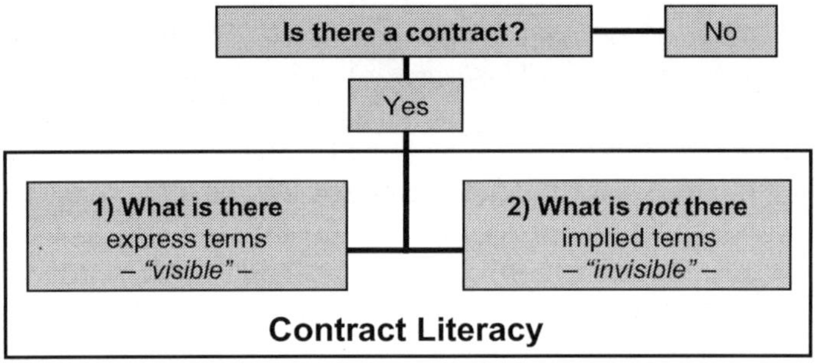

Figure 6.2 Contract Literacy

If we define a contractually literate person as one who can read and write contracts, we should be able, in principle, to include every literate person in that category. Most business people are able to read and write contracts reasonably well; whether they are willing to do so is another matter. Experienced corporate counsel know that the latter is often a problem in practice. Many business people are reluctant to read contracts, either from choice or because of *contract phobia*. The good news is that the phobia is curable.

Understanding what is agreed—the express, "visible" terms—requires a good grasp of the language of the contract in question. Many people around the world these days negotiate and make contracts in a language other than their own native language. The contracting world has been heavily influenced by Anglo-American contract models, not only in cross-border contracting, but also in domestic contracting in many countries. Contracts have been Anglo-Americanized, even where the governing law of the contract is that of a civil law country, the language of which is not English.[16]

Even a person who knows the language well enough to deal with daily business correspondence and routines may not be literate enough to understand the language and contents of contracts—or laws—that are encountered in international business, which demand different literacy skills. Many people have trouble with legal terminology and concepts, such as damages, liquidated damages, and remedies. With the increasing impact of the CISG, it may be worthwhile to brush up one's contract language skills, even for native speakers. The CISG introduced a number of new concepts—and left it to contract drafters and national legislators to define concepts such as Force Majeure and consequential loss, if they wish to use them.[17] In cross-border transactions, in addition to mastering the relevant language and vocabulary, one often needs to master a number of abbreviations, such as the Incoterms trade terms and their correct meaning and use.

The purpose of the Incoterms is to provide a set of international rules for the interpretation of the most commonly used trade terms in foreign trade. Thus, the uncertainties of different interpretations of such terms in different countries can be mitigated.[18] Exhibit 6.1 lists the trade term abbreviations contained in Incoterms 2010.[19]

EXHIBIT 6.1 ICC INCOTERMS® 2010 TRADE TERMS

RULES FOR ANY MODE OR MODES OF TRANSPORT

EXW	ex works
FCA	free carrier
CPT	carriage paid to
CIP	carriage and insurance paid to
DAT	delivered at terminal
DAP	delivered at place
DDP	delivered duty paid

RULES FOR SEA AND INLAND WATERWAY TRANSPORT

FAS	free alongside ship
FOB	free on board
CFR	cost and freight
CIF	cost insurance and freight

Incoterms is a registered trademark of the International Chamber of Commerce (ICC)

In this era of electronic contracting, contracts have become harder to recognize. It is easy to mistakenly believe that e-mail messages and mouse clicks are "non-contractual." Figure 6.2 shows another important requirement for Contract Literacy, namely that of being able to recognize a contract. While this may sound trivial, in everyday corporate life it may not be as easy as it sounds. If a contract is falsely understood solely as a signed piece of paper that has the word "contract" written on it, you might not recognize the contractual aspects of the pre-contract process—such as a bid, a purchase order, a confirmation, service descriptions, work scope definitions, technical specifications, minutes of meetings, and so on. To succeed, you need a process that makes sure all commitments and contracts are recognized and properly dealt with. Appropriate attention must also be paid to requests for proposals, bids, purchase orders, and so on, irrespective of their form and media, as well as to changes made to existing contracts and their attachments.

When you have a basic understanding of the interplay of business, contracts, and the law, you will know how to reallocate rights, obligations, and risks. You may decide to do so in a way different from the default rules that apply. In business-to-business dealings you will want to exercise your freedom of contract, which includes the freedom to choose the law applicable to your contract and the forum in which disputes will be resolved.

Success requires teamwork, with business management in charge

Contract problems or failures cannot be prevented by legal skills or contract drafting techniques alone. Their probability, impact, and significance are dependent on the subject matter and the environment. Technical, financial, operational, and legal issues arise and their early identification, evaluation, and treatment require teamwork.

Before a contract is made, problem prevention requires both performance planning and risk planning. The contract needs to provide clarity as to the roles and responsibilities of the parties, scope of the delivery, services or solutions, its implementation and pricing. The contract should specify details regarding *what, where, when,* and *how.* It also needs to clarify what happens if either party cannot or does not perform: *what if/what if not.*

Experience and research show that the same kinds of issues keep repeating themselves and creating problems in similar contracting situations. Focusing business, technical, and legal resources on such issues and both contractual and business solutions to navigate around them will be well worth the effort. For instance, if technical specifications, work scope definition, or task allocation are unclear, problems will follow. In the words of Mark Grossman, "taking time at the beginning to work out detailed design specs is equally important to both sides of the development deal. It's the only way to be sure everyone's on the same page, that there's been a meeting of the minds as to what the software should do, and how. And that's also the only way both sides will ever be able to walk away from a development project."[20]

Our "hand tool" (Figure 6.3) is designed to prevent unnecessary problems. It lists the trivial-sounding but crucial questions that must be answered when creating or reviewing obligations: who/which party shall do—what—where—when—how—and, last but not least, what if/what if not. This simple "hand tool" has proven to work in practice, both on the sell-side and on the buy-side. If the parties remember to go through the questions and address them when creating, amending, or passing on contractual obligations, a number of potential pitfalls can be avoided. Much more sophisticated tools and checklists exist—yet few are as easy to remember and carry around.

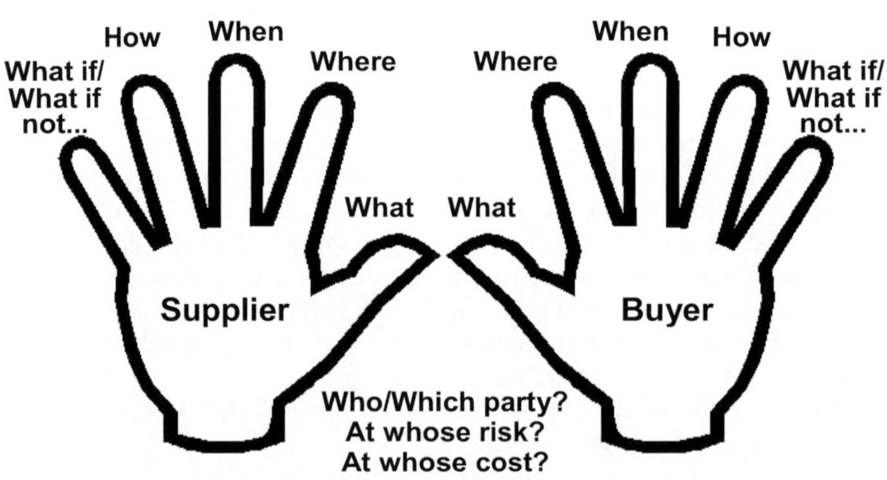

Figure 6.3 Hand tool

Even when not in charge of contract drafting or the contracting process (and remembering that it is wise to rely on experts when appropriate), managers must play a lead role in making contractual choices and being accountable for their business impact. Regardless of the skills of those who craft the contracts, it is up to the project team to fully understand and successfully implement them. Contracts and rules do not make things happen; people do. People in charge of implementing the contract and of doing what the company agreed to do need rules they can access and understand. Language and communication become crucial again.

One aspect of good-quality contracts is their user-friendliness. Most lawyers and business managers tend to agree that contract clarity is important and that contracts should be written in plain English so that they are understandable. From the business point of view, business people are the primary readers of contracts—not judges, courts, arbitrators, regulators, and lawyers. Business people are the ones who should be able to understand and be comfortable with the language and vocabulary used. What the legal professionals are comfortable with should not be the decisive factor.[21]

Many of the choices to be made in contracting are really not as much legal as they are business choices. Putting together good-quality contracts requires teamwork. And it takes time, especially if you are involved in a complex arrangement or a new business model. For contract crafters, the mission is often to create predictability and objective standards for something that does not exist yet. This resembles drawing a map of a future territory that is not there yet. Many questions arise: how much detail do you want to include? How do you frame the issues that arise? What do you include in the contract and what do you leave out?[22] The solutions to these and similar questions are not dictated by the law but are choices that should be made by a team where business decision makers take the lead. So you as a manager must become involved. To succeed, business and legal professionals must become team players, willing to appreciate each other's views and to work together to develop business strategies and solutions to prevent future problems.

If the provisions in your contract or your site practices lead to negative surprises, your company's solicitation, bidding, and contract formation process and documents need to be reviewed. You should also review your project managers' tools and site documentation practices, especially tools and templates for notices and responses. Further, your sales, procurement, project, and site personnel should receive training and support that will help them take the right steps at the right time and in the right manner, and prevent unnecessary problems and unintended liability exposure. When properly designed, your contracting processes and documents will help you prevent disputes from arising and eliminate or reduce their potential impact. They will also help you control and resolve disputes that cannot be avoided.

For those risks that cannot be fully controlled or eliminated, you can build in steps and contractual terms seeking to quickly solve the problem, minimize the losses and preserve business relationships. Although your legal team can assist you here, you need to make sure they collaborate with you and do not focus on limitations of liabilities, indemnities, and similar clauses alone. While these clauses are important and might be included in the current "Top Ten Terms" (the terms companies currently spend most of their time negotiating; see Exhibit 6.2), your legal team will probably admit that these terms represent the wrong agenda and that they should focus on something quite different. Yet they are unable on their own to create a paradigm shift. You should take the initiative so your company can become one of the leaders of the new kind of contracting, focusing on how you and your contracting partner can succeed together rather than preparing to fail.[23]

EXHIBIT 6.2 IACCM TOP TEN TERMS[24]

1. Limitation of Liability
2. Indemnification
3. Price/Charge/Price Changes
4. Intellectual Property
5. Confidential Information/Data Protection
6. Service Levels and Warranties
7. Delivery/Acceptance
8. Payment
9. Liquidated Damages
10. Applicable Law/Jurisdiction

STEP FOUR: CLIMB TO THE BALCONY TO SEE THE BIG PICTURE AND BECOME MORE PROACTIVE

Many managers see contracts as purely legal documents and as a formality with little business impact. When you climb to the balcony you are likely to see contracts and your role in relation to them in a new light, where the main goal is to create and maintain successful business deals and relationships. Aligning expectations of the parties, defining desired outcomes, and allocating tasks clearly are key steps to making this happen. These steps are an important part of the pre-contract stage in the contracting process. The outcome or goal of that process should be successful implementation, rather than signing a document called "contract." The process has other important business implications, including its impact on your brand image.

This step is where you start viewing contracts and contracting more broadly, as management tools that can help you define, shape, and govern successful business relationships. When you understand the strategic and managerial implications of contracts, you will also want to determine the status of your current contracting process and where you want to be. Applying the principles of the proactive approach—which also includes the preventive steps discussed earlier (namely: first, prevent the cause from arising; second, prevent the cause from doing harm; and third, if harm occurs, limit the damage)—you can then use contracts to improve business and prevent problems.

In the words of Tim Cummins, President of the International Association for Contract and Commercial Management (IACCM), "Economic value, cycle times, innovation—all critical weapons in today's highly competitive global economy—are directly influenced by the choice of contract terms. It is clearly time for a more strategic view of contracting policy and practice."[25]

Contracts in a new light: drivers of innovation, sources of value and more

An increasing number of people today are prepared to admit that contracts matter, and not just in litigation or end-game scenarios.[26] While contracts always have a legal dimension, it has been noted that on average, nearly 80 percent of the terms in business-to-business contracts are *not* really areas of significant legal concern—they are the business and financial terms and this includes key documents like Statements of Work, Specifications, and Service Level Agreements.[27]

In a recent paper, *Step-Change: Collaborate to Innovate,* Professor Leslie P. Willcocks and Andrew S. Craig of the London School of Economics name contracting as one of the critical success factors that drive collaboration to innovate. The four fundamental shapers and components of effective collaborative innovation, according to them, are leading, contracting, organizing, and behaving. "Of these, leadership is primary. Leadership shapes and conditions the environment in which requisite contracting, organizing, and behaving can occur. The right kind of contract supports collaborating and is an incentive for the right behavior. The right kind of organization supports teaming amongst the parties and enables high performance."[28]

Contracts as a Source of Value, a recent report by the IACCM, names Lou Gerstner, former Chairman and CEO at IBM, as one of the very few top executives who have seen contracts as fundamentally linked to brand image and who has believed that good contracting—especially in a solutions and services world—confers competitive advantage. The strategy of contracting is, as Lou Gerstner understood, about aligning contract terms and structures with selected market segments and opportunities. It means developing a portfolio of standards that support and enable desired outcomes. For example, a contract to deliver commodities is fundamentally different in its allocation of risks and obligations from a contract to deliver sustained cost reduction, or value-add services or innovation.[29]

Equipped with this new, broader view and with Contract Literacy, you can start playing a key role in marshalling legal and other corporate resources towards using your contracts to increase value creation and the share of that value captured by your company in your future business deals and relationships. From the balcony, it is easy to see that as contracts become increasingly complicated—and critical to business success—it is no longer acceptable to believe that they can be assigned to the legal department alone.

The legal department, however, will be instrumental in providing you as a manager and your staff with the tools you need to form, perform, operate, terminate, change, and otherwise work with contracts. Together as a team you can co-create good-quality contracts that help establish a strong foundation for business success (see Figure 6.4).

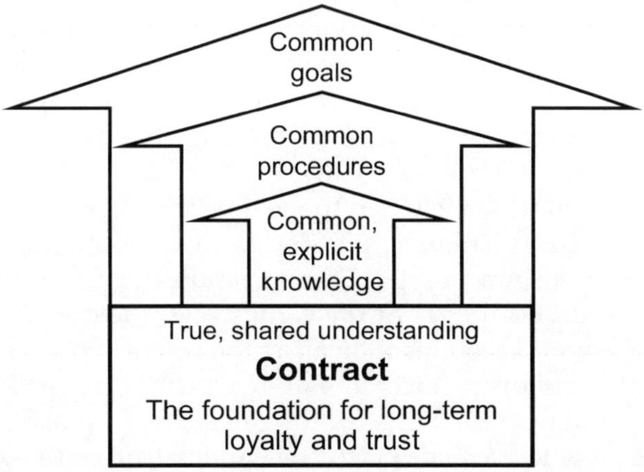

Figure 6.4 Good-quality contracts: foundation for long-term loyalty and trust

Good-quality contracts co-created by management and counsel describe requirements and allocate roles, responsibilities, and risks clearly. They minimize misunderstandings, provide safeguards, and lay the foundation for long-term loyalty and trust. And such contracts will continue to provide guidelines if problems are encountered or if a dispute arises.

Viewed from the balcony, you can now start to see the key role you as a manager play in contracting—and the various crucial functions that contracts can have when you use them as your management tools. You will find that contracts not only present themselves as drivers of collaborative innovation, but also as devices for flexible coordination and control,[30] and as tools for planning,[31] formalization, and sensemaking.[32] Recent research has identified these and several other functions of contracts. The functions frequently mentioned can be summarized as illustrated in Figure 6.5.

Contracts are tools for:

1. managing business, projects, and commitments;
2. creating, allocating, and protecting value;
3. communication, coordination, motivation, and control;
4. sharing, minimizing, and managing risk;
5. problem prevention, dispute avoidance, and dispute resolution.

Good-quality contracts serve as *visible scripts* for parties working together.

Figure 6.5 Functions of contracts

From your balcony perspective, you can see how contracts can work for you as tools to coordinate and manage your business and commitments; to create, allocate, and protect value, whether tangible or intangible (such as IPR); to communicate crucial information inside and between organizations; to motivate; and to allocate decision and control rights.[33] Your contracts also enable you to share, minimize, and manage risk;[34] to prevent problems; and to keep problems from developing into disputes. In case a dispute is unavoidable, contracts provide not only evidence of what has been agreed, but also an effective means to control and resolve the dispute.[35]

One way to look at contracts is to see them as *visible scripts*—blueprints, road maps, or sets of instructions—for collaboration.[36] Seen in this way, contracts serve as tools for *planning* and *managing* business, projects, and relationships, and contracting serves as a process of dialogue and learning.[37] At the early stages, the crafting of a contract then becomes an important initial step in articulating the business plan, in thinking through potential contingencies that may affect it, and in achieving business objectives. Viewed in this way, contracts can help align expectations, encourage innovation, improve supply chain performance, provide adequate protection, and balance risks against benefits.

On the other hand, if your contracts or related processes are too complex or difficult to follow or if their main focus is risk control or allocation, your business units and sales teams might try to avoid them or find ways around them. If this happens, instead of managing risk, you actually create new risk—the risk of unauthorized commitments, unnecessary confrontation, or lost opportunities.[38]

Lean Contracting: a case study from the balcony perspective

In the last 20 to 30 years, a number of changes have occurred that make proposal preparation, contract crafting, and contract management much easier. Today's contract makers have access to tools and technology that one could hardly dream about a generation ago.

Since the 1980s, our contract crafting tools have included commercially available forms, templates, and model documents on disk and later on CD. The early versions of the tools were intended for lawyers. Then came those designed for the public—for instance, consumers' legal software packages offering a "lawyer-in-a-box" (such as self-help wills like Nolo WillMaker) and do-it-yourself legal kits (such as divorce kits and incorporation kits).

Finally, tools that help automate document assembly, proposal preparation, and contract creation became available to anyone. Thus we now have access to technology tools that help automate contracting processes and manage the post-contract performance phase. Document and template automation, combined with contract life cycle management solutions, can increase efficiency, reduce costs and risk, and transform the way we create, track, and manage our contracts.

With all the tools and approaches available to us, it is tempting to ask: why do so many projects still fail? Why do so many problems escalate into disputes and litigation? Why does contracting still take so long? Do our current contracts and processes support and incentivize innovation—or inhibit it?

Despite the existence of all these tools, we still need people to capture, understand, align, and manage expectations. We need people to incentivize innovation and good performance; define requirements, service metrics, and levels; and determine what is in scope and what is out of scope. In a contractual setting, people on delivery teams must be aware of their responsibilities, do what is required of them, and avoid violating their company's agreement. Project managers must orient their organization and suppliers to the project, make sure they are on schedule, review deliverables and invoices, work with changes and notifications, make price adjustments, and so on. People are needed to see that problems don't escalate into disputes and litigation.

While in theory, technology tools make contract creation and management increasingly easy, evolving business needs are not necessarily being met by automating existing processes and documents. The technology tools have the potential to reduce cycle-time and cost, but they do so only if they have been designed and built the right way. Some of them may be too complex, and the related procedures and contracts may be too slow and too bureaucratic, thereby sacrificing innovation, creativity, and speed to control and compliance. Many organizations are still searching for minimalistic yet sound and legally safe ways to set up and manage successful projects and relationships.

The answer to simpler contracting may be found in lean contracting[39] (also known as agile contracting), an approach that applies the simplification principles of lean manufacturing and lean management to contracting, or in the application of Six

Sigma to improve performance—for example to shorten the time to complete contract negotiations. Combined, these approaches have the potential to revolutionize the way that business deals and collaborative ventures are formed and managed.

The in-house legal team at the brewer Scottish & Newcastle Plc (S&N) offers an example. According to Graeme Colquhoun, the Head of UK Legal at S&N, the small team of lawyers at S&N was overwhelmed by paperwork. Often the big legal issues were hard to spot because of the sheer volume of paperwork that passed across the lawyers' desks every day. Sometimes contracts were still being finalized after a project was completed. So S&N needed a new approach. Their lawyers' work in developing what they called "Pathclearer"[40]—and what we call lean contracting—provides a case study of the possibilities when contracts and contracting are viewed from the balcony.

S&N lawyers came to the conclusion that certain terms, such as price and specifications, should always be captured in writing, and that certain types of deals require detailed written contracts. However, they also realized that many other scenarios, such as a long-term relationship between a customer and supplier, call for a "much lighter legal touch." It is very difficult to force a partner to continue with a long-term relationship if the contract ceases to be mutually beneficial, and contracts are "unlikely to offer any real solutions when you are faced with an unwilling contract partner in a continuing relationship. It is almost always better to re-negotiate or simply walk away."[41]

The S&N lawyers identified an intangible yet powerful force in successful continuing business relationships, which they named "commercial affinity." It results from the desire by each party to continue doing business with the other, because it is economically sensible to do so. According to Steven Weatherley, former Head of UK Legal at S&N, "If you are a customer, you have access to a big nuclear button. You have the right to walk away, depriving the supplier of future business. You don't therefore need a myriad of tactical rights and obligations in a contract." "Lawyers," he notes, "are often keen to demonstrate their drafting skills by trying to predict and provide for every conceivable situation. This leads to highly complex lengthy contracts that can only be understood by the lawyers. So the law firms win twice: they get paid for drafting the contract and they get paid each time they have to advise on what it means." Also, drafting detailed written contracts can focus the parties on worst-case scenarios that "can lead to the souring of relationships. ... [C]ontinuing business relationships are like butterflies. They are subtle and hard to capture. When you do try to nail them down, you can kill them in the process."[42]

The new approach has helped make commercial teams at S&N more actively involved in contract negotiations. Further, the speed with which terms can be agreed has meant that S&N is able to seize and realize more opportunities, some of which might have been lost in the quagmire of a more traditional legal approach. In the words of Colquhoun:

> *Relying more on the common law and seeking to create commercial affinity rather than a legal straitjacket, the Pathclearer approach has proved to be effective in improving both the time taken to produce contracts and the effectiveness of these agreements. The commercial teams on both sides remain at the heart of the deal, openly discussing the key commercial concerns and gaining a better understanding of each other's expectations. The result is a more honest and understandable relationship that is founded not on a piece of paper, but rather on the basis of mutual benefit.*[43]

While *lean contracting* and shorter contracts have advantages, they should be used with caution. Certainly, if the situation warrants, a short contract is preferable to an overlong one—yet silence in contracts is not always "golden." All too often, gaps in contracts develop into business and legal problems that are threats to achieving business results and successful business relationships. As we saw in the earlier steps, if something goes wrong and the contract is silent, implied terms and gap-filling legal rules and principles come into play. In order to avoid negative surprises, gaps should be detected and addressed *before* they develop into traps and business and legal problems.

In many cases, a balance needs to be struck between the different (often conflicting) requirements of *lean contracting* on one hand, and clearly articulated responsibilities, liabilities, and remedies on the other; and between the need for certainty on one hand, and flexibility on the other. Contracts must be commercially acceptable, even attractive, so that they generate new business and revenue and help maintain good relationships. At the same time, they must secure compliance with pre-existing and current commitments and applicable laws. They should contain just enough, and not too much, detail; in other words, they should be minimalist yet legally and financially sound.

The key trade-offs often include determining whether and when to use Standard Terms and Conditions and contract templates as opposed to customized contracts.[44] Together with your legal or contracting team you can make the necessary business and legal decisions that can help you put together self-service contracting solutions to allow non-legal staff to generate contracts by completing online interviews, which serve as the basis for contracts that contain the required and correct language.[45]

The contracting puzzle—who has accountability for the pieces to fit together?

In today's business, as the number and complexity of contracts increase, making wise choices requires an understanding of the business opportunities, benefits, and risks inherent in contracts. Unnecessary problems should be prevented at source, and many can be.

Contracts have become important risk management and governance tools. Organizations possess a wide range of contract-related skills and capabilities, yet these are often fragmented. Conscious efforts are needed to transform the skills and knowledge of individuals to organization-level competence.

A growing number of companies recognize that contracts and contracting play a critical role in ensuring that strategy, projects, and commitments are implemented as intended. Many have invested in resources, tools, and technologies that enable them to manage their contracts and contracting processes effectively. Many still lag behind and can improve in these areas. In a number of companies, contracts could be used far more effectively than they are used today, and contract failures could be prevented more often than is done today.

After the way in which you understand contracts shifts from legal rules to business management tools, from the balcony, you can view contracts and contracting through the analogy of a jigsaw puzzle. With a complex project in mind, Figure 6.6 shows contracting as a puzzle of technical, implementation, business, and legal parts, all of which must be consistent and coordinated.

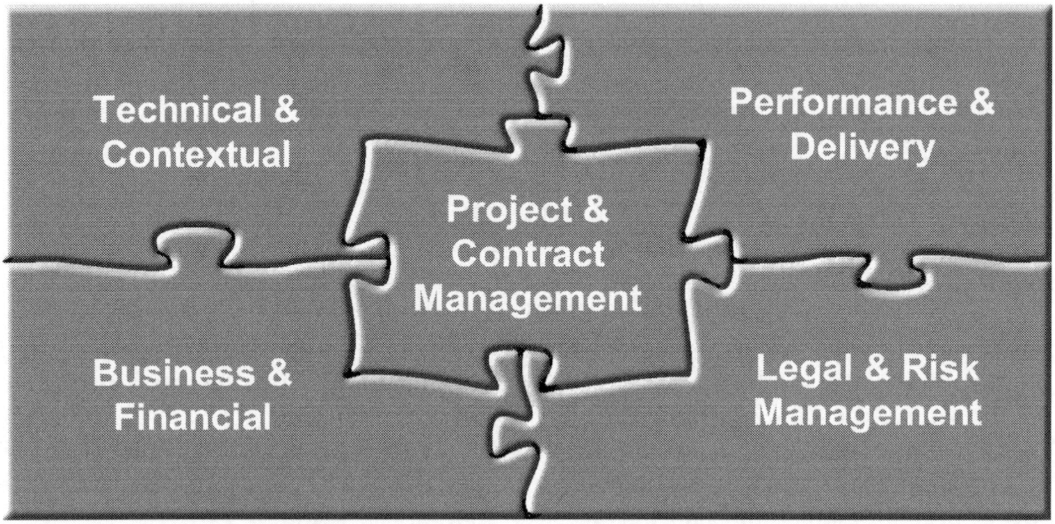

Figure 6.6 The contracting puzzle

If—and only if—correctly assembled, the pieces of the puzzle form a complete, synchronized picture. The ideal contract matches the parties' business needs and reflects their true goals. Such a contract is capable of being implemented within the allotted time, with the resources that have been allocated, and within budget. The designed solution matches the priced solution, which in turn matches the solution that is described—and will be implemented.[46] The supplied solution will meet the customer's requirements, while the project will satisfy the supplier's need for profitability and risk management. The parts of the puzzle fit together and create a successful business deal and relationship.

Further, when making and implementing contracts, a balance needs to be struck between many other differing (and often conflicting) requirements, such as the need for clear rules and certainty on one hand, and flexibility on the other. Contracts must be commercially acceptable and even attractive, so that they generate new business and revenue and help maintain good relationships. At the same time, they must be legally permissible, and secure compliance with pre-existing commitments, applicable laws, and governance regulations. Contracts must be financially sound, improve supply-chain performance, provide adequate protection, and balance risks against benefits.

In our increasingly networked world, it is not always clear who has accountability for the requirements to be prioritized and filled, and for ensuring that all the pieces of the puzzle fit together.

This is something you as the manager cannot expect the various specialist groups to resolve. The strengths of different professional groups must be merged and the various roles and responsibilities must be coordinated. The answer can be a matrix in which each group or function has its own area of responsibility. You can delegate responsibility, but this should be visible in the job description of the person(s) to whom it is delegated. Responsibility is connected to the question of authority and a common understanding is needed regarding both. What matters most is that it is clear to everybody involved and that somebody is in charge of integrating the different areas.

Who, then, is this "somebody" who is in charge of integrating the various skill sets, actions, documents, and interests related to contracts and contracting? The answer varies from one company and one from project to another. The sales, procurement, project, risk, or contract manager can be in charge of a major part of the whole. However, general managers are ultimately responsible for business results, which includes accountability for business contracts and for organizing their implementation.

General managers must take the lead

When properly structured and negotiated, contracts provide a framework for business and relationship management that significantly increases the probability of mutually successful outcomes for all parties, as well as containing the consequences of failure. Our choice of contract terms has a direct and major influence on the financial results of the business. Economic value, innovation, and cycle time improvements can be radically influenced by contracting strategies. Benchmarks and research show that employing the right contract structure and terms is not simply about containing unpleasant risks; it is also—predominantly—about achieving superior economic value from trading relationships. However, realizing this value depends on a shift in the way that contracting is managed and measured.[47]

Many contract managers and lawyers charged with leading contract negotiations today recognize that much of what they do leads to the wrong results. Yet they feel that they lack the empowerment to change things. In the 2008/9 IACCM study of the most frequently negotiated contract terms, 75 percent of respondents (who came from legal, procurement and contracts/commercial groups around the world) acknowledged that today's focus in negotiation does not optimize business outcomes because liabilities, indemnities, liquidated damages, and so on—topping the current list of Top Ten Terms (see Exhibit 6.2)—are all topics that prepare for failure and disagreement.[48] They are at best negative incentives that easily result in an environment of self-protection, constrained information flows, and a culture of blame. Both buy-side and sell-side negotiators feel unable to change the focus because of resistance by internal stakeholders and by "the other side."[49] They need management support.

In its 2008/9 survey, IACCM asked participants to describe not only what they spend most time negotiating today, but also where they think negotiating time should be focused in the future. The "new" Top Ten Terms listed in Exhibit 6.3 are dominated by the need to ensure certainty over the basic intentions of the deal and then to ensure it remains on track and is adjusted in the face of changed conditions or requirements. This revised focus for negotiations presumes that the parties will establish procedures for more open information flows and greater transparency—implying their intent to collaborate and to work together to manage risks and optimize results. Terms such as liability and indemnities occupy the place they should—as last-resort fall-backs in the event that well-crafted intentions become derailed.[50]

EXHIBIT 6.3 IACCM TOP TEN TERMS OF THE FUTURE[51]

1. Scope and Goals
2. Change Management
3. Responsibilities of the Parties
4. Communications and Reporting
5. Service Levels and Warranties
6. Price/Charge/Price Changes
7. Delivery/Acceptance
8. Limitation of Liability
9. Dispute Resolution
10. Indemnification

It is time for a paradigm shift. Managers, lawyers, and contracts professionals must join forces to make it happen. You as a manager must take control of your business through taking control of your contracts—and then lead your organization to make the change happen. But executive support is needed to make the transition to strategic contracting. This support requires a new appreciation of the role of the contract and the resources associated with its creation and management. Since contract terms and policies are so diverse in their organizational ownership, significant change can occur only if—like Lou Gerstner—the CEO understands why strategic contracting is important and mandates the change.[52]

The winners in the networked world will have the ability to make, manage, and adjust commitments faster, more reliably, and more profitably than their competitors. So contracting excellence moves right to the heart of the business. To achieve these goals, the contract process must engender confidence among all its users—internal and external—and must reflect the needs and expectations of the outside world. The quality and integrity of contracting not only drives transactional performance, but also plays a major role in corporate brand image.[53]

Your own and your organization's attitude towards contracts and contracting determines how the opportunities offered by contracts and contracting are used—or whether they are used at all. This involves adopting a view of contracts and the law—subjects that many managers view as dull and boring—as an interesting source of innovative solutions. Decision trees (covered in Chapter 7) and other visual tools, such as the figures in this chapter, are important in engaging people and communicating across professions, borders, and language or culture barriers. This is where you can combine the use of these tools with your business acumen, financial literacy, and your recently-acquired *Contract Literacy*. While your competitors may still think that contracts are a necessary evil, you will know how to use your contracts and contracting process to define and manage successful business relationships, support your ability to make profitable business decisions, and improve performance. You can then start using contracts strategically and benefit fully from proactive contracting as a source of competitive advantage.

Chapter Summary

This chapter has applied the four-step Manager's Legal Plan™ to one of the most important hidden sources of competitive and collaborative advantage: your contracts and contracting. The chapter has shown how your business depends on its ability to make, manage, and deliver on its commitments and contracts. You want your contracts to result in successful transactions and relationships with predictable outcomes and preferably zero disputes. At the same time, you want them to be flexible and ethical. This requires a balancing act requiring both business and legal skills and decisions. When it comes to contracts, you may need to reassess your role so that you can truly seize the opportunities and handle the threats that result from today's global networked economy and the contracts that are an inseparable part of it. And remember that you as a manager must remain in charge. Your contracts and contract disputes are too important to be left to lawyers alone.

Step One: Understand the law: When you understand the law, you will know how to use your freedom of contract. You can actually "make your own law" through your contracts, especially if you are dealing business-to-business. You will know which commitments are legally binding, and how contracts are formed. When you want to understand your rights and responsibilities based on a contract, you will know that reading the document entitled "contract" is seldom enough because your rights and responsibilities depend not only on what the contract says, but also on the "invisible terms" that have an impact. Because the law may write your contract for you, you probably want to provide clarity by express, visible terms. In international dealings, solutions to most of the legal difficulties raised by varying laws and jurisdictions can be provided through contracts.

Step Two: Know how to cope with legal problems and learn from them: A contract, once made, cannot be unilaterally amended. If you encounter a problem after entering into a contract, you have both business and legal decisions to make. Some of the choices were made—knowingly or unknowingly—at the time the contract was entered into, including the choice of forum where the dispute will be resolved. Failure to select a forum in the contract often results in a default option—litigation. If you and your contracting partner disagree and a lawsuit arises, you might decide between "fight or flight"—litigate or settle. Whichever way your dispute is resolved, you will want to use your experience as a learning opportunity for use in future projects and contracts. Legal literature is full of cases related to contract failures that can also prove highly educational. This information is important because research and experience show that dispute resolution would benefit greatly from closer involvement of management and the board.

Step Three: Develop business strategies and solutions to prevent future problems: In order to be in control of your business, you need to be in control of your contracts. When you are, you can develop business strategies and solutions to prevent future problems. Use your contracts and contracting processes to, first, prevent causes of problems from arising, second, prevent the causes from doing harm, and third, if harm occurs, limit the damage. When encountering a legal problem or "negotiating in the shadow of the law," it is important to know—as already stated in Step One—that matters that are *not* expressly agreed upon may still become part of the contract or affect the contract. So you need a basic understanding of the mandatory and non-mandatory legal rules and principles that apply, along with trade usage and practice where relevant. You and your organization need Contract Literacy, which is part of important business knowledge. Equipped with this knowledge, you can start to pay attention to your contract documents and how they are managed—and initiate improvements where needed. When properly designed, your contracting processes and documents will help you prevent causes of claims and disputes from arising and eliminate or reduce their potential impact. Your legal team can assist you here, although you want to make sure your lawyers are not focusing on limitations of liabilities, indemnities, and similar clauses alone.

Step Four: Climb to the balcony to see the big picture and become more proactive: This is where you view contracts broadly, as management tools and not just legal tools, and determine the status of your current contracting practices and goals. Your organization's attitude towards contracts and contracting determines how the opportunities offered by contracts and contracting are used—or whether they are used at all. This involves challenging the conventional wisdom that contracts are legal documents and, instead, adopting a view of contracts and the law as a source of innovative solutions. You want to pay attention not only to your individual contracts and the policies that apply, but also to your entire portfolio of current and future contracts, as well as the contracting process and how it is managed, end-to-end. You want your negotiators to remember that successful implementation, not signing the contract, is the goal.

Taking a proactive approach, you can build quality goals and risk management into your contracting process, while remaining flexible enough to respond to varying customer and legal requirements if needed. For those risks that cannot be fully controlled or eliminated, you can build in steps and contractual terms that allow you to quickly solve the problem, minimize the losses, and preserve the business relationships. Decision trees and other visual tools are useful in communicating more easily across professions, borders, and language or culture barriers. This is where you can combine your business acumen and financial literacy with your recently acquired Contract Literacy. Because your competitors may still think that contracts are a necessary evil, you can achieve competitive advantage through your knowledge of contracts and contracting process, which enables you to define and manage successful business relationships, support your ability to make profitable business decisions, and improve performance.

Notes

1 Blaxill, M. and Eckardt, R. 2009. *The Invisible Edge: Taking Your Strategy to the Next Level Using Intellectual Property*. New York, NY: Portfolio (Penguin Group USA Inc.).

2 *Contracting Capabilities in Industrial Life-Cycle and Service Business*. Research Report. A summarized version in English [Online]. Available at: http://yliopisto.joensuu.fi/oikeustieteet/siviili/CCC Research Report.pdf [accessed: August 1, 2010], 2. The multidisciplinary Corporate Contracting Capabilities research project studied contracting methods and capabilities in Finnish firms in 2006–2008 under the leadership of Professor Soili Nystén-Haarala, one of the Nordic pioneers involved in building a bridge between contract law in the books and contracting in practice. See, for example, Nystén-Haarala, S. 1998. *The Long-Term Contract: Contract Law and Contracting*. Helsinki: Kauppakaari Oyj/Finnish Lawyers' Publishing.

3 See generally Siedel, G.J. and Haapio, H. 2010 (in press). Using Proactive Law for competitive advantage. *American Business Law Journal*, 47(4), Winter, Special Issue "Law as a Source of Strategic Advantage." Available as Working Paper at: http://ssrn.com/abstract=1664561 [accessed: August 1, 2010]. The article uses a contracting example to illustrate the opportunities that contracts and the law offer to create new value and innovate in areas often neglected by managers. See also

Pohjonen, S. 2009. Law and Business—Successful Business Contracting, Corporate Social Responsibility and Legal Thinking. *Tidskrift Utgiven av Juridiska Föreningen i Finland (JFT)*, No. 3–4, pp. 470, 477 [Online]. Available at: http://www.helsinki.fi/oikeustiede/omasivu/pohjonen/Law%20and%20Business.pdf [accessed: August 1, 2010].

4 Haapio, H. 2006. Business success and problem prevention through proactive contracting, in *A Proactive Approach*. Scandinavian Studies in Law, Volume 49, edited by P. Wahlgren and C. Magnusson Sjöberg. Stockholm: Stockholm Institute for Scandinavian Law, 149–94; Haapio, H. 2007. An ounce of prevention ... Proactive legal care for corporate contracting success. *JFT* (Tidskrift utgiven av Juridiska Föreningen i Finland), 1, 39–68; Pohjonen, S. 2006. Proactive contracting: in contracts between businesses, in *IUS GENTIUM*, Vol. 12, Spring, 155–83; and Rekola, K. and Haapio H. 2009. *Industrial Services and Service Contracts. A Proactive Approach*. Helsinki: The Federation of Finnish Technology Industries, 67.

5 See, for instance, Cooper, P.J. 2003. *Governing by Contract. Challenges and Opportunities for Public Managers*. Public Affairs and Policy Administration Series. Washington, DC: CQ Press, which discusses the tools managers need to form, operate, terminate, or transform contracts amidst a complex web of intergovernmental relations.

6 For the differences between contracts for goods as opposed to services and resource- (task) driven and results- (outcome) driven service descriptions, see, for example, Rekola and Haapio 2009, 37 and 108.

7 Brown, L.M. 1955. *How to Negotiate a Successful Contract*. Englewood Cliffs, NJ: Prentice-Hall, Inc., vii.

8 See, for example, Groton, J.P. and Haapio, H. 2007. *From Reaction to Proactive Action: Dispute Prevention Processes in Business Agreements*. International Association for Contract and Commercial Management EMEA Academic Symposium, London, 9 October 2007. Available at: http://www.iaccm.com/loggedin/library/nonphp/Paper 7—From Reaction to Proactive Action—Dispute Prevention Processes in Business Agreements.pdf [accessed: August 1, 2010].

9 See Wallgren, C. 2006. ADR and business, in *ADR in Business—Practice and Issues Across Countries and Cultures*, edited by J.C. Goldsmith et al., Alphen aan den Rijn: Kluwer Law International, 13–19 and Guillemin, J-F. 2006. Reasons for choosing alternative dispute resolution, in J.C. Goldsmith et al., 21–52.

10 Groton and Haapio 2007, 1.

11 See, for example, Wallgren-Lindholm, C. 2010. Bringing Arbitration Closer to Company Management and Boards: Can Arbitral Institutions Further This Aspiration?, in *Between East and West. Essays in Honour of Ulf Franke*, edited by K. Hobér, A. Magnusson and M. Öhrström. New York, NY: JurisNet LLC; and Villareal, E. 2006. *ADR in the United States—A Practical Guide*, in J.C. Goldsmith et al., 137–46.

12 Standards Australia 1999. *Guide to the Prevention, Handling and Resolution of Disputes*, AS 4608-1999. This Standard was revised in 2004 through the approval of AS 4608-2004, *Dispute management systems*.

13 See Office of Government Commerce (OGC) 2002. *Dispute Resolution Guidance*. Norwich: Office of Government Commerce [Online]. Available at: http://www.ogc.gov.uk/documents/dispute_resolution.pdf [accessed: August 1, 2010].

14 Groton and Haapio 2007, 7. See also Groton, J. and Smith, R.J. 2010. *Realistic Risk Allocation: Allocating Each Risk to the Party Best Able to Handle the Risk*. New York, NY: International Institute for Conflict Prevention & Resolution (CPR) [Online]. Available at: http://www.cpradr.org/Portals/0/0/Docs/CPR%20Realistic%20Risk%20Allocation%20in%20Construction%20Disputes.pdf [accessed: August 1, 2010].

15 See Chapter 7. See also Wallgren-Lindholm 2010 and Villareal 2006.

16 For specific problems and solutions related to Anglo-American contract models and civil law governing law, see the web pages of the related research project at the University of Oslo, http://www.jus.uio.no/ifp/english/research/projects/anglo/ [accessed: August 1, 2010].

17 Pace Law School Institute of International Commercial Law has launched a Lexical Initiative for International Commerce (LIIC) in an effort to minimize misunderstandings due to multiple interpretations of commercial language. For the LIIC and the International Sales Law Thesaurus Project, see Pace Law School 2010. *Lexical Initiative for International Commerce (LIIC). Simplifying the Path for Cross-Border Transacting* [Online]. Available at: http://web.pace.edu/page.cfm?doc_id=35536 [accessed: August 1, 2010].

18 United Nations Economic Commission for Europe (UNECE) 2000. *Abbreviations of Incoterms Alphabetic Code for Incoterms 2000.* Recommendation No. 5, 4th Edition, ECE/TRADE/259, adopted by the United Nations Centre for Trade Facilitation and Electronic Business (UN/CEFACT) Geneva, May 2000 [Online]. Available at: http://www.unece.org/cefact/recommendations/rec05/rec05_ecetrd259.pdf [accessed: August 1, 2010], 3. For The Golden Rules of Incoterms, see pages 6–7 of the same reference.

19 International Chamber of Commerce (ICC) 2010. *Incoterms® 2010.* ICC publication No. 715. Paris: ICC Publishing SA.

20 For instance, in software development contracts, design specifications, flexible pricing, and performance standards tend to become frequent points of contention. See Grossman, M. 2010. Software Development Contracts, Grossman Law Group [Online]. Available at: http://www.ecomputerlaw.com/articles/show_article.php?article=2005_software_development_contracts [accessed: August 1, 2010].

21 For companies working in many different countries, language creates other challenges as well. Some companies localize and translate their contracts for each area where they do business. Others rely on one model contract in one language in all their dealings, trusting that the people—external and internal to the company—will somehow master or translate the text.

22 This book is not a manual on contract drafting and, for obvious reasons, it cannot deal with the details of, for instance, scope of work, remuneration models, payment terms, key performance indicators, warranties, or remedies for non-performance. There are numerous sources on model contracts, and you can find them both online and offline. Many companies have their own contract forms and clause libraries for their people, along with checklists and guidance that will help avoid overlooking something that ought to be covered. There are both free and fee-based sources of contract forms and sample contracts on the Internet. For a list of web sites where you will find contract forms, among others, see http://www.findlaw.com/16forms/collections.html. For drafting CISG contracts and documents, see McMahon, J.P. 2004. *Drafting CISG Contracts and Documents and Compliance Tips for Traders—Guide for Managers and Counsel* [Online]. Available at: http://www.cisg.law.pace.edu/cisg/contracts.html [accessed: August 1, 2010]. For a checklist of the main issues to be considered when drafting service descriptions, see Rekola and Haapio 2009, 153. For information on sample contracts, Standard Terms and Conditions, and other materials that are commercially available related to contracts for the sale of industrial goods and services, see Webliography in Rekola and Haapio 2009, 164–80.

23 See International Association for Contract and Commercial Management (IACCM 2009a). The top negotiated terms: Negotiators admit they are on wrong agenda. *Contracting Excellence*, July [Online]. Available at: http://www.iaccm.com/contractingexcellence.php?storyid=923 [accessed: August 1, 2010]. The results have been substantially confirmed in a corresponding survey undertaken by the IACCM in December 2009–March 2010, to which more than

1,000 organizations contributed. See International Association for Contract and Commercial Management (IACCM) 2010. Top Terms—Contract Negotiations As A Source Of Value. *Contracting Excellence*, April/May, Special Edition [Online]. Available at: http://www.iaccm.com/userfiles/file/CE_April2.pdf [accessed: August 1, 2010].

24 International Association for Contract and Commercial Management (IACCM) 2009a.

25 International Association for Contract and Commercial Management (IACCM) 2009b, *Contracts as a Source of Value* [Online]. Available at: http://www.iaccm.com/loggedin/library/nonphp/New_values_in_contracting_v2.pdf [accessed: August 1, 2010], 6.

26 See, for example, Smith, D.G. and King, B. 2007. *Contracts as Organizations*. University of Wisconsin Legal Studies Research Paper No. 1037. March [Online]. Available at: http://ssrn.com/abstract=969816. [accessed: August 1, 2010], with references. See also Vlaar, P.W.L. 2008. *Contracts and Trust in Alliances. Discovering, Creating and Appropriating Value*. Cheltenham: Edward Elgar.

27 Cummins, T. 2003. *Contracting as a Strategic Competence*. International Association for Contract and Commercial Management (IACCM) [Online]. Available at: http://www.iaccm.com/library/nonphp/contracting.pdf [accessed: August 1, 2010].

28 Willcocks, L.P. and Graig, A.S. 2009. *Step-Change: Collaborate to Innovate*. Reading: Logica [Online]. Available at: http://www.logica.com/~/media/Global%20site/Factsheets/Thought%20pieces/Outsourcing%20-%20Collaborating%20to%20Innovate%20-%20White%20Paper%20-%20Final.ashx [accessed: August 1, 2010], 16.

29 International Association for Contract and Commercial Management (IACCM) 2009b, 4.

30 Salbu, S.R. 1997. Evolving contract as a device for flexible coordination and control. *American Business Law Journal*, 34(3), 329–84.

31 For planning (and non-planning) through contracts, see Haapio, H. 2008. Innovative contracting, in *A Proactive Approach to Contracting and Law*, edited by H. Haapio. Turku: International Association for Contract and Commercial Management and Turku University of Applied Sciences, 105–52, with references.

32 Vlaar, P.W.L. 2006. *Making Sense of Formalization in Interorganizational Relationships: Beyond Coordination and Control*. Ph.D. Thesis. ERIM Ph.D. Series Research in Management. Erasmus Research Institute of Management (ERIM), RSM Erasmus University/Erasmus School of Economics, Erasmus University Rotterdam [Online]. Available at: http://hdl.handle.net/1765/7326 [accessed: August 1, 2010].

33 For the business functions of contracts, see, for example, Argyres, N.S. and Mayer, K.J. 2007. Contract design as a firm capability: An integration of learning and transaction cost perspectives. *Academy of Management Review*, 32(4), October, 1060–77 [Online]. Available at: http://journals.aomonline.org/inpress/pdf/done/221.pdf [accessed: August 1, 2010]; Argyres, N.S., Bercovitz, J. and Mayer, K.J. 2007. Complementarity and evolution of contractual provisions: An emprical study of IT services contracts, *Organization Science*, 18(1), January–February, 3–19; Eckhard, B. and Mellewigt, T. 2006. *Contractual Functions and Contractual Dynamics in Inter-firm Relationships: What We Know and How to Proceed*. University of Paderborn, Working Paper No. 88. January 8 [Online]. Available at: http://ssrn.com/abstract=899527 [accessed: August 1, 2010]; Vlaar 2006; Vlaar 2008; Bogetoft, P. and Olesen, H.B. 2004. *Design of Production Contracts: Lessons from Theory and Agriculture*. Copenhagen Business School Press; Roxenhall, T. and Ghauri, P. 2004. Use of the written contract in long-lasting business relationships. *Industrial Marketing Management*, 33(3), April, 261–8; Poppo, L. and Zenger, T. 2002. Do formal contracts and relational governance function as substitutes or complements? *Strategic Management Journal*, 23(8), 707–25 [Online]. Available at: http://www.olin.wustl.edu/faculty/zenger/smj2002.pdf [accessed: August 1, 2010];

and Salbu 1997, with references. In Roxenhall, T. 1999. *Affärskontraktets användning.* [The use of the written Business Contract]. Doctoral thesis no. 77. Företagsekonomiska institutionen. Uppsala: Uppsala universitet, the author explores three Swedish case studies to determine how written contracts are used as a means of communication to control the company's own staff as well as the staff of the opposite party, and to coordinate the supply and production activities of both parties. In Pruth, M. 2000. *Kontrakt som styrmedel i TPL-samarbeten—Existerande funktioner och utveckling av nya principer.* [Contracts as Management Tools in Third-Party Logistics Alliances—Existing Functions and Development of New Principles]. Göteborg: Handelshögskolan vid Göteborgs Universitet, the author investigates logistics alliances. His empirical study shows that logistics contracts work as management tools supporting operative efficiency, development, and change; they formalize the common objective and motivate behavior by incentive structures.

Contracts can further be used for various other purposes not reflected here, including the protection of confidential information, allocation of decision and control rights, and exclusion or minimization of tort liability. For using contracts to make a company's supply chain commit to sustainability and other corporate values, see Sorsa, K. 2008. Responsible business—How to make the supply chain commit to it?, in *Proceedings of the International Association for Contract and Commercial Management (IACCM) International Academic Symposiums on Contract & Commercial Management*, London, UK, November 9, 2007 and Arizona, USA, April 7, 2008 [Online]. Available at: http://www.iaccm.com/loggedin/library/nonphp/Paper%208%20-%20Responsible%20Business%20-%20How%20to%20Commit%20the%20Supply%20Chain%20to%20it.pdf [accessed: August 1, 2010]. For the contractual allocation of intellectual property rights and control rights to customized products based on an empirical analysis of Finnish small and medium-sized firms, see Paija, L. 2003. *Distribution of Intellectual Property Rights and the Development of Technology Suppliers.* Keskusteluaiheita—Discussion papers, no. 844. Helsinki: ETLA, Elinkeinoelämän tutkimuslaitos/The Research Institute of the Finnish Economy and Paija, L. 2004. *Allocation of Control Rights to Customised Products: Empirical Analysis of Finnish SMEs.* Keskusteluaiheita—Discussion papers, no. 918. Helsinki: ETLA, Elinkeinoelämän tutkimuslaitos/The Research Institute of the Finnish Economy.

34 See, for example, Mahler, T. 2010. *Legal Risk Management—Developing and Evaluating Elements of a Method for Proactive Legal Analyses, With a Particular Focus on Contracts.* Doctoral Thesis, 1 February 2010, Faculty of Law, University of Oslo and Haapio, H. 2007. Contractual risk management: not just a matter for lawyers! *Risk Consulting,* 2, 22–4 [Online]. Available at: http://www.if-insurance.com/web/industrial/SiteCollectionDocuments/Risk%20Consulting/rm2_2007s1-32eng.pdf [accessed: August 1, 2010].

35 See Step Three. See also Salbu 1997; Groton and Haapio 2007; Groton, J.P. 2008. The "up front" prevention, control, and early resolution of disputes: Dispute prevention and management lessons that businesses can learn from the construction industry, in *A Proactive Approach to Contracting and Law,* edited by H. Haapio. Turku: International Association for Contract and Commercial Management and Turku University of Applied Sciences, 153–71; and Groton, J.P. 2007. Zero disputes? Learn from the construction industry! *Contracting Excellence,* December [Online]. Available at: http://www.iaccm.com/contractingexcellence.php?storyid=373 [accessed: August 1, 2010], with references.

36 Haapio, H. and Haavisto, V. 2005. Sopimusosaaminen: tulevaisuuden kilpailutekijä ja strateginen voimavara. [Contracting capabilities: Emerging source of competitive advantage and a strategic resource]. *Yritystalous—Leader's Magazine* 2, 7–15.

37 See, for example, Pohjonen, S. and Visuri, K. 2008. Proactive approach in project management and contracting, in *A Proactive Approach to Contracting and Law*, edited by H. Haapio. Turku: International Association for Contract and Commercial Management and Turku University of Applied Sciences, 75–95; Argyres, N.S. and Mayer, K.J. 2004. Learning to contract: Evidence from the personal computer industry. *Organization Science*, 15(4) July–August, 394–410; and Argyres et al. 2007. See also Jennejohn, M. 2007. *Collaboration, Innovation, and Contract Design*. Columbia Law and Economics Working Paper No. 319. June 8 [Online]. Available at: http://ssrn.com/abstract=1014420 [accessed: August 1, 2010], where the author re-conceptualizes contracting as an effort, *inter alia*, to establish a pragmatic learning process between collaborators. In this article's sister paper, Jennejohn, M. 2006. *Governing Innovative Collaboration: A New Theory of Contract*. 22 October, 2006 [Online]. Available at: http://ssrn.com/abstract=937127 [accessed: August 1, 2010], the author addresses contract interpretation and related prescriptions.

38 Cummins, T. 2008. Taking the law out of contracts—and putting lawyers into the contracting process, in *A Proactive Approach to Contracting and Law*, edited by H. Haapio. Turku: International Association for Contract and Commercial Management and Turku University of Applied Sciences, 97–104. The source further adds that it is likely that the quality of interactions and the ease of doing business will count more and more in defining your reputation.

39 See, for instance, Cummins, T. 2006. Lean contracting: What might it look like and why does it matter? *IACCM Newsletter*, November [Online]. Available at: http://www.iaccm.com/newsletters.php?id=52 [accessed: August 1, 2010] and Toolanen, B. 2008. *Lean Contracting. Relational Contracting Influenced by Lean Thinking*. Doctoral Thesis. 2008:41. Division of Structural Engineering. Department of Civil and Environmental Engineering. Luleå University of Technology [Online]. Available at: http://epubl.luth.se/1402-1544/2008/41/LTU-DT-0841-SE.pdf [accessed: August 1, 2010].

40 Colquhoun, G. 2007. A clearer way to deal. *The Journal*, January, 45 [Online]. Available at: http://www.journalonline.co.uk/Magazine/52-1/1003773.aspx [accessed: August 1, 2010]. See also Weatherley, S. 2005. Pathclearer—A more commercial approach to drafting commercial contracts. *PLC Law Department Quarterly*, October–December, 39–46 [Online]. Available at: http://www.iaccm.com/loggedin/library/nonphp/pathclearer article pdf.pdf [accessed: August 1, 2010]. Additional materials related to the Pathclearer approach, including a range of the simplified contract templates that Scottish & Newcastle plc is using and an audio recording in which IACCM President Tim Cummins interviews Graeme Colquhoun and Steven Weatherley, can be accessed through the IACCM Resources Executive Library at: http://www.iaccm.com/loggedin/library/index.php (for members only) [accessed: August 1. 2010].

41 Weatherley 2005, 40 and 42.

42 Weatherley 2005, 42, 44 and 45.

43 Colquhoun 2007.

44 In Argyres and Mayer 2007, the authors discuss these trade-offs and contract design capabilities for commercial contracts from a managerial perspective. Here as well as in Argyres and Mayer 2004, the authors draw on several examples from actual contracts to illustrate how firms learn how to use contracts to manage their interfirm relationships over time. See also Mayer, K.J. and Weber, L. 2009. *Unpacking Contract Capabilities: Shaping Behavior by Implementing Appropriate Contract Framing*. Atlanta Competitive Advantage Conference Paper, February 25 [Online]. Available at: http://papers.ssrn.com/sol3/papers.cfm?abstract_id=1349247 [accessed: January 3, 2010] and Weber, L. and Mayer, K.J. 2005. *Building Contract Capabilities with Standard Form Contracts: Selecting the Content, Usage, and Negotiating Party*. Paper for a seminar held at the Center for Research in Economics and

Strategy (CRES), Olin School of Business, Washington University, on October 5, 2005 [Online]. Available at: http://www.olin.wustl.edu/cres/research/calendar/files/Contract Templates Weber Mayer Wash U.doc [accessed: August 1, 2010], where the authors develop a series of propositions to help guide firms in their use of standard form contracts.

45 For an example, see the case study offered by Cisco on managing their contracting process for non-disclosure agreements, known as NDA Central, presented in Quinn, B.C. and Adams, K.A. 2007. Transitioning your contract process from the artistic to the industrial, *ACC Docket*, December, 61–72 [Online]. Available at: http://adamsdrafting.com/downloads/Quinn.Adams.ACCDocket.Dec07.pdf [accessed: August 1, 2010]. See also Walker, G., Allan, G. and Colliss, J. 2008. *NDAs—Streamlining the Process Using Technology and Smart Negotiation* [Online]. Available at: http://www.acc.com/chapters/sfbay/upload/IP NDA Program Materials 5-21-08.pdf [accessed: August 1, 2010].

46 See also Garrett, G.A. and Kipke, R.J. 2003. *The Capture Management Life-Cycle. Winning More Business*. Chicago, IL: CCH Incorporated, 106–8.

47 International Association for Contract and Commercial Management (IACCM) 2009b, 2. For research related to contracting capabilities, see Report mentioned in Note 2; Nystén-Haarala, S. (ed.) 2008. *Corporate Contracting Capabilities. Conference Proceedings and Other Writings*. University of Joensuu Publications in Law, No. 21; and, in the context of commercializing intangibles, Lee, N. 2008. From tangibles to intangibles—Contracting capability for intangible innovation, in Nystén-Haarala 2008, 33–50 [Online]. Available at: http://ssrn.com/abstract=1350337 [accessed: August 1, 2010].

48 See http://www.iaccm.com/loggedin/library/nonphp/2008_Top_Negotiated_Terms.pdf [accessed: August 1, 2010] and Note 23 above.

49 International Association for Contract and Commercial Management (IACCM) 2009a.

50 International Association for Contract and Commercial Management (IACCM) 2009a.

51 International Association for Contract and Commercial Management (IACCM) 2009a.

52 International Association for Contract and Commercial Management (IACCM) 2009b, 10.

53 Cummins 2008, 98.

CHAPTER 7 Tools and Resources to Achieve Competitive Advantage: Benefit from Your Legal Resources and Management Tools While Creating an Ethical Culture

Earlier chapters of this book describe the Manager's Legal Plan™ and illustrate how the plan can help create competitive advantage in contexts varying from product liability to intangible assets and contracting. This concluding chapter will address general concerns that create opportunities for competitive advantage across a broad range of legal matters. The chapter encompasses three types of resources: (1) legal resources that can help you seize competitive advantage; (2) management tools that are useful when you work with law-related business matters; and (3) resources that enable you to create an ethical corporate culture. In each of these areas, many companies have developed specific ways to address legal problems. But they may have overlooked big picture issues that become apparent with a trip to the balcony.

Legal Resources

This section first reviews conventional strategies for developing and using legal resources. Then it turns to new opportunities for using these resources for competitive advantage.

CONVENTIONAL BUSINESS STRATEGIES FOR DEVELOPING AND USING LEGAL RESOURCES

In a world where law touches every aspect of business operations and decision making, you can benefit greatly from access to high-quality legal resources. According to an article in the *Harvard Business Review:* "A decade of growth in the scope, nature, and complexity of government regulation has catapulted attorneys into daily business operations to an unprecedented degree. The equally rapid rise in consumer, shareholder, employee, and competitor litigation has forced prudent managers to include legal advice as an essential element of business planning and decision making."[1] Recognizing the importance of sound legal advice, companies face two fundamental questions relating to their legal resources (see Figure 7.1). First, should the company develop an in-house legal staff or rely on outside lawyers? Second, how can the company control legal costs?

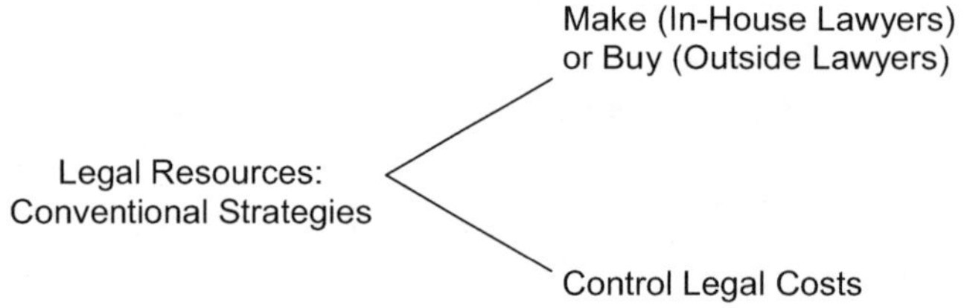

Figure 7.1 Legal resources: basic concerns

Make or buy legal services?

The first question is essentially a make or buy decision: Should you create your own legal resources inside the company or buy outside legal resources? As discussed in earlier chapters, the legal environment in which business operates contains a number of threats that can be neutralized through a combination of legally savvy management and sound legal advice. A later part of this chapter will discuss the key role that in-house lawyers can play in creating value and developing new capabilities.

While your company can always buy legal services when needed, an in-house law department is more likely to be a strong ally in your journey towards using the law for competitive advantage. Even a small company will benefit from having an in-house counsel, who may perform multiple roles (for example, combining the roles of in-house counsel and chief financial officer, in-house counsel and contract manager, or in-house counsel and human resource director).

The value of an in-house law department is demonstrated by surveys of senior executive satisfaction with legal services. For instance, a survey of CEOs and other senior executives, reported in *Corporate Counsel*, concluded that 67 percent ranked their law department's performance as "excellent," while only 15 percent gave this rating to their outside lawyers. Among the top reasons why these executives have an in-house law department: in-house lawyers understand the company better than outside lawyers and they participate in strategic planning.[2]

What credentials should you look for in hiring in-house lawyers? Graduation from a reputable law school and experience in dealing with business law issues are important attributes. Membership and active involvement in a professional association also signal the potential for success as an in-house counsel. The membership of the US-based Association of Corporate Counsel (ACC), founded in 1982, is a diverse mix of more than 25,000 in-house lawyers employed by over 10,000 organizations in more than 70 countries.[3] The European Company Lawyers Association (ECLA), created in 1983, in turn, is the umbrella organization for 22 company lawyer associations in Europe and represents more than 32,000 individual company lawyers.[4]

Many corporate lawyers are also members of the International Bar Association (IBA), established in 1947, which has a membership of more than 40,000 individual lawyers and

197 bar associations and law societies spanning all continents.[5] In addition to the lawyers' associations, many general counsel and corporate lawyers have joined the International Association for Contract and Commercial Management (IACCM), established in 1999, whose membership consists of over 16,000 members and an extended network of more than 6,500 corporations from more than 120 countries, including most of the Global 500.[6]

Membership in the ACC, IBA, IACCM, or one of the national associations belonging to ECLA provides in-house counsel with benchmarking, networking, education, and other opportunities that help increase the value that they add to their companies.

What mechanisms are available to control legal costs?

As discussed in Chapter 1, cost control is essential to achieving competitive advantage. In-house lawyers, of course, have primary responsibility for controlling in-house legal costs. An especially important example is the use of alternative dispute resolution (ADR), which is covered later in this chapter.

In-house lawyers also play an important role in evaluating the quality and cost of the outside legal services that are necessary even when your company has established a strong in-house department. Among the alternatives to traditional hourly billing that have been developed in recent years are the following:[7]

1. *Flat Rate.* You agree to pay the law firm a fixed amount for a transaction or other legal service, such as $100,000 for a trial. A variation of the flat rate is project billing, whereby a flat fee is charged for a specific assignment, such as drafting a contract. Another variation is incentive billing, whereby the law firm receives a bonus beyond the flat rate for specified results.
2. *Fee Cap.* The law firm charges you an hourly rate but the total bill will be capped at an agreed-upon amount.
3. *Blended Rate.* Law firm partners normally receive an hourly rate that is higher than junior lawyers. With a blended rate, you pay a single hourly rate somewhere between the partner and junior lawyer rates, regardless of who does the work.
4. *Defense Contingency Fee.* Contingency fees, traditionally used in the US in hiring plaintiffs' attorneys, can also be used by companies when they hire defense attorneys in certain countries. The law firm's compensation then depends on the case results. For example, the firm might receive a percentage of the amount saved in litigation.
5. *Requests for Proposals (RFP).* You invite several law firms to bid on a particular project. For instance, New York Life Insurance Co. asks firms competing for its business to submit a bid after providing the firms with an RFP that includes an analysis of past legal expenses.[8]
6. *Legal Audits.* You can hire an outside organization to audit the billings from your law firm. According to an article in *Risk Management,* the best of "the legal cost control methods available to risk managers ... remains a law firm audit from a carefully chosen vendor."[9]

However, the use of these alternatives can create tension between in-house and outside lawyers. The alternatives have also produced mixed results. Often some basic principles applicable to the procurement of any services will go a long way. First, you want to choose the provider of the service carefully—and, where it matters, identify the specific lawyers within the firm who will do the work. Then you will want to define the project precisely. Do you need a written report or is verbal advice enough? If you do not want long memoranda, say so. If you need clear advice directly to the point, say so. And you can always ask for an estimate in advance and identify check points to make sure everyone is on the same page as the work progresses.

NEW PERSPECTIVES ON LEGAL RESOURCES

The two questions just discussed (in-house versus outsourced legal resources and controlling costs) apply to every business function, not just law. But the attention devoted to these questions, especially the cost control issue as applied to legal resources, might cause you to overlook broader issues that create powerful opportunities to use legal resources to achieve competitive advantage. These broader issues cluster around the four questions reflected in Figure 7.2: Are your company lawyers focused on your customers? Are your in-house counsel using best practices adapted from other areas of your business? Do they help you create more value and engineer new opportunities? Can the law department be developed into a profit center? After addressing these questions, this section will close with a checklist for evaluating the quality of your law department.

Figure 7.2 Legal resources: new concerns

The customers of your company lawyers

Customer focus is important for any business function. In the corporate legal community, for instance, there has been considerable debate over the following question raised by a participant in a panel discussion of corporate lawyers: "I report to the president, who reports to the CEO of our Parisian parent. We have a board of four directors. But who is my client? Is my client the president? Is my client 'the company'? Is my client the executive staff?"

Corporate counsel often disagree on the answer to this question. For instance, one panelist responded, "My client is the president." Another answered, "The shareholders." Still another panelist stated, "My client is the corporation."[10] According to the American Bar Association's Model Rules of Professional Conduct, the correct—although still fuzzy—answer is that a lawyer hired by an organization (say, your company) represents the organization.

This issue has practical implications that relate, for instance, to attorney client privilege—the rule that in many countries protects communications between attorney and client from involuntary disclosure when these communications relate to legal advice.

Some executives "erroneously believe that corporate counsel personally represents them when they speak with corporate counsel on matters relating to their corporate responsibilities." This belief could lead "to personal liability. ... [and] to employees being offered up in sacrifice to the greater corporate good."[11]

Understanding whom the corporate counsel represents is important to both lawyers and managers, but the problem is that another stakeholder—the customer—is sometimes completely ignored. Because competitive advantage requires that companies create value for their customers or co-create value with them, the "big C" *Clients* of your lawyers are your company's customers, even though the lawyers' client in a narrower legal sense is the corporation. In a market-oriented company, your lawyers—like everyone—must focus on the customer.

Some companies take this idea very seriously. For example, picture yourself as a young lawyer who has just graduated from a prestigious law school near the top of your class. You are hired by the law department at McDonald's Corporation and look forward to becoming an expert on the legal intricacies of franchise law and site acquisition. Your first assignment? Put on your apron and flip hamburgers for two weeks in a McDonald's® restaurant. Your next assignment? Attend McDonald's training program, Hamburger University™, where you will supplement your Juris Doctor degree with a Bachelor of Hamburgerology degree. As Shelby Yastrow, former General Counsel for McDonald's, notes, "Every lawyer on our litigation team spends hours in our restaurants, because we sometimes have to explain why a licensee is not being renewed or not getting another restaurant. We have to understand how the business is run, so we get in there and cook hamburgers."[12]

Once you begin your work as a McDonald's lawyer, your education about the business continues, as you will be asked to serve on projects that have little or nothing to do with the law. Again according to Shelby Yastrow, this experience will "give you a better understanding of the company, but much more importantly will demonstrate that you are a business person who happens to bring something extra to the table, namely legal talent, not a technocrat who is more interested in the nicety of the law than in corporate profits."[13] The McDonald's legal philosophy is symbolized by the fact that the company motto of "Quality, service, and cleanliness" (QSC) is reflected on lawyers' notepads, which state: "Less Esq., more QSC. More burgers, less BS."[14]

Similar approaches used by other companies include placing legal staff on-site (known as co-location) to encourage them to develop business judgment, and bringing outside counsel into the company for one-year internships so that they better understand the business.[15]

Certain risks arise when the distinction between legal advice and business advice becomes blurred. For example, the business advice provided by lawyers is not protected by attorney-client privilege. But McDonald's, while doing everything possible to maintain the privilege, opts to retain intense focus on the customer. Again quoting Shelby Yastrow: "I am there for the same reason everybody else is: to sell hamburgers, open restaurants, and get a return for our shareholders."[16]

Using best practices from other areas of your business

The traditional philosophy regarding the law department was that, because of the complexity and uncertainty inherent in the law, you can't manage lawyers using conventional approaches. As a CEO once joked, the law department is the only one with an unlimited budget—and each year the department exceeds its budget.[17] While the law department does face unique challenges, your big-picture perspective from the balcony should enable you to identify opportunities to improve management of the department in ways that makes your company more competitive.

Consider, for example, the challenge faced by the DuPont law department. In 1991, the department handled close to 1,200 cases and the caseload was increasing at a rate of 20 percent to 40 percent annually. To handle this volume of cases, DuPont attorneys worked with around 350 law firms across the US. As DuPont attorneys struggled to handle this huge caseload without dramatically increasing legal costs, they received a mandate from the DuPont CEO. He advised them that the company must cut expenses by $1 billion and the law department had to share in the cost cutting.[18]

The first reaction of DuPont's in-house attorneys to this mandate was fairly conventional. After benchmarking other law departments, they called the company's outside law firms and told them to reduce their fees.

But DuPont attorneys soon realized that reducing fees would not accomplish their cost-cutting goals, so they turned to a more radical approach. When they examined business practices within the company, they discovered that the procurement staff was able to obtain volume discounts and improve quality by reducing the number of suppliers. Using this basic concept, the attorneys developed a strategy called the DuPont Legal Model that is based on strategic partnering with its outside law firms. According to DuPont attorney Daniel Mahoney, "The hallmark of these relationships [with outside firms] is a shift from simple cost-cutting, which will negatively affect law firm profits and ultimately attorney-client relationships, to one of value enhancement where the client and the law firm share in the benefits of efficient, results-oriented legal services."[19]

Here are the key elements of the original DuPont implementation plan:

1. Reduction of the number of law firms from around 350 to 34 so-called Primary Law Firms (PLFs).[20]
2. Use of technology to improve communication and share knowledge among the PLFs.
3. Process redesign to develop systematic approaches to case management.
4. Performance metrics to measure success in reducing costs and improving quality.
5. Training that leverages the knowledge of in-house and outside attorneys.[21]

Not everyone initially appreciated the benefits of the plan. As one attorney noted during a training session, "If we were interested in numbers we would be accountants."[22] But the results were impressive. According to DuPont General Counsel Thomas Sager, the company reduced legal expenses by an estimated $72.5 million from 1994 to 1997. The law department was also able to cut its caseload in half, while reducing cycle time from 39 to 22 months.[23]

The plan produced a win-win result in that PLFs also benefit from improved cash flow, reduction in marketing costs, positive publicity, networking opportunities, and technology and information advantages.[24] According to James Leader, a partner in one of the PLFs, "We win, too, not only because of the guaranteed business, but because DuPont has helped us to improve technology, referred other clients, and encouraged us to cooperate with other law firms in ways we never would have imagined a few years ago."[25]

In order to remain in the forefront of the changing legal environment, the DuPont Legal Model was later revised to include these strategies and initiatives:

- improving productivity through Six Sigma;
- improving Proactive & Preventive Legal Care^{SM};
- developing Legal Practice Groups (subject-matter networks organized to work collaboratively by sharing resources, information, work product, and best practices);
- applying the model to patent and trademark law firms.[26]

The revised plan, called the DuPont's Proactive & Preventive Legal Care^{SM} program, was created "to help provide a competitive edge for DuPont by capitalizing on changes in the law, anticipating and minimizing future legal risks, and identifying best practices for managing current liabilities. At its core, this program asks DuPont Legal and its PLFs to work together to contribute to the client's bottom line through creative business solutions. DuPont believes the more lawyers know about their client's business, the better they can spot future legal issues that will bring value to the client."[27]

Sometimes it is hard for legal departments to demonstrate the value they bring to the business because no one tracks such information. According to James D. Schomper, corporate counsel for DuPont Legal, a recovery initiative that started in 2004, has shown highly favorable results exceeding $100 million in recoveries every year. For 2008, for example, the team set its goal at $100 million, but as of the second quarter of 2008, it had already exceeded $140 million.[28] A "Recovery" is defined here as any recoupment in the form of cash (royalty payments, settlements, adjustments), products, services, or other quantifiable rights obtained through intervention of legal professionals outside of the normal course of business. Recovery opportunities can include breaches of contract (for example, a customer's failure to meet purchase requirements or supplier poor performance), interest on late payments, rebate violations, collecting past due payments, and overpayments or overbilling. Opportunities also can be found in patent and trademark infringements, product counterfeiting, and other IP violations. "DuPont is not necessarily seeking candidates for litigation. Many recoveries are successfully resolved through negotiation and arbitration."[29]

The DuPont Legal Model illustrates the potential benefits to your company when the law department uses best practices developed in other areas of the company. The model takes a business-focused and results-oriented approach to law, and, at the same time, helps law firms and corporate law departments improve the quality, cost, and efficiency of legal services. The DuPont example also demonstrates that proactive lawyers working in corporations do not have to wait for an assignment to solve a problem; they can take the initiative and facilitate the creation of practices and procedures that help clients to achieve their objectives, foster fruitful long-term relationships, and avoid negative surprises. By applying a proactive approach, they can help their clients and co-workers to become more successful, which makes the lawyers more valuable to the business units and the corporation. Working together as strategic partners, proactive lawyers and their clients can give the corporation a competitive edge and establish a strong legal foundation for its business.

Just as the best practices adopted by other areas in a company usually incorporate the latest technology, technology also has the potential to transform traditional lawyer-client relationships. Contract drafting serves as a powerful example. Today anybody—lawyer or not—can have access to comprehensive commercial off-the-shelf automated forms, templates, clause libraries, and web-based self-service solutions for RFP and proposal preparation and contract creation. Some resources are hosted on the provider's server, others in-house. Organizations can now move from manual drafting to automated contract assembly, and can develop and use their own computer-based drafting systems.[30] Organizations can also automate their templates and make them available through their intranet.

In addition, comprehensive contract lifecycle management solutions exist that are designed to simplify management of all aspects of the contracting process. From the first step—for example, when a salesperson requests a term sheet from a customer—through contract creation, negotiation, performance, compliance, and risk management, the user can control and monitor the process and track all relevant data.[31] An Internet search using terms like "automated document assembly," "enterprise contract management," "contract lifecycle management," or "contract management solutions" will produce thousands of results. White papers and webcasts abound on implementing and selecting such solutions. And there are technology tools in the market that can convert project and contract documents to an easier-to-read format.[32]

Companies have also come to realize that the legal education of their employees is important to achieving competitive advantage. As a result, companies like Lucent Technologies have created online courses on business law for employees. According to Lucent attorney Philip Crowley, employees who understand legal issues "are more likely to recognize business situations that call for a lawyer's expertise."[33]

Computer-based collaboration is also important to corporate counsel, especially given the impact of globalization of the law. Cisco Systems, for instance, has created Legal Exchange, which enables, say, an attorney in Asia, to obtain immediate advice from Cisco attorneys around the world. Other uses of technology include legal self-diagnostic programs that enable employees to obtain legal advice after answering a series of questions, and online auctions to select outside law firms.[34]

Cisco Systems, which uses thousands of non-disclosure agreements each year, has also developed a system known as NDA Central that non-legal Cisco personnel can use to draft the agreements. Its automated solutions have allowed Cisco to handle the contract process much more efficiently than it would have otherwise. Cisco's experience shows that when a comprehensive and innovative contract process is used, the rewards can be significant.[35]

From cost center to profit center—from risk engineers to opportunity engineers

In the past, many corporations perceived their legal departments as cost centers, a necessary evil. At best, lawyers were perceived to be gatekeepers or risk engineers helping the company stay out of legal trouble. A fresh, proactive approach to the role of lawyers and legal departments can change the old picture. With a new mindset, you can marshal your legal resources to a new direction, letting them help you create more value and engineer new opportunities.

Earlier chapters have explored the role that law, intellectual property rights (IPR), and contracts can play in enabling your company to gain competitive and collaborative advantage. In the words of Ben Heineman, former General Electric (GE) General Counsel, the GE law department's Six Sigma program was designed to "creatively enhance revenue and profit for the business unit we're working with."[36] This can be your new goal too.

Let's take the example of contracting. Your competitors may view contracting at worst as a mundane task that someone has to do and at best a risk management effort to protect your company against unlikely events. They probably focus their contracting and legal resources on drafting and negotiating limitations of liabilities and indemnities.[37] What if you saw opportunities where others see only costs and risks? What if you focus on *transaction opportunities* instead of *transaction costs*, while automating many of the "mundane" tasks? To do this, you need to change management attitudes so that those involved in contracting can grow from transaction risk engineers to transaction opportunity engineers.

Opportunity Engineering is a relatively new concept with great potential in the field of Proactive Law and Proactive Contracting. It is based on the view that you can systematically engineer your opportunities, create an engineered growth portfolio, and engineer the financial returns of your business investments much as you can engineer your products. A key concept of Opportunity Engineering is making uncertainty work *for* you rather than *against* you.[38] In their book *Unlocking Opportunities for Growth,* Alexander B. Van Putten and Ian C. Macmillan of the Wharton School of the University of Pennsylvania show how the concept can be applied to various areas of business—for instance, selection and management of R&D projects, mergers and acquisitions, and joint ventures and alliances. They also discuss how Opportunity Engineering can provide value when you design, monitor, and guide contract negotiations by allowing you and the other side to unbundle contract clauses by pricing them explicitly as options and to sell them as such.[39] Working together with your contract and legal resources, you can develop new ways of collaborating, learning, and sharing with your customers and other companies. You can also design new kinds of transactional interfaces, including contracts that lead to competitive and collaborative advantage and contribute to the success of your company's profit centers.

Through concepts such as Opportunity Engineering, law departments can contribute to the success of profit centers. But can you also develop your law department into a profit center in its own right? According to intellectual property consultant Julie Davis, "It's not enough that [law departments] keep their company out of legal trouble; they must now think of ways to contribute to the bottom line and increase shareholder value."[40] When *Corporate Counsel* magazine convened an advisory group (called LD21) of leading corporate counsel to examine the role of the law department in the twenty-first century, one of their conclusions was that: "Many law departments can become profit centers by using their resources to build new customer relationships."[41]

As we saw in Chapter 5, many companies' intangible assets are currently underutilized and generate little or no value. Others are adopting a more aggressive posture toward intellectual property, and their IP management and legal departments have helped to transform this attitude into action. Not only do they attack those who infringe upon their IPR, they also help identify, protect, and market intellectual property (IP) that would otherwise waste away on the company shelf.

As a manager, you can and should participate in IP value creation. After you climb to the balcony and inventory your IP, you can work with in-house legal and IP management to determine the value and strengths of your IP portfolio as well as possible problems. You can then marshal your resources toward the required direction. If you lack in-house legal or IP resources, you can hire outside experts. Consulting firms and law firms have recently established new practice groups focusing on, for example, *IP monetization*. For law firms, this is a natural outgrowth of their IP litigation and business law services. The new goal: to help companies like yours benefit from the strength and value of their IP and develop and implement strategies to monetize it. As discussed in Chapter 5, the Manager's Legal Plan™ that is designed to maximize the value of your IP will enable you to move toward this goal.

The quality of your law department

The importance of law in gaining competitive advantage has resulted in newfound respect for the law department. As Jack Foltz, former Vice President and General Counsel of the Sun Company, puts it: "I remember a time when I would walk into a room full of engineers, accountants, and marketers and they would look at me as if I was their daughter's first date. That no longer happens. Admit it or not, they know that when the in-house counsel arrives on the scene, he or she is not there to be a nay sayer but to help them strike a balance between business initiatives and the law."[42] A survey of Fortune 500 CEOs conducted by Heidrick & Struggles in 2000 confirmed this observation, concluding that the general counsel's adviser role dominates the other two roles (legal and managerial) and a key skill in serving as an adviser is the ability "to accomplish business strategies and objectives."[43]

The key role that corporate lawyers play in your business success makes it imperative that you have a set of criteria for evaluating and developing the law department. One benchmark is General Electric. The following questions, drawn from a list of the GE law department's best practices, can serve as a checklist when you review your law department.[44]

- *Are you hiring the best talent?* You should look for lawyers who understand your business and who are able to explain the complexities of law in terms that you understand.
- *Are your lawyers focused on business strategy?* GE attorneys, for example, gain business knowledge through assignments in the company's divisions. According to one GE attorney, "GE is like a graduate school in business."[45]
- *Are your lawyers well trained?* Using a model inspired by GE's famed Crotonville training center, GE lawyers attend courses taught by experts from GE and business schools.
- *Does your law department maximize its use of technology?* Like other functions within GE, the law department does its work online, with an intranet that includes a "knowledge bank" that avoids replication of work.
- *Does your law department control its budget?* Despite the company's size, GE's legal costs as a percentage of revenue are lower than the national median. A key factor in budget control at GE is an early dispute resolution (EDR) program that attempts to resolve litigation by settlement, mediation, or arbitration.

If you can answer yes to these questions, you have access to a law department that will enable you to achieve competitive advantage. The mission of this twenty-first century department, as summarized by the *Corporate Counsel* LD21 committee of prominent corporate counsel in Exhibit 7.1, reflects the themes in this chapter and throughout the book.

EXHIBIT 7.1 THE LAW DEPARTMENT MISSION[46]

- Serving as gateways, rather than gatekeepers, law departments will function proactively to bring legal and risk consideration issues into business strategy discussions.
- Lawyers will be members of division and corporate management committees who add value by focusing attention on business opportunities made possible by changes in laws and regulations.
- Law departments will provide online resources that enable all employees to understand how to comply with laws and regulations and manage legal risk.
- Law departments will focus on helping companies harvest greater value from intellectual property.

Management Tools for Addressing Legal Aspects of Business

Although the law plays an important role in achieving competitive advantage, your corporate lawyers should not make business decisions for you. Law is just one of myriad concerns that must be factored into your decisions. Business decisions made entirely from a legal perspective, which tends to be risk averse, might not produce the results that your shareholders expect in an entrepreneurial business world.

Your dilemma is that, in making business decisions, you must deal with the considerable complexity and uncertainty inherent in the law. This section will first describe a management tool called *decision tree analysis* that is especially useful in making law-related business decisions. In fact, this tool is recommended for use whenever you are faced with a complex decision that relates to any aspect of your business, including (as discussed later in this chapter) ethical decisions. Following the discussion of decision tree analysis, a more specific set of tools, collectively called "alternative dispute resolution" (ADR) will be reviewed, along with the importance of systems design.

DECISION TREE ANALYSIS

Chapter 5 discusses the many uses of IP law, including an attack on your competitors who infringe on your IP rights. Assume that you manage a small software company based in the US.[47] After licensing your software to another company, you discover that the licensee has violated the licensing agreement by producing its own version of your software. You bring suit, expecting to win $6 million in damages, after deducting $300,000 for legal expenses. The licensee has just offered you $1.5 million to settle the case.

In making a management decision whether to settle the case, you ask your corporate attorney to provide an analysis of your chances for success if you reject the settlement and proceed to trial. The attorney advises you that the key questions in the litigation are the following:

- Is the licensee's software substantially similar to your software? The attorney advises you that your chances of success on this issue are better than even.
- Did the licensee have access to your software before developing its software? The attorney thinks that it is likely that you will prevail on this issue.

- Is your copyright on the software valid? The attorney thinks it highly probable that the court will decide that it is.

Given this analysis, would you settle for $1.5 million or risk $300,000 by going to trial in an attempt to recover $6 million? In making this decision, you will want to answer two questions. First, what are your overall chances for success if you go to trial? Second, can a value be placed on the litigation, given the uncertainty of winning at trial? Unfortunately, it is difficult to answer these questions based on your attorney's analysis. For instance, in an exercise similar to this case that one of the authors has used with hundreds of managers and MBA students, their estimates of overall chances for success range from 10 percent to 95 percent.

Decision tree analysis involves a three-step process in which you build a model of your decision. This model enables you to determine both the likelihood of winning at trial and the value of the litigation. The first step is to draw a diagram of the decision in the form of a tree on its side. This diagram enables you to visualize and distinguish events that can be controlled (decisions) from uncertain events. As Figure 7.3 illustrates, squares are used to represent decisions (in this case, your decision whether to continue litigating or to accept the settlement offer) and circles are used to depict uncertain events (here, the issues that must be decided in court).

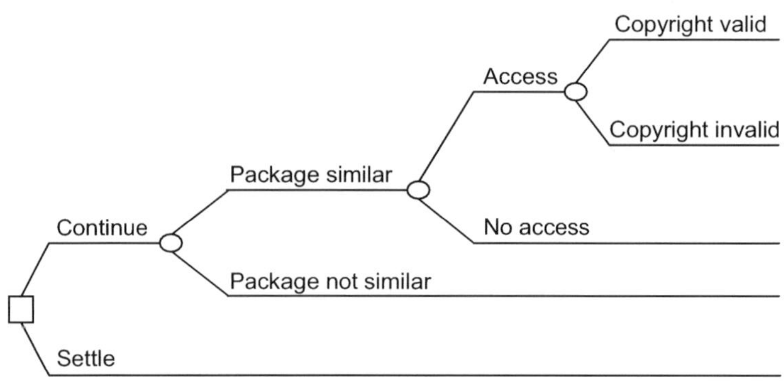

Figure 7.3 Decision tree diagram

The second step in building a model of the decision is to assign values to the endpoints of each branch on the tree. The "win" endpoint in Figure 7.4 has a value of $6 million, while the "lose" endpoints have a negative $300,000 value. Although not depicted on this tree, circles and additional branches could be added at other "win" endpoints to reflect the uncertainty of the amount of damages that the court will award.

The third step is to assign probabilities for each uncertain event. This requires conversion of the attorney's verbal statements to numbers. In this case, we assume that the attorney tells you that the "better than even" statement regarding the similarity issue means a 60 percent chance of success. The "it is likely" statement regarding the access issue means a 70 percent chance of success and the "highly probable" statement means an 80 percent chance of success. The decision tree in Figure 7.4 includes these probabilities.

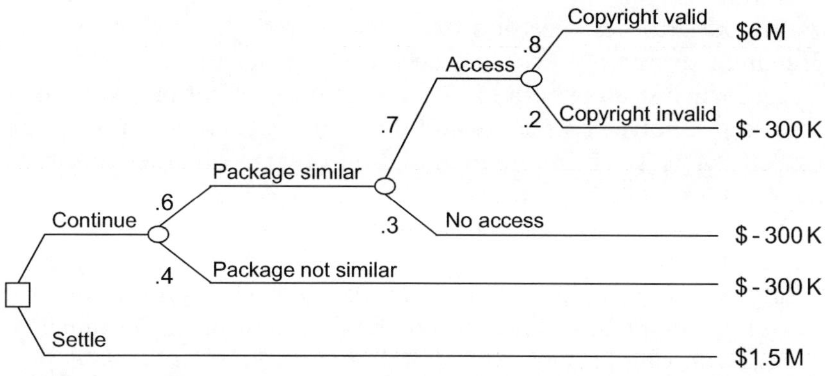

Figure 7.4 Decision tree with endpoint values and probabilities

After developing the model in Figure 7.4, you are ready to use it to answer your questions. For instance, you can calculate the overall chance for success if you go to trial by multiplying the win probabilities along the "win" path. As Figure 7.5 shows, there is a 34 percent chance that you will be successful at trial. Furthermore, you can calculate the value of the litigation by "folding back" the tree. This requires calculating a weighted average for each uncertain event, moving from right to left. For example, the weighted average of the copyright validity issue is $4.7 million, the sum of .8 × $6 million and .2 × –$300,000. The end result shown in Figure 7.5 is an expected value of $1.8 million. Thus, if you "played the averages," you would continue with the litigation because this amount is greater than the settlement offer.

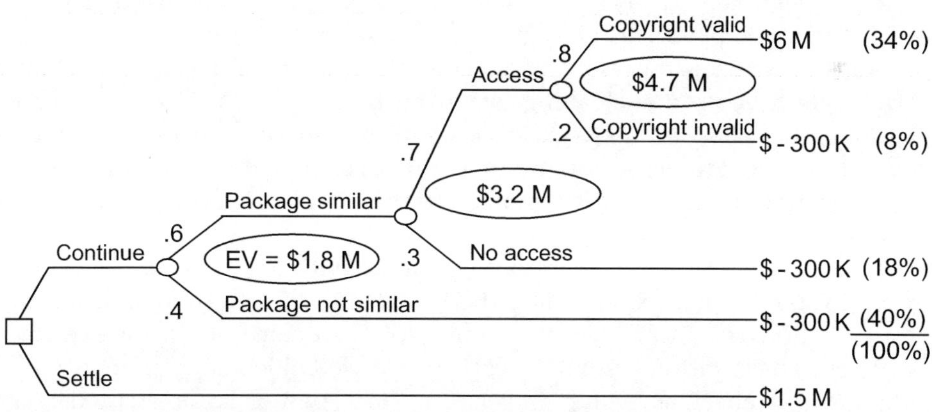

Figure 7.5 Overall probability of success and expected values

The decision tree is a powerful tool that enables you to make a number of management decisions relating to legal issues, such as how to maximize the use of limited financial resources and how much to pay expert witnesses who could improve your chances for success. But even if you stop at Step One and don't use the model for quantitative analyses, the picture of the decision in decision tree form is useful when discussing complex, multi-issue matters with your attorney. Decision trees can be used for a variety of legal decisions beyond settlement decisions, such as a decision whether to proceed with a merger, and are also useful when dealing with marketing, finance, operations, and other matters beyond the law that involve complexity and uncertainty. Commercial software produced by Vanguard, TreeAge, TreePlan, SmartDraw, and other companies simplifies the use of decision tree analysis by managers.

In addition to decision trees, other visualization tools such as flowcharts, mind maps, and time lines can be used to make better business/legal decisions. They have the capability of enabling people from different professions and backgrounds to quickly see the big picture as well as the details—for example, to communicate and evaluate a proposed transaction or relationship, assess its risks and opportunities, and create tools to control the risks. In the context of knowledge visualization, *strategy visualization* has been developed into a fine art, one of its aims being to activate and engage employees. Why not use the same approach in developing legal strategy or contracts? As a result, complexity can be simplified, ideas and statements become clearer, communication becomes more effective, and people can become more motivated to contribute toward better decision making. Here, you as the manager again must take the lead because, with few exceptions,[48] lawyers are typically accustomed to conveying their thoughts and ideas using words only.

ALTERNATIVE DISPUTE RESOLUTION

Many companies have decided that traditional court proceedings are too costly, slow, rigid, and unpredictable. So they have started to look for alternative methods to resolve business disputes. Collectively, these methods are called ADR. As noted previously, GE's EDR program is an important factor in its budget management. According to Brackett Denniston, GE's Senior Vice President and General Counsel, ADR has saved "millions of dollars" for the company.[49] Other companies also recognize that traditional litigation might not be the most cost-effective process for resolving disputes. Because of its impact in reducing legal costs, ADR might have another meaning within law firms: "alarming drop in revenue."[50]

In addition to legal costs, managers incur significant opportunity costs when they are involved in litigation. Studies show that in a mid-sized company, "the disruption factor of a typical patent infringement case amounts to the loss of about six to eight months of new product development."[51]

Two basic models are used to resolve disputes outside of court: mediation and arbitration. In some countries, including the US, ADR is deemed to include arbitration; in others, it is not. The International Chamber of Commerce (ICC), for example, has separate Rules for Arbitration and for ADR: these Rules complement one another.[52]

Mediation is, in effect, a negotiation between the disputing parties assisted by a third party, the Neutral, also called the mediator. An arbitrator (or in some cases a panel of arbitrators) is authorized to make a legally binding decision. Unlike litigation, arbitration gives the parties the right to select the arbitrator(s) or the appointing institution, allows them to avoid public hearings, and may substantially lower their costs. In international dealings, many prefer arbitration, because of the easier cross-border enforcement of arbitral awards.[53]

The mini-trial illustrates an effective ADR procedure developed from the mediation model. In the first mini-trial, Telecredit sued TRW for $6 million, claiming patent infringement.[54] For almost three years, the case languished in the court system, the two companies exchanged around 100,000 documents, and they spent close to $500,000 in legal fees. After realizing that their legal costs would continue to mount over the coming years, they developed an out-of-court "mini-trial" process to resolve their dispute.

During the mini-trial, attorneys for each side presented their case to two executives, the President of Telecredit and the Vice-President of TRW, both of whom had authority to settle the case. A neutral party (a retired judge who was an expert on patent law) moderated the process. Following the presentations, the two executives met for 30 minutes and resolved the dispute. Among the benefits of this mini-trial: (1) an opportunity for each executive to hear the case as presented by the opposing attorney; (2) an estimated $1 million savings in legal fees; and (3) a chance to resolve the dispute in a manner that preserved the business relationship between the companies, as opposed to the win-lose scenario that characterizes litigation.

The parties must usually agree to use arbitration, mediation, and related ADR methods. Otherwise, the dispute will go to court. You can include separate clauses for mediation and arbitration in your business contracts, or you might use a combination. Several dispute resolution service providers have rules and model clauses that you can use—but you should do so with caution. Here, especially in the international arena, (unless you have pre-approved contract clauses) you do not want to make choices on your own or draft clause language without consulting a competent advisor. You also should be proactive: incorporate not only dispute resolution but also dispute prevention and control principles and techniques into all business relationships. This includes having in place a process for controlling the impact of unanticipated events and problems.[55]

In addition to contracts, you as the manager have two other key tools that can help you implement alternatives to litigation: ADR policy statements and suitability screens.

An alternative dispute resolution policy statement

In the IP scenario that was used earlier in this chapter to illustrate decision tree analysis, the defendant offered to settle the case for $1.5 million. In working with managers, we have discovered that their typical reaction to a settlement offer like this is that the person who offered settlement must have a weak case. Research has shown that most people "reactively devalue" proposals simply because they are made by the other side.[56] An ADR policy statement is an important tool for avoiding reactive devaluation because if a company is on record as preferring to avoid litigation, it can make such an offer without undercutting its own position. The best-known statement, the Corporate Policy Statement on Alternatives to Litigation©, also known as the ADR Pledge, was developed by CPR, the International Institute for Conflict Prevention and Resolution. This pledge, which has been adopted by over 4,000 operating companies, is shown in Exhibit 7.2.

EXHIBIT 7.2 CPR CORPORATE POLICY STATEMENT ON ALTERNATIVES TO LITIGATION©[57]

____

COMPANY

We recognize that for many disputes there is a less expensive, more effective method of resolution than the traditional lawsuit. Alternative dispute resolution (ADR) procedures involve collaborative techniques which can often spare businesses the high costs of litigation.

In recognition of the foregoing, we subscribe to the following statements of principle on behalf of our company and its domestic subsidiaries:

In the event of a business dispute between our company and another company which has made or will then make a similar statement, we are prepared to explore with that other party resolution of the dispute through negotiation or ADR techniques before pursuing full-scale litigation. If either party believes that the dispute is not suitable for ADR techniques, or if such techniques do not produce results satisfactory to the disputants, either party may proceed with litigation.

____

CHIEF EXECUTIVE OFFICER (Signature), Print Name

____

CHIEF LEGAL OFFICER (Signature), Print Name

____

DATE

From alternative dispute resolution to early dispute resolution: suitability screens and early case assessments

As stated in Chapter 6, in many companies, the focus is shifting from ADR to EDR.[58] Companies like GE and Xerox have developed suitability screens, which are checklists used to determine whether mediation, arbitration, or litigation is suitable for use in resolving a particular dispute. These checklists include factors such as the business relationship between the companies, the effect of negative publicity, the effect on other cases, the nature of the legal and factual issues, the amount of damages at stake, and the legal costs.[59]

In an article entitled *General Electric's integrated conflict-management system,*[60] Elpidio (PD) Villareal, GE's former Counsel—Litigation & Legal Policy, and co-authors present the EDR System GE's legal department launched in 1998, partly in response to GE's company-wide Six Sigma initiative. The System identifies criteria for future conflict prevention and resolution efforts and provides a mechanism for the company to effectively evaluate and quickly resolve matters. At the same time, according to the authors, the system allows the legal department to maintain quality in the dispute resolution process. The EDR system includes guidance on early case assessment (ECA), dispute resolution method selection, periodic and after-action reviews, and conflict management training and support.[61]

GE's Early Warning System (EWS) was designed to mitigate risk and avoid future litigation. An EWS enables GE lawyers to be more proactive because it helps them anticipate litigation trends. It also helps them identify and resolve disputes at their earliest possible stages. EWSs—sometimes referred to as legal smoke detectors—promote teamwork among legal and business functions and allow the legal department to expand its view of the world. Instead of focusing on providing the legal perspective, the department can focus on the business and help avoid future litigation. The lawyers are essentially reclaiming the role of counselors and advisers and providing the business-driven value that a company requires.[62]

CPR has recently published ECA Guidelines designed to help businesses decide early on how to manage disputes, including identifying key business concerns, assessing risks and costs, and making an informed choice or recommendation on how to handle the dispute.[63] While formal ECA programs vary from organization to organization, they typically provide a vehicle for companies to proactively reduce the expense, volume, and time necessary to resolve conflict. The programs put uniform processes in place to obtain reliable information so matters can be effectively evaluated and quickly resolved. According to Villareal and his co-authors, ECA programs focus on conflict and its resolution as part of an overall business process. This means viewing conflict and litigation in terms of the company's general profitability, rather than in a vacuum.[64]

Another trip to the balcony

A trip to the balcony will allow you to gain perspective on how the individual pieces fit together as a dispute resolution system. The dispute resolution system depicted in Figure 7.6 is generic. Moving from left to right, the starting point is a company-wide policy statement similar to the one in Exhibit 7.2. The system includes two suitability screens for use during contract negotiations or, if there is no ADR clause in a contract, after a dispute arises. The first screen helps you decide whether to use binding or non-binding processes and the second enables you to select one of the two binding processes, litigation or binding arbitration.

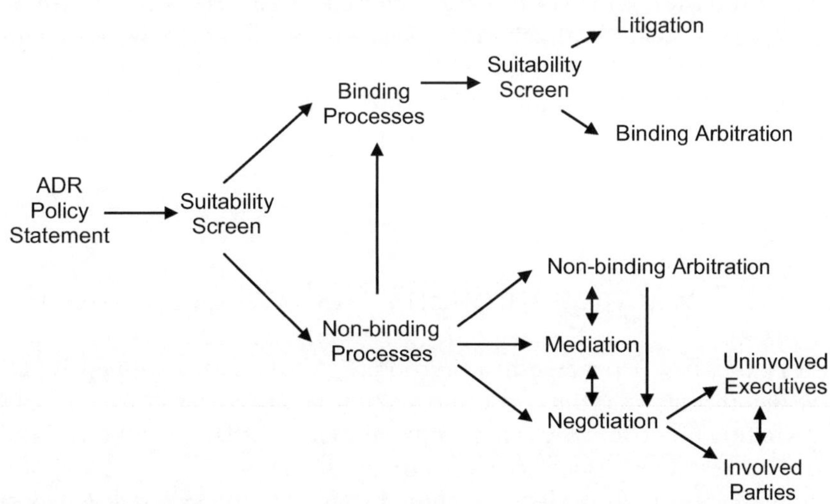

Figure 7.6 Dispute resolution system

The non-binding path embodies several fundamental principles of systems design.[65] For instance, you should start with the options that are lower in cost and give the disputing parties more control. These options also enable the parties to resolve the dispute in a manner that builds on their interests, as opposed to litigation or binding arbitration, which focus on who is "right" in a legal sense. And the system includes loopbacks. For instance, after receiving a non-binding decision from an arbitrator, the parties can loop back to negotiation or mediation.

Dispute resolution represents a specific type of contract negotiation. You should also consider your approach in reviewing contract negotiations in general. Too often, companies focus on the short-term results of a negotiation (Did we make a deal? How much did we pay?) and do not review the manner in which the negotiation was conducted (for instance, did we try to craft an agreement that satisfies the interests of the other side, as well as our own interests?).[66]

A focus on short-term contract results can harm relationships with your suppliers and customers. For instance, a major reason for the success of the DuPont Legal Model is that, rather than simply forcing cost reductions on outside law firms (a result that might look impressive in the short term), the DuPont law department developed a solution that takes into account the interests of the outside law firms.

Including in your contracts appropriate techniques for handling disputes will direct any disputes into channels where they can be dealt with constructively. In many cases their mere availability encourages the parties to act more forthrightly with each other and resolve their disputes without the necessity of using the prescribed techniques.[67]

In any kind of dispute resolution, management involvement is crucial, both in the decision to adopt ADR techniques and then in their implementation. You as a manager know how to analyze complex situations and decide what action to take. Do not remain distant if court or arbitral proceedings begin. Why give up control of business matters when the law and lawyers enter the picture? It is still your business. Remain in charge and do not assume that your contribution is no longer needed unless requested. Experienced legal practitioners realize that resolution of business disputes benefits from closer involvement of management and the company's board.[68] As noted by Jean-Francois Guillemin, General Counsel of Bouygues, ADR is unlikely to succeed without full management commitment on the part of all the companies involved.[69]

Remember to choose your counsel with care: "a good lawyer is not one who knows how to stalemate or filibuster, but one who can ideally bring both his client and the other side together and lead this team into finding constructive solutions that add value in the future for all parties."[70]

Competitive Advantage through an Ethical Corporate Culture

Does business ethics pay? Does an ethical corporate culture create competitive advantage? Studies have determined that these questions are difficult to answer because of problems in deciding whether one company is more ethical than another and whether a company's profitability is a result of ethical conduct or other factors. Nevertheless, a survey of academic studies published in 1999 concluded that "33 studies showed a positive link between corporate ethics and profit, 14 showed no effect or were inconclusive and only five suggested a negative relationship."[71]

It is logical that an ethical corporate culture creates an environment that is conducive to gaining competitive advantage. As Harvard Professor Lynn Paine notes, "the economic case for corporate ethics has both a negative and a positive aspect. ... The negative case for ethics focuses on risk management and cost avoidance, [and] the positive case emphasizes innovation, productivity gains, and revenue enhancement."[72]

An example of the cost avoidance case for ethical business behavior is the $340 million fine that Daiwa Bank had to pay for its delay in disclosing over $1 billion in losses as a result of unauthorized trading by one of its employees.[73] The positive aspect of corporate ethics is illustrated by findings reported in a KPMG's Organizational Integrity Survey.[74] The survey concluded that a commitment to business integrity helps companies attract and retain both good employees and customers. For instance, among employees who felt that their management acted ethically, 81 percent would recommend their companies to recruits and 80 percent believe that their customers would recommend their companies to others. Among employees who felt that their management did not act ethically, the percentages dropped to 21 percent and 40 percent respectively.

Recognizing the link between an ethical culture and competitive advantage, most companies have embraced business ethics management in recent years. Research on ethics programs frequently distinguishes between a compliance approach and an integrity approach.[75] The compliance approach is said to be lawyer-driven, with an emphasis on preventing legal liability. The integrity approach is management driven, with a goal of encouraging responsible conduct that extends beyond avoiding liability.[76] Although the compliance approach predominates over the integrity approach,[77] Professor Paine forcefully argues for an integrity approach, noting that "legal compliance is unlikely to unleash much moral imagination or commitment."[78] As noted by former Securities and Exchange Commission Chairman Richard Breeden, "It is not an adequate ethical standard to aspire to get through the day without being indicted."[79]

While there may be a theoretical distinction between compliance and integrity approaches, studies have shown that in practice most companies combine both approaches.[80] As noted in a BP report on ethical conduct, "There are two generic approaches to codes of ethical conduct in business. The first is based on rules and compliance. The second is value based ... We use a balanced mix of both approaches, with a strong emphasis on the personal responsibility of individuals to exercise judgment in a manner consistent with our values."[81]

USING THE MANAGER'S LEGAL PLAN™ TO LINK LAW, ETHICS, AND PROFITS

Despite the common use of codes of conduct, there is disturbing evidence that employee ethics programs are often unsuccessful. The Association of Certified Fraud Examiners estimates that US organizations lose $400 billion each year as a result of their employees' criminal or unethical behavior.[82] US stores lose over $2 billion more annually through employee theft than they do through shoplifting.[83] And the KPMG survey concluded that 76 percent of employees have observed violations of company standards or the law over the past year. Around 50 percent of employees believe that the misconduct is serious enough to cause their organizations to "significantly lose public trust."[84]

Clearly there is a disconnect within many organizations between the company's code of conduct and actual conduct in the workplace. A possible reason for this disconnect is that, by focusing on law and ethics in developing and implementing their codes, companies overlook profits, a third force that is the end result of competitive advantage and a key component of a free society. Professor Tim Fort has developed a three-part ethical context for business decisions that draws on the works of philosophers from a variety disciplines, including William Frederick, Michael Novak, and F.A. Hayek.[85] As illustrated in Figure 7.7, the three parts are ethics, law, and profits.

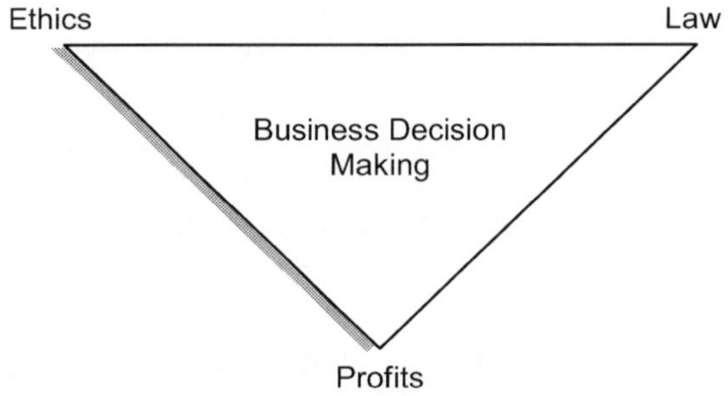

Figure 7.7 The ethical context for business decisions

Studies have emphasized the importance of corporate culture in ethics management: "To achieve desired outcomes, concerns for ethics and legal compliance must be baked into the culture of the organization."[86] In other words, "executives cannot just descend from some ethical mountaintop with a couple of stone tablets and expect immediate compliance."[87] Yet that is exactly the impression that many employees have when ethics programs focus on the first two points on the triangle while ignoring the third.

What process can managers use to incorporate the third point of the triangle, the profit motive, into an ethical corporate culture? The Manager's Legal Plan™, with its emphasis on moving to the balcony to see the big picture and become more proactive, is a useful tool in accomplishing this goal. Exhibit 7.3 provides examples, drawn from earlier chapters, of how legal concerns are closely linked to business concerns and opportunities. For example, what starts as a legal concern, such as product liability, is transformed into a broad business opportunity, in this case developing new products that meet customer needs.

EXHIBIT 7.3 SEEING THE BIG PICTURE AND BECOMING MORE PROACTIVE

Legal Concerns	Business Concerns and Opportunities
Product Liability	Develop new products that meet customer needs.
Wrongful Discharge	Secure access to key talent.
Environmental Regulation	Meet customer needs while preserving the environment for future generations.
Protection of Intellectual Property	Encourage innovation and co-creation with your stakeholders.
Risk Allocation through Contracts	Use contracts to build successful relationships with those in your business network.

The business concerns listed in Exhibit 7.3 dovetail with the subjects addressed in corporate codes of conduct, such as safe products for customers and environmental protection. By using the Manager's Legal Plan™ to address these concerns not merely as ethical values or legal requirements but instead as a source of competitive advantage, you have an opportunity to "bake them into the culture" in a manner that allows your employees to understand their importance in economic terms.

Even when employees understand the importance and linkages between law, ethics, and economics in your company culture, they still need practical tools that will enable them to make specific decisions on an everyday basis. A decision tree, discussed earlier in this chapter, is ideal for this purpose. The tree in Figure 7.8 has been adapted from the work of Professor Constance Bagley of Yale University.[88]

As this tree illustrates, your first question is whether the proposed course of action is legal. If not, the proposal should be dropped immediately. Assuming legality, the second question is whether the proposal creates shareholder value.

If it doesn't make economic sense and is unethical, the decision to reject the proposal is easy. But if the proposal doesn't make economic sense and is ethical, the decision is more difficult because you might decide, for example, to proceed as a matter of corporate social responsibility.

Finally, if the proposal does make economic sense and is ethical, the decision to proceed is easy. And if the decision makes economic sense but is unethical, the proposal should be rejected.

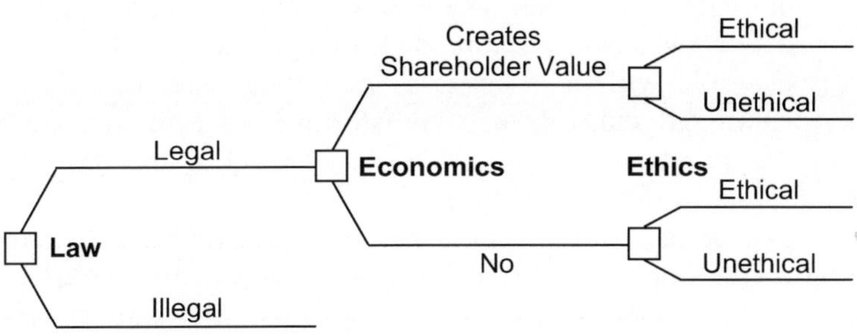

Figure 7.8 A values-based decision tree

Many guidelines are available for your use in deciding whether a proposal is ethical. These include your company's code of conduct, an analysis of costs and benefits of the decision to stakeholders, and trying to visualize what someone with high ethical standards whom you admire would do.

You can also use simple guidelines such as "newspaper" or "family" tests, as described succinctly by legendary investor Warren Buffet: "... I want employees to ask themselves whether they are willing to have any contemplated act appear the next day on the front page of their local paper—to be read by their spouses, children, and friends ..."[89] Stated another way by Tim Solso, CEO of global power company Cummins, "Ask yourself if you would be embarrassed to have your family members learn of your actions or have them reported on the front page of the local newspaper. If so, then don't do it."[90]

DISPUTE PREVENTION

In closing this section on ethics, one value deserves special mention because of its role in guiding your interaction with company lawyers as you work together on legal matters. This value is dispute prevention. *Dispute prevention* is a term that has been used for many years with a variety of meanings. From a Proactive Law point of view, the meaning can be crystallized into a guide for management conduct: "It is often more important to predict what people will do than to predict what a court will do. ... Winning a lawsuit can be ruinous."[91] As Voltaire reputedly put it, "I was never ruined but twice: once when I lost a lawsuit, and once when I won one."

The dispute prevention philosophy tracks closely themes that are emphasized in the bestselling management book of all time, *In Search of Excellence*:[92] stay close to your customers and be obsessed with service and quality. These themes, which lie at the heart of quality programs, are especially important in today's market-driven, customer-focused world.

One of the authors once stayed at a Marriott hotel the night before making a corporate presentation that had been scheduled for early the next morning. The front desk was asked to provide a wake-up call, which was never made. Fortunately, an alarm clock had been set and he arrived for the presentation on time. But having recalled reading in *In Search of Excellence* that the Marriott CEO is intensely customer focused and personally reads every complaint, he decided to test the system by filling out a hotel complaint card and noting the problem with the wake-up call. Three weeks later, the letter in Exhibit 7.4 was received from the Marriott president. What had been an unpleasant experience was transformed into a pleasant memory of a CEO who cared enough about customers to respond to their complaints (even though the author's last name is misspelled in the letter!).

Contrast this example with a recent case involving a major utility company. A company lineman removed a fuse from a transformer box, which turned off a traffic signal. A few minutes later, two cars collided at the intersection, resulting in the death of the 12-year-old daughter of one of the drivers.

Apparently the company took a traditional approach to the accident, which is to focus on legal rights in court, rather than on the feelings of the victim's parents. In a newspaper article about the accident, a company representative stated that the company owed no duty to warn that the traffic light wasn't working. The company's main duty, he said, was "to protect its own workers." The article went on to point out that the executive "expressed no sympathy for the accident victim."[93]

According to one expert, "The single greatest cause for adverse litigation is when the victims feel the company doesn't really care."[94] The father of the victim in this case, upset after reading the comments of the company representative, decided to sue the company. Even then, the utility company attorney did not express regret over the daughter's death. When the case proceeded to trial, the parents' attorney asked the jury for $10 million in damages. After the jury awarded $37 million ($17 million for the decedent's father and $20 million for her mother), the case was appealed and the final award was reduced to "only" $10 million.[95]

This case provides a lesson in the philosophy that should touch every aspect of your attempt to use law for competitive advantage. As stated earlier, this philosophy focuses more on what people will do than on what a court will do. The Russian author Alexander Solzhenitsyn once expressed the following concern about the Western world: "Whenever the tissue of life is woven of legalistic relations, there is an atmosphere of moral mediocrity,

EXHIBIT 7.4 LETTER FROM MARRIOTT PRESIDENT[96]

Marriott
corporation

INTERNATIONAL HEADQUARTERS
Marriott Drive
Washington, D.C. 20058

J. Willard Marriott, Jr.
President

April 22, 1985

Mr. George Seidel
76 Peter Coutts Circle
Stanford, California 94305

Dear Mr. Seidel:

It was truly disappointing to learn about the problem you had with our wake-up service. Please accept my sincere apologies.

I have forwarded your comments to our Dallas/Ft. Worth Airport Marriott and I have asked our General Manager to give prompt attention to the matter.

Thank you for taking the time to write. I hope you will allow us another opportunity to serve you soon so that we may regain your complete confidence.

Sincerely,

Bill Marriott

J. W. Marriott, Jr.

paralyzing man's noblest impulses."[97] By adopting a dispute prevention philosophy, you not only have a chance to prevent expensive litigation, you also have the opportunity to exercise a "noble impulse" by expressing genuine sympathy to those who have suffered loss or injury.

Chapter Summary

After defining competitive advantage and noting problems with conventional management approaches to the law, Chapter 1 describes a plan that enables you to use the law to seize competitive advantage—the Manager's Legal Plan™. Chapters 2 to 6 illustrate how you can use this plan to seize competitive advantage in varying contexts. This closing chapter examines three general concerns—legal resources, management tools, and the role of ethics and values—that will enable your company to gain competitive advantage as you deal with a broad range of legal issues.

Conventional strategies for developing and using legal resources involve two fundamental questions: Should the company develop an in-house legal staff or rely on outside advisors and how can the company control legal costs? In answering the first question, in-house law departments generally play a key role in creating value and providing higher perceived quality. With regard to cost control, the chapter describes several alternatives to traditional hourly billing.

In focusing on these two questions, companies overlook several larger concerns. First, in a market-driven company, lawyers, too, must focus on value creation and on the external customer to provide the best advice to their internal clients. As part of their training, for example, McDonald's attorneys flip hamburgers in the company's restaurants. Second, law departments must be vigilant in using best practices developed by other functions in the company. An example is the DuPont Legal Model, which has added value while substantially reducing legal costs. Third, companies should consider opportunities for law departments to work with IP and other managers to become opportunity engineers and profit centers. The chapter also provides a checklist to use in evaluating the quality of a company's law department.

Following discussion of legal resources, the chapter turns to tools that managers can use to address business/legal problems. Decision tree analysis is an all-purpose tool that can be used to make decisions relating to law and other functional areas. In making settlement decisions, for example, decision tree analysis provides a more scientific approach than conventional decision making.

Another set of tools relates to ADR, which includes a variety of processes based on arbitration and mediation models. Tools available to managers include contractual dispute prevention and control, the ADR policy statement, and suitability screens. Even when immersed in a business dispute situation, managers should remember to go to the balcony to observe the big picture business issues and remain in charge. For example, from the balcony you can see how specific tools can be incorporated into a framework using principles of systems design.

The chapter closes with an examination of the role of ethics in gaining competitive advantage. The conventional approach is to develop an ethics program based on a lawyer-driven compliance strategy or a management-driven integrity strategy. Use of the Manager's Legal Plan™ provides an opportunity for companies to link ethics, values, and economics in a way that creates competitive and collaborative advantage.

Notes

1 Handler Chayes, A., Greenwald, B.C. and Paisner Winig, M. 1983. Managing your lawyers. *Harvard Business Review*, January–February, 84.

2 Gordon, M. 2001. Execs like you better. *Corporate Counsel*, July, 24.

3 Association of Corporate Counsel (ACC) 2010. *About ACC* [Online]. Available at: http://www.acc.com/aboutacc/index.cfm [accessed: October 11, 2010].

4 European Company Lawyers Association (ECLA) 2010. *ECLA* [Online]. Available at: http://www.ecla.org/documents/eclaJune.pdf [accessed: October 11, 2010].

5 International Bar Association (IBA) 2010. *About the IBA* [Online]. Available at: http://www.ibanet.org/About_the_IBA/About_the_IBA.aspx [accessed: October 11, 2010].

6 International Association for Contract and Commercial Management (IACCM) 2010. *About IACCM, Facts & Figures* [Online]. Available at: http://www.iaccm.com/facts.php [accessed: October 11, 2010].

7 Ricker, D. 1994. The vanishing hourly fee. *ABA Journal,* March, 69. This article describes the first four alternatives in greater detail.

8 Dooley, L. 1999. Law firm "beauty contests" lose allure as companies turn to RFPs. *Corporate Law Weekly,* November 25, 854.

9 Marquess, J.J. 1999. Legal fee audits: A cost control primer. *Risk Management*, February, 29.

10 Role of the General Counsel, 1995. *ACCA Docket*, September–October, 60 and 62.

11 Rice, P.R. 1998. *Corporate Attorney-Client Privilege: Study Reveals Corporate Agents Are Uninformed; What They Don't Know Can Destroy the Privilege* [Online]. Available at: http://www.acc.com/vl/public/Article/loader.cfm?csModule=security/getfile&pageid=147094&page=/legalresources/resource.cfm&qstring=show=147094&title=Corporate%20Attorney%2DClient%20Privilege%20Survey%20Overview [accessed: August 1, 2010].

12 Ask the General Counsel, 1996. *ACCA Docket,* January–February, 39.

13 Ask the General Counsel 1996, 39.

14 Ask the General Counsel 1996, 42. For a reader not familiar with the abbreviations, Esq. stands for Esquire, a title used by attorneys in the US, QSC stands for "Quality, service, and cleanliness," and BS stands for bullshit!

15 2001. Lawyers in the trenches. *LD21*, Spring, 16; 2001. People like us. *LD21*, Spring, 29.

16 Ask the General Counsel 1996, 42.

17 Banks, R.S. 1983. Companies struggle to control legal costs. *Harvard Business Review*, March–April, 168.

18 1995. The reengineering process: Two case histories. *ACCA Docket*, September–October, 20. The summary of the development of the DuPont Legal Model is drawn from this article.

19 Mahoney, D.B. 1996. When pruning is in order. *Business Law Today*, July–August, 50.

20 Sager, T.L. 1997. Toward a common goal. *ACCA Docket*, July–August, 13. This article describes the first four elements of the DuPont plan.

21 The reengineering process: Two case histories 1995, 24.

22 Sager, T.L. and Boccuti, G.G. 1997. Achieving the common goal: DuPont's performance metrics. *ACCA Docket*, September–October, 20–21.

23 Mahoney 1996, 14.

24 Mahoney 1996, 16 and 18.

25 Barrett, P.M. 1997. Tiny firm prospers paring fees DuPont's way. *Wall Street Journal*, December 31, B1.

26 DuPont 2010a. *The DuPont Legal Model Leaps Ahead.* Dupont Legal Model [Online]. Available at: http://www.dupontlegalmodel.com/onlinelibrary_detail.asp?libid=127 [accessed: August 1, 2010].

27 DuPont 2010a.

28 Creative counsel. The 2008 IC-10, 2008. *Inside Counsel,* September, 46–67 [Online]. Available at: http://www.insidecounsel.com/assets/article/1832/46-68_IC0908_coverstory.pdf [accessed: August 1, 2010].

29 See DuPont 2010b. *The Recovery Initiative.* DuPont Legal Model [Online]. Available at: http://www.dupontlegalmodel.com/ourinitiatives_Recovery.asp [accessed: August 1, 2010].

30 For computer-based drafting, see, for example, Chapter 20 in Paris, C.E.C. 2004. *How to Draft for Corporate Finance.* Looseleaf/Cdr edition. Practising Law Institute; and Quinn, B.C. and Adams, K.A. 2007. Transitioning your contract process from the artistic to the industrial. *ACC Docket,* December, 61–72 [Online]. Available at: http://adamsdrafting.com/downloads/Quinn.Adams.ACCDocket.Dec07.pdf [accessed: August 1, 2010].

31 Quinn and Adams 2007.

32 See, for example, McNair, D. 2005. Contractual risk identification, assessment and management system for the owner. *Contract Management in Practice,* 2(9), November/December, 136–40.

33 Voorhees, M. 1999. Learning the law with a mouse. *National Law Journal,* November 22, B10.

34 2001. Getting in shape. *LD21,* Spring, 7; 2001. Dawn of the machine age. *LD21,* Spring, 25; 2001 Virtual competition. *LD21,* Spring, 28.

35 Quinn and Adams 2007.

36 2000. GE and the art of "systematic common sense". *Corporate Counsel,* August, 51.

37 See International Association for Contract and Commercial Management (IACCM) 2009. The top negotiated terms: Negotiators admit they are on wrong agenda. *Contracting Excellence,* July [Online]. Available at: http://www.iaccm.com/contractingexcellence.php?storyid=923 [accessed: August 1, 2010]. For the "Top Ten Terms," see Exhibit 6.2.

38 van Putten, A.B. and MacMillan, I.C. 2009. *Unlocking Opportunities for Growth. How to Profit from Uncertainty While Limiting Your Risk.* Upper Saddle River, NJ: Wharton School Publishing. Foreword and Chapters 1 and 5.

39 van Putten and MacMillan 2009, 115.

40 2001. The profit center. *LD21,* Spring, 16.

41 Nowlan, S.E. 2001. The law department ... transformed. *LD21,* Spring, 4.

42 Foltz, J.L. 1996. Laws of reality. *ACCA Docket,* May–June, 48.

43 Aman, C. 2000. What CEOs really think of GCs. *Corporate Counsel,* November, 23.

44 Hall, K. 2001. What would Ben do? *Corporate Counsel,* March, 58–62.

45 Hall 2001, 58.

46 Nowlan, S.E. 2001. Gatekeeper to gateway. *LD21,* Spring, 3. Reprinted with permission from the Spring 2001 edition of the *LD21* © 2010 ALM Media Properties, LLC. All rights reserved.

47 This example is adapted from Siedel, G.J. 1986. The decision tree: A method to figure litigation risks. *Bar Leader,* January–February, 18.

48 As regards *visualizing legal information,* the few exceptions include the pioneeering work of Dr. Colette R. Brunschwig, who wrote her doctoral thesis on *Visualisierung von Rechtsnormen—Legal Design* [Visualization of Legal Norms] in 2001, and a growing group of researchers and practitioners who follow her footsteps. In their article "Doing deals with flowcharts," in *ACCA Docket*'s 2001 October issue, Henry W. Jones and Michael Oswald discussed various benefits of visualization, with examples, and the technology tools available to help attorneys and others to use flowcharts to add value and improve productivity and efficiency. Katri Rekola, Helena Haapio, and Henry W. Jones have explored the opportunities of visualization in contracting further in IACCM's

Contracting Excellence magazine. See Rekola K. and Haapio, H. 2009. Better business through proactive productization and visualization of contracts. *Contracting Excellence,* 2(5), June/July, 17–19 [Online]. Available at: http://www.iaccm.com/userfiles/file/CE_2_5_press_C2(1).pdf [accessed: August 1, 2010]; and Jones, H.W. III 2009. Envisioning visual contracting: why non-textual tools will improve your contracting. *Contracting Excellence,* 2(6), August/September, 27–31 [Online]. Available at: http://www.iaccm.com/userfiles/file/CE_2_6_press_new.pdf [accessed: August 1, 2010].

49 Hechler, D. 2001. GE's juggling act. *National Law Journal,* July 23, A16.

50 Cavenagh, T.D. 2000. *Business Dispute Resolution.* Cincinnati, OH: West Legal Studies in Business, 186.

51 Center for Public Resources (CPR) 1982. *Corporate Dispute Management 1982.* New York, NY: Bender, 338. CPR is now the International Institute for Conflict Prevention and Resolution.

52 Wallgren, C. 2006. ADR and business, in *ADR in Business—Practice and Issues Across Countries and Cultures,* edited by J.C. Goldsmith et al., Alphen aan den Rijn: Kluwer Law International, 3–19. At page 7, the author states that outside the US ADR does not usually include arbitration.

53 A judgment of a *court* may not be recognized or enforced in a foreign country. Many countries—at the time of going to print 145 countries—are parties to the Convention on the Recognition and Enforcement of Foreign Arbitral Awards, also known as the New York Convention. For the current status of signatories, see United Nations Commission on International Trade Law (UNCITRAL) website at: http://www.uncitral.org/uncitral/en/uncitral_texts/arbitration/NYConvention_status.html [accessed: August 1, 2010].

54 Siedel, G.J. 1992. The use of mini-trials to resolve construction disputes, in *Construction Conflict Management and Resolution,* edited by P. Fenn and R. Gameson, London: E & FN SPON, 356.

55 For the continuum of dispute prevention, control and resolution techniques and how to incorporate them into your business agreements, see Groton, J.P. and Haapio, H. 2007. *From Reaction to Proactive Action: Dispute Prevention Processes in Business Agreements.* International Association for Contract and Commercial Management EMEA Academic Symposium, London, 9 October 2007, Available at: http://www.iaccm.com/loggedin/library/nonphp/Paper 7—From Reaction to Proactive Action—Dispute Prevention Processes in Business Agreements.pdf [accessed: August 1, 2010]. See also Groton, J. and and Smith, R.J. 2010. *Realistic Risk Allocation: Allocating Each Risk to the Party Best Able to Handle the Risk.* New York, NY: International Institute for Conflict Prevention & Resolution (CPR) [Online]. Available at: http://www.cpradr.org/Portals/0/0/Docs/CPR%20Realistic%20Risk%20Allocation%20in%20Construction%20Disputes.pdf [accessed: August 1, 2010].

56 Bazerman, M. 1998. *Judgment in Managerial Decision Making.* New York, NY: Wiley, 129.

57 © 2010 International Institute for Conflict Prevention & Resolution, 575 Lexington Avenue, New York, NY 10022; (212) 949-6490, www.cpradr.org. Reprinted with permission of CPR. The CPR Institute is a nonprofit initiative of 500 general counsel of major corporations, leading law firms and prominent legal academics whose mission is to install alternative dispute resolution (ADR) into the mainstream of legal practice.

58 Wallgren-Lindholm, C. 2010. Bringing Arbitration Closer to Company Management and Boards: Can Arbitral Institutions Further This Aspiration?, in *Between East and West. Essays in Honour of Ulf Franke,* edited by K. Hobér, A. Magnusson and M. Öhrström. New York, NY: JurisNet LLC; and Villareal, E. 2006. *ADR in the United States—A Practical Guide,* in J.C. Goldsmith et al., 137–46.

59 Cronin-Harris, C. 1997. *Building ADR Into the Corporate Law Department: ADR Systems Design.* New York, NY: CPR Institute of Dispute Resolution, 105–7.

60 Villarreal, E., Paquin, J.D. and Boyens Victor, J. 2004. General Electric's integrated conflict-management system. *ADR Choices*, Fall, 1 and 4–5 [Online]. Available at: http://www.dri.org/ContentDirectory/Public/Newsletters/0001/2004%20ADR%20Choices%20Fall.pdf [accessed: August 1, 2010].

61 See also DeGroote, J. 2009. *Early Case Assessments: More On The ECA Toolkit From PD Villareal.* Resourceful Internet Solutions, Inc. [Online]. Available at: http://www.mediate.com/articles/DeGrooteJbl20091130.cfm [accessed: August 1, 2010].

62 Villarreal et al. 2004, 4–5.

63 International Institute for Conflict Prevention & Resolution (CPR) 2009. *Early Case Assessment Guidelines* [Online]. Available at: http://www.cpradr.org/PracticeAreas/EarlyCaseAssessmentGuidelines/tabid/412/Default.aspx [accessed: August 1, 2010].

64 Villareal et al. 2004, 4. For an overview of an ECA framework as implemented at Schering-Plough Corporation, see Villareal 2006, 142–6.

65 Ury, W.L., Brett, J.M. and Goldberg, S.B. 1988. *Getting Disputes Resolved: Designing Systems to Cut the Costs of Conflict*. San Francisco, CA: Jossey-Bass, 42.

66 Ertel, D. 1999. Turning negotiation into a corporate capability. *Harvard Business Review*, May–June, 61.

67 Groton and Haapio 2007, 6.

68 Wallgren-Lindholm 2010.

69 Guillemin, J-F. 2006. Reasons for choosing alternative dispute resolution, in *ADR in Business—Practice and Issues Across Countries and Cultures*, edited by J.C. Goldsmith et al., Alphen aan den Rijn: Kluwer Law International, 25.

70 Wallgren 2006, 5.

71 Donaldson, T. 2000. Adding corporate ethics to the bottom line. *Financial Times*, November 13, supplement, 4.

72 Paine, L.S. 2000. Does ethics pay? *Business Ethics Quarterly*, 10(1), 319–330.

73 Kaplan, J.M. 1996. Why Daiwa Bank will pay $340 million under the sentencing guidelines. *ETHIKOS*, May–June, 1.

74 KPMG 2000. *2000 Organizational Integrity Survey*, 4.

75 Trevino, L.K., Weaver, G.R., Gibson, D.G. and Toffler, B.L. 1999. Managing ethics and legal compliance: What works and what hurts. *California Management Review*, 41(2), 135.

76 Paine, L.S. 1994. Managing for organizational integrity. *Harvard Business Review*, March–April, 113.

77 Trevino et al. 1999, 137.

78 Paine 1994, 111.

79 Paine 1994, 111.

80 Trevino et al. 1999, 137.

81 BP 2000. Environmental and Social Review 2000 [Online]. Available at: http://www.bp.com/liveassets/bp_internet/globalbp/STAGING/global_assets/downloads/E/Environmental_and_social_report_2000.pdf [accessed: August 1, 2010], 12.

82 Gibeaut, J. 1999. Getting your house in order. *ABA Journal*, June, 66.

83 Coleman, C. 2000. As thievery by insiders overtakes shoplifting, retailers crack down. *Wall Street Journal*, September 8, A1.

84 KPMG 2000, 2.

85 Fort, T.L. 1997. How relationality shapes business and its ethics. *Journal of Business Ethics*, 16(12/13), 177. Available at: http://hdl.handle.net/2027.42/42517 [accessed: August 1, 2010].

86 Trevino et al. 1999, 145.

87 Gibeaut 1999, 70.

88 Bagley, C. 2003. Forethought: The ethical leader's decision tree. *Harvard Business Review*, February, 18.

89 Berkshire Hathaway Inc. *Code Of Business Conduct And Ethics* [Online]. Available at: http://www.berkshirehathaway.com/govern/ethics.pdf [accessed: August 1, 2010], 1.

90 Rwangen, 2009. Character matters, part II. *Implement Improvement,* The Lighthouse—An E-Newsletter, January [Online]. Available at: http://implementimprovement.com/?p=484 [accessed: August 1, 2010].

91 International Institute for Conflict Prevention & Resolution (CPR) 1982, xxviii. Dispute prevention is a natural part of the Proactive/Preventive Law agenda. See, for example, Dauer, E.A. 1988. Corporate legal health: Preventive Law dictates going to root causes to prevent claims from arising. *Preventive Law Reporter*, September: "The first rule of Preventive Law: it is not sufficient to predict what courts will do. If we are to avoid ever getting to court, we need to be able to predict what *people* will do. Litigation law is mostly law. Preventive Law is mostly facts. And the critical time for preventive lawyering is when those facts are first being born. As a lawyer speaking to business people, I would have one request of them: Please let us be involved in the making of those facts."

92 Peters, T.J. 1983. *In Search of Excellence*. New York, NY: HarperCollins.

93 Oliphant, J. 1999. Florida Power gets expensive lesson in corporate sensitivity. *Corporate Law Weekly*, May 13, 28.

94 Oliphant 1999, 28.

95 *Goldberg v. Fla. Power & Light Co* [2005] 899 So. 2d 1105.

96 Copyright © Marriott International, Inc. All rights reserved. Reprinted with permission of Marriott International, Inc.

97 Solzhenitsyn, A. 1978. Decline of the West. *Time*, June 19, 33.

Index

FSC
www.fsc.org
MIX
Papier | Fördert gute Waldnutzung
FSC® C083411

Kolibri 360 GmbH
Ferdinand-Jühlke-Straße 7
99095 Erfurt, Deutschland
produktsicherheit@kolibri360.de